Cambridge Opera Handb

Richard Wagner
Tristan und Isolde

Wagner's *Tristan und Isolde* occupies a singular position in the history of Western culture. What Nietzsche called the 'terrible and sweet infinity' of its basic nexus of longing and death has fascinated audiences since its first performance in 1865. At the same time, its advanced harmonic language, immediately announced by the opening 'Tristan chord', marks a defining moment in the evolution of modern music. This accessible handbook brings together seven leading international writers to discuss the opera's genesis and the libretto's relationship to late Romantic literary concerns, to present an analysis of the Prelude, the music of the drama itself, and Wagner's innovative use of instrumental timbre, and to illustrate the production history and reception of the music-drama into the twenty-first century. The book includes the first English translation of Wagner's prose draft of the libretto, a detailed discussion of Wagner's orchestration, and rare pictures from important and influential productions.

Arthur Groos is Avalon Foundation Professor in the Humanities at Cornell University, where he has taught since 1973. A member of the departments of German Studies, Medieval Studies, and Music, his musical interests focus on issues of music and culture, and opera, especially Wagner, Puccini, and modern opera. His books include *Giacomo Puccini: La bohème* (with Roger Parker, 1986) and *Romancing the Grail: Genre, Science, and Quest in Wolfram's Parzival* (1995), as well as the collections *Reading Opera* (1988), *Madama Butterfly: Fonti e documenti* (2005), and seven other edited volumes. Founding co-editor of the *Cambridge Opera Journal*, he has served on the editorial/advisory boards of *JAMS* and *Opera Quarterly*. He is also general editor of *Cambridge Studies in Opera*, and co-editor of *Transatlantische Studien*.

Published titles in this series

Ludwig van Beethoven: *Fidelio* by Paul Robinson
Vincenzo Bellini: *Norma* by David Kimbell
Alban Berg: *Lulu* by Douglas Jarman
Alban Berg: *Wozzeck* by Douglas Jarman
Hector Berlioz: *Les Troyens* by Ian Kemp
Georges Bizet: *Carmen* by Susan McClary
Benjamin Britten: *Billy Budd* by Mervyn Cooke and Philip Reed
Benjamin Britten: *Death in Venice* by Donald Mitchell
Benjamin Britten: *Peter Grimes* by Philip Brett
Benjamin Britten: *The Turn of the Screw* by Patricia Howard
Claude Debussy: *Pelléas et Mélisande* by Roger Nichols and Richard Langham Smith
C. W. von Gluck: *Orfeo* by Patricia Howard
Leoš Janáček: *Kát'a Kabanová* by John Tyrrell
Claudio Monteverdi: *Orfeo* by John Whenham
W. A. Mozart: *La clemenza di Tito* by John Rice
W. A. Mozart: *Così fan tutte* by Bruce Alan Brown
W. A. Mozart: *Don Giovanni* by Julian Rushton
W. A. Mozart: *Die Entführung aus dem Serail* by Thomas Bauman
W. A. Mozart: *Idomeneo* by Julian Rushton
W. A. Mozart: *Le nozze di Figaro* by Tim Carter
W. A. Mozart: *Die Zauberflöte* by Peter Branscombe
Giacomo Puccini: *La Bohème* by Arthur Groos and Roger Parker
Giacomo Puccini: *Tosca* by Mosco Carner
Richard Strauss: *Arabella* by Kenneth Birkin
Richard Strauss: *Elektra* by Derrick Puffett
Richard Strauss: *Der Rosenkavalier* by Alan Jefferson
Richard Strauss: *Salome* by Derrick Puffett
Igor Stravinsky: *The Rake's Progress* by Paul Griffiths
Giuseppe Verdi: *Falstaff* by James A. Hepokoski
Giuseppe Verdi: *Otello* by James A. Hepokoski
Richard Wagner: *Der fliegende Holländer* by Thomas Grey
Richard Wagner: *Die Meistersinger von Nürnberg* by John Warrack
Richard Wagner: *Parsifal* by Lucy Beckett
Richard Wagner: *Tristan und Isolde* by Arthur Groos
Kurt Weill: *The Threepenny Opera* by Stephen Hinton

Richard Wagner
Tristan und Isolde

Edited by

ARTHUR GROOS

CAMBRIDGE
UNIVERSITY PRESS

CAMBRIDGE UNIVERSITY PRESS
Cambridge, New York, Melbourne, Madrid, Cape Town,
Singapore, São Paulo, Delhi, Tokyo, Mexico City

Cambridge University Press
The Edinburgh Building, Cambridge CB2 8RU, UK

Published in the United States of America by Cambridge University Press, New York

www.cambridge.org
Information on this title: www.cambridge.org/9780521437387

First published 2011
Printed in the United Kingdom at the University Press, Cambridge

A catalogue record for this publication is available from the British Library

Library of Congress Cataloguing in Publication data
Richard Wagner: Tristan und Isolde / edited by Arthur Groos.
p. cm. – (Cambridge opera handbooks)
Includes bibliographical references and index.
ISBN 978-0-521-43138-5
1. Wagner, Richard, 1813–1883. Tristan und Isolde. 2. Wagner, Richard, 1813–1883. 3. Opera – 19th century. I. Groos, Arthur.
II. Title. III. Series.
ML410.W1A295 2011
782.1–dc22

2010037296

ISBN 978-0-521-43138-5 Hardback
ISBN 978-0-521-43738-7 Paperback

Contents

Contributors

JOHN DEATHRIDGE is King Edward Professor of Music, King's College London.

THOMAS GREY is Professor of Musicology, Stanford University.

ARTHUR GROOS is Avalon Foundation Professor in the Humanities, Cornell University.

STEVEN HUEBNER is James McGill Professor of Musicology, McGill University.

JOSEPH KERMAN is Professor of Musicology Emeritus, University of California, Berkeley.

JÜRGEN MAEHDER is Professor of Musicology at the Freie Universität Berlin.

STEWART SPENCER currently works as a translator.

Illustrations

General preface

This is a series of studies of individual operas, written for the serious opera-goer or record-collector as well as the student or scholar. Each volume has three main concerns. The first is historical: to describe the genesis of the work, its sources or its relation to literary prototypes, the collaboration between librettist and composer, and the first performance and subsequent stage history. The history is itself a record of changing attitudes towards the work, and an index of general changes of taste. The second is analytical and it is grounded in a very full synopsis which considers the opera as a structure of musical and dramatic effects. In most volumes there is also a musical analysis of a section of the score, showing how the music serves or makes the drama. The analysis, like the history, naturally raises questions of interpretation, and the third concern of each volume is to show how critical writing about an opera, like production and performance, can direct or distort appreciation of its structural elements. Some conflict of interpretation is an inevitable part of this account; editors of the handbooks reflect this, by taking up their own critical position. A final section gives a select bibliography and guides to other sources.

Introduction

Tristan and Isolde, the actual opus metaphysicum of all art.
Nietzsche, 'Richard Wagner in Bayreuth', *Untimely Meditations*

But I am still looking for a work with as dangerous a fascination, with as terrible and sweet an infinity as *Tristan*, – I look through all the arts in vain.
Nietzsche, 'Why I am so clever', *Ecce homo*

Friedrich Nietzsche's comments on *Tristan und Isolde* foreground two elements of its fascination: the intimation of philosophical depths not usually associated with opera, and the 'terrible and sweet infinity' of its musical-poetic language. Wagner himself would certainly have agreed also about the work's singularity: on the day of the second performance he proclaimed in a letter to King Ludwig II that 'nothing similar of this kind can be compared with our *Tristan*, as it will reverberate and resound today'. As if to underscore the assertion, he supplemented the conventional date of 13 June 1865 with another time-reckoning: 'the second day of *Tristan*'.[1] Almost a century and a half into the Age of *Tristan*, almost everyone would agree on the unparalleled intensity and impact of this particular opera, though some might also attempt to resist the vortex of its attraction with distancing tactics made possible by postmodern approaches to the past.

The singular position of *Tristan und Isolde* in Western culture also presents challenges for an opera handbook. We set out with the presupposition that a work as extraordinary and influential as *Tristan* would require a variety of strategies: providing information, of course, but also making sources available in English and – especially – interpreting the opera. The next section, for example, posed the first challenge: a musical synopsis of *Tristan und Isolde*, unlike the overview of a conventional number opera, might be as arduous to read as it would be to write. Indeed, tracking *Tristan*'s narrow complex of themes might – to borrow a phrase from Vladimir Nabokov – prove as difficult as 'looking for allusions to aquatic mammals in *Moby Dick*'.[2] In the event, I decided to provide a translation of Wagner's own prose synopsis (the first in English, to my knowledge), which will enable beginners to familiarize themselves with the plot, and experienced listeners to spot the nascent libretto or to note details that Wagner later changed in the process of versification and composition.

The genesis of the opera has been recounted many times in the standard literature and also in recent monographs by Roger Scruton and Eric Chafe.[3] For this handbook John Deathridge chose to focus on two salient but often-overlooked 'facts' of this rich complex: the economic constraints that compelled Wagner to produce the score on something resembling an assembly-line schedule (without possibility of revision), and the opera's relationship to the *Wesendonck Lieder*, and thus to a fascinating but often misunderstood nexus of biography and cultural practices. The libretto has also frequently been discussed, usually in the form of a comparison with its Middle High German source, Gottfried von Straßburg's *Tristan*, but its significance for the opera remains largely unexplored. The libretto chapter attempts to rectify this neglect, making a case for it as a literary text in its own right, one that also engages in a highly sophisticated intertextual dialogue with major texts and genres of German literary culture.

Three chapters pursue diverse approaches to understanding *Tristan und Isolde* as a music-drama. Joseph Kerman's rigorous 'close reading' focuses on the Prelude to Act I and the resonances of its initial measures at crucial points of the ensuing action. Thomas Grey suggests ways in which *Tristan* might be interpreted through structural oppositions – between the visible and invisible, what is heard and what is silent – which are foregrounded through acousmatic effects at the beginning of each act, and lead to a conflation of sensory perceptions in the Act II love-duet that is resolved only with Isolde's death. Jürgen Maehder examines Wagner's use of timbre and innovations in compositional technique that underlie his creation of a 'knowing orchestra', capable not only of elucidating the inner life of the protagonists with a music of presentiment and recollection, but also of providing instrumental sounds with a history of their own.

The last chapters are devoted to the extraordinary reception history of *Tristan und Isolde*. Steven Huebner pursues its musical traces, especially the 'Tristan' chord, from Wagner's own *Meistersinger* to later Romantic music and modernism, simultaneously examining the methodological problems involved in identifying and interpreting those traces. Even though the opera lacks the political, historical, and religious dimensions so appealing to theatre directors of *Der Ring des Nibelungen*, *Die Meistersinger*, and *Parsifal*, Stewart Spencer's history reveals that *Tristan* has nonetheless stimulated a wide variety of interpretative responses, ranging from the realism of early stagings to abstract, symbolist, and mythic revisions in the twentieth century, and even the alienated domesticity of recent productions. The bibliography aims to give readers access to basic areas of *Tristan* scholarship, from studies of the medieval myth to presentations of the opera's genesis, controversial elements such as the 'Tristan' chord and the Prelude, secondary literature on the opera in general, and studies of its performance and reception history.

Two chapters have appeared previously in the following publications: Chapter 1 in John Deathridge, *Wagner Beyond Good and Evil* (Berkeley, CA: University of California Press, 2008), 117–32; Chapter 3 in Joseph Kerman, *Write All These Down: Essays on Music* (Berkeley, CA: University of California Press, 1994), 335–49. I would like to conclude with warm thanks to my collaborator-friends for their co-operation and patience.

Synopsis: Wagner's prose draft (1857)

The following synopsis presents Wagner's complete prose draft for *Tristan und Isolde*, the last stage before the elaboration of the verse libretto. Wagner's manuscript has the date 20 August 1857 on the upper right of the first page; a letter of 25 August to Eduard Devrient announces that he has just 'put it down on paper'.[1] Readers will notice familiar libretto lines already imbedded in the prose, but also intriguing divergences, such as the suggestion at the end of Act III that the music Isolde hears during her Transfiguration is an 'alte Liebesweise' ('ancient love melody').

Act I

On the foredeck of a large sea-going ship, closed off like a tent and richly hung with tapestries to represent a cabin erected for Isolde. In the middle are curtains that can be opened. *Isolde* on a couch, her face pressed into the cushions. *Brangaene*, sympathetic and concerned, on a foot-stool in front of the couch. A song from the mast above: 'The heart longs to go westwards, the voyage goes eastwards – a good breeze, easy voyage, calm sea; blue streaks reveal the distant coast of Cornwall, coming ever nearer.' – *Isolde* starts up: *Brangaene* should check on their progress and open the curtains; she is suffocating. *Brangaene* opens the curtains wide: one can see the length of the ship to the helm, and over the stern out to sea and the horizon. Upstage, a small group of sailors at the helm; still further back, at the stern, stands *Tristan* with his arms folded, gazing into the sea. *Brangaene* reports that blue streaks of land can be seen in the distance, probably the coast of Cornwall, which they could reach before evening. *Isolde*: 'Nevermore! The sea should swallow them up!' – *Song* from the mast: 'Safe journey, calm sea!' Isolde 'longs for a storm to hurl the ship into the depths and destroy all living things on it!'

Brangaene, extremely concerned, embraces her mistress: 'She has indeed suspected trouble. Cold, mute, and pale, Isolde boarded ship, listlessly brooding throughout the long voyage; sleepless with a distraught gaze. The faithful servant has almost died of growing anxiety. Now let the storm break. Oh, if only she would finally speak and reveal what is tormenting her.' – *Isolde*, turned away from her, fixes her gaze for a long time on *Tristan*, whom she espies at the furthest end of the ship. Disjointed phrases with sinister and cryptic allusions to her situation. What does Brangaene think of Tristan? – *Brangaene*: praises him and his deeds, his great propriety. *Isolde* mocks her: Tristan is cowardly and timid; he does not even dare to pay his lady the respect due her; he knows very well why he does not dare approach her – fear of punishment for his treachery. – 'Hear him yourself – go there and present my compliments; say that his lady requires his attendance.' – *Brangaene* obeys hesitantly. While *Isolde* follows with her gaze, she approaches Tristan and greets him: he suppresses an upsurge of emotion and listens to her calmly. When she has finished her message, *Kurwenal* leaps up irately and asks *Tristan* for permission to answer in his stead. *Tristan*: what would he answer? – *Kurwenal* gives a haughty response: Tristan is master here and no-one else. Does she know who he is? Lord of Parmenie, and the lawful heir to Marke's kingdom, which he has generously ceded to Isolde: what does it matter to a supremely rich man such as he? Indeed, he is bestowing Isolde on his uncle; – so who here is lord and who servant? *Tristan* tries to restrain him. – *Brangaene*: what should she bring back as his answer? *Tristan* politely but firmly expresses his regret at being unable to obey Isolde's command. While *Brangaene* hesitantly returns, Kurwenal sings after her, as if mocking and very loudly, so Isolde can also hear it, a song celebrating Tristan's battle with the Irishman Morolt, who once came to claim the ancient tribute from Marke's kingdom. Tristan fought and killed him on a desolate island, and – generous as always – he sent the braggart's head back home to Ireland. Embarrassed, *Tristan* has tried to restrain him; he doesn't let him finish and dismisses him rebukingly; Kurwenal descends sullenly into the hold near the helm. Tristan remains as before. – –

Isolde has heard the song: she commands *Brangaene* to close the curtains, gives herself over to the most intense grief, and demands to know exactly what Tristan answered. Brangaene reports reluctantly, but with a sense of personal insult. *Isolde* asks about the minutest details, Tristan's facial expressions, etc., then if she considers all this courageous? Brangaene should know everything, and learn that he is merely afraid of Isolde, nothing more than a cowardly, bragging knave. With the greatest emotion and in the most intense agitation she relates what transpired between them. – Mortally ill from a poisoned wound, alone on an empty skiff, he once landed in Ireland. She and her mother took pity on him, treated and healed him – does she still remember Tantris? *Brangaene* answers in the affirmative, and has always thought she recognized him again in Tristan. – *Isolde* relates how she came across his sword while he lay on his sickbed, and found in it a notch that perfectly matched the splinter her mother had removed from the slain Morolt's skull. Thus she identified the murderer of the Irish hero, and – mindful of her oath of vengeance – seized the sword and rushed to slay Tristan; but then took pity on the wretched invalid (here she clearly reveals how a powerfully awakened attraction prevented her). She concealed the incident from her mother and father and, once he was fully recovered, let Tristan escape unpunished; he had sworn eternal gratitude and loyalty to her. But how has he rewarded her now? After a series of battles, in which he broke Ireland's dominion over Cornwall and England, Tristan at last convinced his lord to sue for Isolde's hand. Out of disdain he led the wooing expedition himself, easily obtained peace and reconciliation from her parents, whose power he had humbled, and acquired her from them as a wife for Marke. Weak and concerned about themselves, seeing only the advantage of peace, her father and mother acquiesced without consulting her – thus she has now been sold as hostage to someone who formerly paid tribute to the Irish. And for all this she has Tristan to thank, whom she once had in her power, but whose life she spared. *Brangaene* is shocked; she did not suspect that Marke's proposal was so repugnant to her. *Isolde* pours out her heart in despair at the ignominious fate of being given in marriage to the ageing king; all the pride that once filled every Irishman lives on only in her; she alone feels the disgrace that she alone must suffer. But she will never become Marke's chattel. She must have revenge, and Tristan's blood must be spilt: she has heard how, after she mercifully released him unharmed, he bragged about her beauty upon his return and aroused the king's desire for her – that miserable, base pander, who still mocks her like a servant-girl being taken to market but fears to meet her face to face. – *Brangaene* attempts to put the situation in a different light. Surely, Tristan has only acted out of loyalty towards his king, and since she as successor to the Irish throne will also become queen of Cornwall and England, Tristan has actually elevated her to the highest rank. Could he have shown his thanks any better for her clemency back then? King Marke is praised as noble, generous, and virtuous. She will be happy at his side. When Isolde fiercely turns away, Brangaene continues by consoling her that she cannot fail to be loved by Marke, since even if he were the coldest of men, she knows a means to kindle the most passionate love in him. Misinterpreting Isolde's aversion, she confides that the queen, considering the risk of marriage for a couple disparate in age and unacquainted with each other, has entrusted her with a love-potion, which she is to administer secretly to Marke. *Isolde* flies into a rage, shows her abhorrence of winning a husband by such means, laments her mother's weakness and praises the former strength of purpose that taught her the art of preparing not only healing potions, but also the most deadly ones. She once prepared such a poisoned draught for her in case the most extreme peril threatened her honour. The poor woman did not realize that she herself was putting her daughter into a situation where no love-potion but only a death-potion could save her. Isolde orders *Brangaene* to bring the chest in which the potions are locked up; she obeys with anxious reluctance. She opens it and Isolde examines the two vials, removes the one containing the poison, and gives it to Brangaene to do with as she will command.

Loud shouts from without announce the approach of land. Isolde's growing agitation. *Kurwenal* enters through the curtains and delivers Tristan's command that the ladies prepare to disembark before evening; the coast is only a few hours away; Marke will certainly come to meet them, since a pennant of joy announcing the success of the bridal quest is flying from the mast. Isolde, at first recoiling with a shudder at the news, responds to *Kurwenal*'s impertinent, half-surly tone with a hastily assumed composure and measured dignity, requesting Tristan to appear before her immediately. Kurwenal should ask him if he finds it proper to land in such discord with his king's bride, if he does not fear the reproaches that Marke would have to make him on that account? *Kurwenal* is about to answer haughtily – she continues in a more intense tone that he should inform Tristan that she wishes to land in Cornwall at peace with him; he will surely know what they need to reconcile between themselves; she is ready to make peace with him beforehand. Isolde's expression, dignity, and intense pallor change *Kurwenal*'s attitude; he hesitates, scarcely believing he can make his lord comply. In response to the question whether he thinks his lord is afraid of her he flares up and promises Tristan's prompt appearance. – *Isolde*: 'He's coming! I know it!' She orders Brangaene to prepare the drink of reconciliation to offer Tristan from a most precious wine that seafarers once brought them from Italy: but in the chalice she should pour the contents of the vial that she has indicated. *Brangaene*, horrified, refuses to obey. *Isolde* implores her by their long-standing affection not to be disloyal, now that mother and father have abandoned her, and she has no other relations. She threatens to throw herself into the sea immediately if she refuses to obey. *Brangaene*: if you want to die, I will keep faith with you, but consider that your fate drags mine along with it: I will perish with you.

Tristan enters. – *Isolde*, extremely upset, staggers to her seat. *Tristan* bows respectfully. Long, silent pause. *Tristan*: 'Lady, your wish is my command.' *Isolde* says she is pleased at long last to see the person into whose protection she has been entrusted, so that she may know in whose hands she is. Why has he never approached her? *Tristan* responds, barely intelligibly and cryptically, that an oath binds him. Could she respect him if she did not find him faithful? *Isolde*: whose trust could he have betrayed by paying his respects to her? *Tristan*, evasively, where he was raised it is the custom for a match-maker to avoid the bride on the return journey. *Isolde*: for what reason? *Tristan*: ask the custom. *Isolde*: since he is so decorous, doesn't he consider how proper it would be to be reconciled with his lady before he hands her over to the king? *Tristan* knows of no fault that requires atonement. *Isolde*: must I remind you, Sir Tantris, that a debt of blood is still pending between us? She tells him how she once recognized him as Morolt's murderer and raised the avenging sword over his head. Or does he think because she spared the patient's life then out of pity that she had forgotten her oath of revenge? What if she had only spared the invalid in order to cut him down in the flower of his strength? And what if she thought that the time had now come when she, having the conqueror of the Irish before her, proud and happy to be taking the last crown-jewel of Ireland to his lord, didn't regard him in her heart any more highly than a pebble on the beach? Now, when he, having refused the crowns of Cornwall and England, was throwing a third crown to the person he deigned, on a whim, to make king of the world? What would he say if it now occurred to her to demand payment for the long-standing blood-guilt? *Tristan* makes a proud gesture. *Isolde* is pleased at his pride; she has almost thought him timid and cowardly for not daring to approach her. *Tristan* has not imagined that she was still angry with him about the blood-guilt. *Isolde* – but about some recent one? Aren't you aware of another debt to me? *Tristan*, meaningfully, not you? – *Isolde*: but to Marke your feudal lord? *Tristan*: I have served him, loyal and true. *Isolde*: when you wooed me for him? – She turns away from the silent man with deadly bitterness and bids Brangaene to prepare the potion. – 'As you were true to your duty, so shall I be to my oath. I once swore revenge for Morolt's death; only atonement can avert vengeance. Since you have proven yourself so useful to your lord that he would show me little affection if I took vengeance on you for elevating him, I now offer you reconciliation.' (She has observed Brangaene and directed her with a peremptory expression; now she demands the chalice from her; tremblingly, she hands it over.) (From without shouts of the crew: a stronger wind, speeding up the journey.) *Isolde* holds the chalice. 'Do you hear the shouts? Time is short: in a few moments you will be standing before King Marke; wouldn't it be better to appear before him completely reconciled with me? So that when you hand over his bride to him you can say: lo, sire, though I slew her uncle, wrested land and crown from her, bought her from her relatives, (and) now lead her to your bed, she bears no grudge towards me. Without anger or gall, like a little dove, she forgave me: don't you just adore my good fortune?' *Tristan* impetuously snatches the chalice from her hand. 'I know Ireland's queen and her black arts: she brewed medicinal potions, balms that heal all wounds, even the most deadly. Whatever the properties of this potion you offer me, I drink it in expiation of all guilt.' *Isolde* vehemently: drink to it. – *Tristan* drinks; *Isolde* wrests the chalice from him and drinks the remainder, exclaiming: 'This for you, traitor!' *Brangaene*, in desperation, has leaned over the rail. – *Tristan* and *Isolde* look silently at each other in growing confusion. Increasing agitation; they clutch convulsively at their hearts, shyly hide their glances from each other, then look at each other again with growing fervour. Finally an almost simultaneous cry: 'Tristan!' 'Isolde!' They fall into each other's arms in the full ardour of love. From without, shouts of the crew: Hail King Marke! – *Brangaene*, horrified, rushes towards the embracing couple. She reproaches herself for deliberately exchanging the potions, without suspecting what new and unforeseen misery she would create. Renewed shouts. They start up suddenly, barely in control of their senses: they seem to have lost all memory. Where were they? What were they dreaming? Where has their mortal enmity gone? Tristan! Isolde! O bliss! O supreme blessedness! 'I am yours alone!' 'Yours alone! – the world forgotten, everything vanquished – only Tristan und Isolde!' The curtains are opened wide, the ship is filled with companions and sailors (on the masts); all waving their hats over the side: Hail, King Marke! Hail Cornwall! – (*Brangaene*) *Kurwenal* reports that the King is casting off from land towards the ship in a richly decorated barge. *Tristan*: which king? Marke? What does he want? *Isolde*: 'What dream? Brangaene, you wretch! What potion?' *Brangaene*: 'The love-potion!' *Isolde* stares aghast in front of her, but soon turns with rapidly returning ardour towards Tristan – 'Tristan' – 'Isolde!' 'Hail, King Marke!' 'Kill me!' She faints into his arms. Brangaene rushes over: 'O most piteous fate!' *Tristan*: 'O most lamentable delight!' 'Help the queen!' – 'Hail! King Marke!' – *The curtain falls rapidly*.

Act II

An orchard. In front is Isolde's chamber with steps leading up to it. Through the open door one can see into the dimly lit interior. Bright, pleasant, moonlit night. Sounds of hunting, at first loud, then fading into the distance. On the steps *Brangaene*, leaning against the doorway, watches the retreating pack of hunters. *Isolde*, ardently excited, stepping out of the chamber – 'Can you still hear them? I think the sound has already died away.' She fervently longs for the moment that will bring Tristan into her arms. *Brangaene*, serious and concerned, attempts to restrain her impetuosity. Isolde's reproaches. Brangaene suspects treachery: she finds this suddenly arranged hunt at night suspicious. *Isolde* dispels all concerns. She knows only one tribulation, separation from Tristan: anything that would avert this, even death, would not terrify her. *Brangaene* reproaches herself as the cause of their unprecedented distress as well as her own disgrace in exchanging the potion. I wanted to prevent your death, and have only changed it into a suffering that will kill us all. – *Isolde* calms her down, praising her action; she has revealed what was destined to be made manifest: death and Tristan, Tristan and life – a higher power has decided. Therefore hurry, open the gate for Tristan. Brangaene hesitates. Isolde besieges her again – finally she leaves, promising to watch faithfully on the tower.

Tristan rushes in. Long, passionate embrace. A flood of long-restrained emotions. Utmost jubilation of delight. Praise of night for falling on their happiness after the torments of the day. They sink down on a flowery bank – gradual calming of stormy passion to more gentle tenderness. Reproach of day as the bringer of all suffering for the lovers. Each outdoes each other in complaining who might have suffered more on account of day. Tender reproaches. *Isolde*: it was day when you villainously wooed me for Marke. – *Tristan*: it was day that blinded me, pointing out honour as the treasure of the world, deceiving me with false appearances to seek empty things. *Isolde*: how did day deceive you into betraying me? *Tristan*: it seduced me with its brazen glitter to disclose your image in the chaste night of my heart; I praised you loudly before all the people, arousing desire and envy. Everyone clamoured for you as queen to get even with me for my good fortune and fame. Good Marke, who had adopted the orphan as his own son, had promised him his kingdom and possessions and sworn never to marry. Because of this, and because he was successful at everything, people envied him; the courtiers prevailed on the king to marry: Isolde was befitting as his queen, and Tristan should woo her because no-one else dared undertake the voyage on account of the long-standing blood-guilt. Now everyone believed that I would refuse, and thus they hoped to show that I was self-centred, concerned only with my own advantage. I stepped forward and volunteered for the voyage, renouncing my inheritance on behalf of Marke's future offspring; thus did I pay homage to my day-sun, honour and fame. *Isolde*: And you sacrificed me to increase your honour and fame? *Tristan*: blame day for blinding me to revel in presumption. *Isolde*: should I blame day for inciting me to death and revenge? He showed you to me only as a malefactor, as my most callous, malicious enemy. Even if I wanted to see you differently, as I harboured you in the nocturnal depths of my heart, my image of you remained bright and glaring so that I only saw in you a mortal enemy. *Tristan*: 'When you handed me the death-potion, night dawned sublimely in me, I lost consciousness, and wanted to plunge to my death, to belong to you there forever.' *Isolde*: But alas! It was the love-potion, which abducted you from night, and lovingly gave you a false day? *Tristan*: O rapture, hail to this potion! Through death's portals it opened up the blissful realm of night to me, where I would otherwise have groped aimlessly around. Now everything that ever deceived me has disappeared. – *Isolde*: But day revenged himself.

We had to do him penance for your sins. You had to surrender me to the king and yield to the constellation of day, leaving me alone in barren splendour. How did I endure it? *Tristan*: Oh, now we were dedicated to night; day could separate but not deceive us any more. We laugh at its vain glare: fame and honour, fleeting motes of dust in the sun, disperse; their lie revealed itself before the profound secret confided to us by night, uncovering even the deception of loyalty and friendship. Day may now hold us under duress, but it no longer deludes us: to the night-sighted it is barren darkness. One desire only lives in me by day, the longing for holy night! – Descend, O night of love! Take me up unto your bosom! Let me forget that I am alive; extinguish the world before my gaze! If I am aware of myself, how impoverished I am! If I have lost myself entirely, how rich I am! If I die becoming blind in ecstasy; if I no longer see the world, then I myself am the world, the most love-sacred life. If the sun no longer shines, she has hidden her warmth in my breast; then the stars of ecstasy shine for me! Heart on heart! Mouth on mouth! Dying – I am the ruler of the world! – Mutual intensification of the most sublime ecstasy and rapture. Intoxicating presentiment of death. – Never to awaken again! Desire for death! – Silence. *Brangaene*'s watch-song: profound sorrow! Be afraid of waking! Warning. – *Isolde* considers the admonition – Sorrow! *Tristan*: 'Let me die!' *Isolde*: sadly tender reproaches. *Tristan*: how could we die? What of us could be killed that would not be love? Are we not completely, only love? Can our love ever end? Could love ever desire to love love no longer? – If I wanted to die now, would love die then, since we are only love? – *Isolde*: but it is we who love each other; Tristan and Isolde, – I and you? If Tristan died? *Tristan*: then wouldn't only that disappear which prevents me from loving you forever? *Isolde*: 'Tristan's dying is only thinkable along with Isolde's death!' *Tristan*: 'Then we would have died in order to love each other. No day could ever separate us again: if its anxious gleam never awakened us again, the night of love would always shelter us; could there be a higher bliss than this, completely free of all anguish?' *Brangaene*'s more anxious warning. – *Tristan* hears it: who calls us to awaken there? *Isolde*: 'Death! (– *Tristan*: let me die! –) (*Tristan*:) he wakens us.' *Tristan*: 'Day is not yet dawning, eternity is assuredly still ours.' *Isolde's* growing concern for Tristan, which he calms through further raptures. Should we flee the fate that has brought us to an eternity free of waking? Isolde, death joined us together; at its portals we drank love: dedicated to death, forever loving, endlessly living, let us embrace so we may never part! Heightened ecstasy. Further, supreme intoxication – most fervent embrace. – (Day). *Brangaene's* scream. Marke, Melot, and some courtiers enter rapidly. (A brief fight beforehand – *Kurwenal* retreating downstage in front of the intruders.)

Isolde sinks down horrified on the flowery bank. *Tristan* – holding his coat in front of her with his arm extended, as if to protect her, remains with his eyes fixed on the intruders as if petrified. – Long silence. *Tristan*, dully: 'Dreary day has dawned!' – *Marke*, speechless with the terrible shock. *Melot*, to him: 'Tell me, was I not loyal? My spying glance was right – I have honestly defended your honour!' *Marke*, not turning his gaze from Tristan: 'You did? Melot?' *Brangaene* has rushed up and attends to Isolde. *Kurwenal* positions himself behind Tristan. *Tristan*, as before: 'Spectres of the day, why are you leering at me? Disperse, you sun-dreams!' – *Marke* – with a deeply grieved, trembling voice: 'This, Tristan, to me? Where have loyalty, honour, fame and every exalted virtue gone – since Tristan betrayed me? Why the uncounted favours, honour, power and greatness that you won for me, in order to reward yourself with my deepest disgrace? (Pauses – no response.) Were my thanks not enough for you? Wasn't it enough that everything you won for me I left to you as your inheritance? I loved you so much that I never wanted to marry again after my young wife died without children. When everyone prevailed on me, when you yourself requested me to, I resisted with every ruse in order to keep faith with you. But in spite of all my resistance you forced me to take a wife, threatening to leave my kingdom otherwise. You brought this glorious woman to my attention, you brought her to me at the greatest risk: who could call her his own without calling himself blessed? Why then, since through this possession you made my heart more feeling than ever before, did you wound me most terribly where you had made it most sensitive? Why deflect me from my straightforward path, where I never knew suspicion, never mistrusted my friend, making me susceptible to this poison that goaded me to steal away and spy on him? Why inflict on me this hell that no heaven can redeem, this disgrace that no misery can ever expiate? Why, Tristan? Why did you do this to me?' *Tristan*: 'O king, that I cannot tell you – and what you ask, you can never know.' – (He turns to Isolde, who has opened her eyes to look longingly to him). 'Wherever Tristan now goes, Isolde, will you follow him? It is not a land where the sunlight shines: for me the earth is waste and bare, I have expended all my estates and possessions on it. I mean the dark realm of night, from which my mother once sent me, when she conceived me in death and bore me in death. Love was death for her; let it also be a refuge for our love: – Tristan now departs for the wondrous realm of night; will Isolde follow him?' *Isolde*: 'I had to follow you when you wooed me for a foreign land; now that you want to lead me into your own domain, where could I flee, since your land spans the realms of all the world? Where Tristan is at home, there is Isolde's hearth! Show her the way so she may faithfully follow you!' – He blows a soft kiss on her forehead. – *Melot* gives a furious start – 'Traitor!' *Tristan* draws his sword. 'Who stakes his life against mine?' He fixes his gaze on Melot. 'He was my friend, he loved me by all that was dear; no-one was more concerned for my honour and reputation; he egged my foolish heart on to impetuousness; he led the crowd that pressed me for the sake of fame to woo Isolde for the king. The sight of you, Isolde, enflamed him as well; he betrayed me to the king out of jealousy. You have been chosen, wretched friend, to show me the path on which I will lead you, O queen! – Defend yourself, Melot!' He rushes towards Melot, discards his sword, and is wounded. *Kurwenal* catches the falling Tristan in his arms. Isolde falls upon his breast. *Marke*, who attempted to restrain Melot: 'Traitor, Melot! What have you done!' *Brangaene* at Marke's feet. The curtain falls rapidly.

Act III

Tristan's ancestral castle in Brittany. A castle garden surrounded on the right by the banqueting hall, on the left by a parapet with a look-out to survey the ocean, which is suggested by cliffs in the distance. Upstage, the castle-gate – ramparts – badly cared for, heavily over-grown. – *Tristan*, stretched out sleeping on a couch in the shade of a linden tree. *Kurwenal* sitting by his head, bent over him in anguish. – From without are heard the pipes of a shepherd, whose upper torso appears at the rampart; he looks sympathetically at them and calls softly to Kurwenal, 'Isn't he awake yet?' *Kurwenal* shakes his head: if he awakened, it would only be in order to take leave forever, unless his one and only healer appeared first – whether the shepherd can see anything yet on the ocean? *Shepherd*: 'Then you would have heard a different tune, as merry as I can play. I haven't seen anything yet. Tell me: what ails our lord?' – *Kurwenal*: 'That you can never know. Keep a sharp look-out, and don't ask me questions!' *Shepherd* leaves sadly and plays his melancholy tune. – *Kurwenal* (notices the growing restlessness of the sleeping Tristan), crying, places his head on his lap. *Tristan* (calls softly, without moving) opens his eyes, and raises his head a little: 'Who's playing that ancient melody? Why does it awaken me? Where am I?' – *Kurwenal* starts up in shock, rejoices greatly to see his friend alive again, to hear his voice. *Tristan*: 'Kurwenal? You? Where was I? What happened?' *Kurwenal*: 'This is your ancestral castle, don't you recognize the shepherd's tune?' He attempts to revive youthful memories. In response to Tristan's astonished questions, he responds that the loyal people have maintained his ancestral castle, in spite of the fact that he once gave everything away to set out for distant adventures: – *Tristan*: 'Where did I go?' – *Kurwenal*: 'Ah, to Cornwall, where you found good fortune and won great honour.' – 'How did I get back?' *Kurwenal* relates – painfully and reluctantly – how he carried the wounded man away on his shoulders, boarded a ship and sailed with him to their homeland. Here he should now recover – this is his true homeland, and the sun under which he grew up. *Tristan*: 'Whatever you think, I know differently, but I cannot tell you. Even if I awakened in Kareol, I was not there: – but where I was I cannot tell you. I saw neither the sun, nor land, nor people – but what I saw I cannot tell you. I was where I have always been, where I am eternally going: – in the wide realm of world-night (the most divine forgetting): only one knowing is ours there: divine oblivion. I have not found it yet, for a longing drove me back again into the light. I had to surface from the night of gods to see the harsh day that still shines on Isolde.' *Kurwenal* buries his head. *Tristan* with growing intensity: – 'Isolde – alas! Only in her can I die. Only Isolde can redeem me! Day grows on me, pale and anxious. – Horror awakens in me: Deception and delusion rouse my brain and show me that I live: Isolde –, alas! Isolde herself becomes a delusion for me! Where is Isolde – where am I not to be near her? Accursed day, why do you shine harshly on my misery; when will you fall, night of love that will take me to Isolde?' – *Kurwenal*, deeply moved, consoles him, – he will see her for certain, and soon – if she still lives? *Tristan*: 'Isolde not still live? How could I have seen day again, if it didn't still shine on her. Oh, she lives, and I had to awaken in order to summon her.' *Kurwenal* relates what he has done. Since Tristan lay as if dead, and the wound that the villainous Melot inflicted seemed incurable, he had sent a faithful vassal across the sea to England to request cures from Isolde (she would certainly come herself if she could escape); she should know now that only she could save him, and he was awaiting her return hourly. *Tristan*: 'She's coming! She's coming! O hasten to the look-out! Kurwenal, o you most loyal friend! Look out to sea, watch for the joyous pennant that announces Isolde's approach.' He hears the sad tune of the shepherd. 'What does that sound mean?' *Kurwenal*: 'That no ship can be seen yet; the faithful shepherd is watching from the cliff; a happier melody will let me know if the ship approaches.' *Tristan*: 'The melody sounds longing and lamenting: – (Isolde isn't coming yet!) Now it's coming back to me that I often heard it as a boy. I heard it pierce the evening air forebodingly when I first heard of my father's death; and it sounded more forebodingly when my mother's fate was made known to me. When he begat me, my father passed away, when she bore me my mother died – the lamenting melody sounded then too; it echoed deep in my heart and asked: for what purpose, then, were you born? To yearn to die? To live – to yearn – to yearn and – not be able to die? Now it summons my helper– can she bring me peace? Is there a balm to cool my yearning (for death)? She once healed a mortal wound, but only to give me then a poisoned draught! The wound healed, but my heart bled – the poison coursed burning through my veins, rushes furiously from heart to brain: oh, this anguish, what balm can release me from it? No death can deliver me: night casts me back into day, showing my suffering to the sun again! How the glowing mid-day sun scorches: no cooling, no refreshment for the parched! – Who am I, miserable wretch, to suffer these pains! (Once I could laugh in the daylight, chase motes in the sunshine.) Why am I the one your laughter no longer deceives, bright day? – That terrible potion, oh, woe is me! I brewed it myself!! From my father's distress and my mother's pangs, from the tears of love and the wounds of death, terrible magic, endless suffering – living to die, dying to live! Accursed love, let me go!' – He sinks back in a faint. *Kurwenal*, who has attempted unsuccessfully to restrain him and stood by horrified, cries out and bends over him, wailing. He cries loudly to him. – *Tristan* opens his eyes again. Kurwenal, you called; dear Kurwenal, how can I reward your loyalty? You never left me where I fought and suffered; where I was mistaken, where I was defiant, you were helping at my side; you helped me serve Marke as well as betray him: now, once more, dear friend, help me for the last time, help me die! To the look-out, friend, you *must* see the flag now: call to me that Isolde draws near, this one thing more, and I will bequeath everything I ever acquired to you! – *Kurwenal* hesitates. *Tristan* with heightened urgency: 'Can you hesitate to announce Isolde's approach? If only I could hear once more the joy that Isolde draws near! Isolde! Alas, Isolde! – Oh let me go! Look, I am strong, I no longer need your help: look, how it enlivens and supports and sustains me: Isolde's approach raises me up! – over there! To the look-out! Sluggish friend! Can't you see the ship yet?' – A joyful tune by the shepherd resounds in the distance. *Kurwenal*, who was reluctant to leave Tristan, jumps up suddenly and climbs the look-out. 'A ship coming (from Cornwall) from the north: gallantly it steers towards us: how the sail swells: it hastens, it flies –' *Tristan* interrupts with questions – 'The pennant?' – *Kurwenal*: 'Hail! The bright pennant of joy is flying!' *Tristan* rises higher and higher from his couch, loudly rejoicing. Growing rapture of anticipation. 'Do you see her?' *Kurwenal*: 'The ship just disappeared behind the cliffs.' *Tristan*: 'Are the rocks dangerous? I know that the breakers rage there; I have seen many a ship founder there. Who is at the helm?' *Kurwenal*: 'The best seaman!' *Tristan*: 'Do you see them again?' – 'Not yet' – 'They are lost!' – *Kurwenal*: 'No! Ahoy! They are clear! Heading toward the safe harbour!' – *Tristan*: 'To the shore, Kurwenal! Fly, help them land! Carry her up here in your arms! Is it really she?' – 'She's waving! – ha, with a bold leap she leapt ashore!' – 'Help her!' *Kurwenal* rushes down. – *Tristan* picks himself up from his bed – 'Why do I hesitate? I am bursting with my former strength: – Isolde nears! O bliss, – she valiantly defied every danger! To me! To her! Eternal salvation!' He hears Isolde's voice calling him: He leaps up in the most horrible excitement, staggering towards her as she enters. They meet in the middle of the stage. A loud cry of rapture. He sinks down slowly, lifeless, in *Isolde's* arms. She holds him: 'Tristan! Tristan!' (Then she gives a muffled cry and collapses over him.) *Kurwenal*, the *steersman*, the *shepherd* stand by, speechless. – *Isolde* (slowly coming to) attempts to awaken him: he should only live one brief hour! It is I – I came to save you! – Listen to me! – the wound – where? –: she is terrified! His eyes are lifeless, his heart silent! Not one moment of life left for her? His breath? – Expired! No greeting for the faithful one? – An outbreak of despair! Moving lament! Too late – no balm can bring him back! – She sinks in a faint over him. Tumult from below. *Kurwenal* on the look-out: a second ship in the harbour. *Brangaene* rushes onstage. *Marke* with his retinue following her! She: 'Isolde' – He: 'Tristan!' – Horror at the sight. Too late. *Brangaene* attends Isolde. – *Marke*: 'Awake, you unfortunate ones. Up, my Tristan! Must you also betray your friend even now when he comes to prove his loyalty?' *Isolde* regains consciousness in the arms of Brangaene, who attempts to revive her with the good news she brings: when she became aware of Isolde's sudden, secret departure, she hastened to Marke, revealed her guilt and the secret of the potion to him; he set out, quickly boarding a ship, to catch up with her and take her to Tristan himself. *Marke*: 'Why do this to me, Isolde! What I could not understand was revealed to me: I hastened after you to make you happy: but who can fathom this horrible misfortune!' *Isolde* does not hear them: she gazes at Tristan's features, which seem to her to come to life again: his eye beams at her, his heart beats, but so marvelously that only she is aware of it: – his breath wafts towards her; do you hear the blessed melody resounding to me in the sweet wafting? – ancient love-melody – last farewell – rising raptures. Flowery fragrances of delight arise, swell to an ocean of sweet-smelling waves: a melody surging ever higher – she is transported by bliss, rushes into the sea to drown, to forget! Supreme release, redemption! – She sinks down, blissfully transfigured and dies. The bystanders are profoundly moved. Marke blesses them.

1 *Public and private life: on the genesis of* Tristan und Isolde *and the* Wesendonck Lieder

JOHN DEATHRIDGE

Abandoning the monument to love

The fact that *Tristan und Isolde* had deep personal roots is now an ineradicable part of its history. Wagner first conceived it in 1854 at a time when he was almost wholly dependent on the patronage of a rich Swiss businessman, Otto Wesendonck, who not only advanced large sums of money to pay off his debts, but also provided him with a house close to his imposing estate in Zurich that was promptly named the 'Asyl' by its grateful and impecunious recipient, then still a political refugee from Germany with a price on his head. Wagner responded, practically from the start of their acquaintance in 1852, by falling head-over-heels in love with Otto's attractive wife, Mathilde Wesendonck, who seems to have reciprocated with genuine affection that stretched, but cautiously did not overstep, the limits of upper-middle-class decorum. For his part, Wagner was smitten, his love for his patron's wife inevitably coming into painful conflict with his genuine loyalty and gratitude to his patron – a conflict similar, as biographers never fail to point out, to that between Tristan's passion for Isolde and his loyalty to his protector King Marke.

The situation left an indelible mark on the conception of *Tristan*, though at first with only a few hints at the disconcerting nihilism that was to become a major part of the final work. In a famous letter to Liszt from December 1854, Wagner wrote:

> Since I have never enjoyed in life the actual happiness of love, I want to erect another monument to this most beautiful of all dreams, in which, from beginning to end, this love is going to satisfy its hunger properly for once. I have worked out a *Tristan and Isolde* in my head – the simplest and at the same time most full-blooded musical conception. Then I'll cover myself over with the 'black flag' flying at the end so I can – die.[1]

Wagner's mention of the black flag – a detail of the Tristan legend among the first to catch his attention – suggests that he originally had a different idea of the opera's outcome. Wrapping the black flag in ironic quotation marks, too, spoke volumes. In the legend, Tristan lies sick and incurable in the care of his wife, Isolde of the White Hands, while they await the arrival by ship of another Isolde, the Irish princess and wife of King Marke, whom Tristan secretly loves and whose powers alone can heal his wound. If the ship is flying a white flag, Isolde is on board; if the flag is black, she is not. As the ship comes into view, it is flying a white flag, whereupon Isolde of the White Hands, jealous of her husband's dependence on King Marke's wife, tells him the flag is black. Mistakenly believing that he will never again see the Isolde he really desires, Tristan dies of grief. The coded message to Liszt, fully aware of his friend's tangled emotional and financial state, could not have been clearer: the beautiful dream of love, beyond the pale of a loveless marriage with my wife Minna, to whom I, Richard Wagner, am publicly bound ethically and legally, can at least be conjured up in a work of art, even though I will never enjoy the sight of the white flag, concealed for ever from me by the public bond to my lawful spouse.

The subsequent development of *Tristan und Isolde* in Wagner's imagination gradually transformed the shadowy dilemma of his unhappy marriage and its petty jealousies into a wider examination of the tragedy of the human self as he saw it. The 'beautiful dream of love', in other words, developed into a conundrum far beyond the confines of Wagner's private world: how can some of the most beautiful and ecstatic love music ever written exist alongside a nightmare of delusion and its resolution in death? The trivial modern phrase 'to die for' used to express the succumbing to culinary bliss suddenly became appallingly literal. In the summer of 1856 Wagner wrote to August Röckel for the first time about the subject of Tristan and Isolde – a not insignificant fact in the light of their serious intellectual companionship dating from the 1840s and their participation in the 1849 Dresden Revolution. He talked of a concept 'in my head', describing it with a single, starkly-worded phrase: 'love as terrible torment' ('die Liebe als furchtbare Qual').[2] Egon Voss has rightly said that the phrase, and those like it in prose sketches for the opera written down shortly after this letter, leave no doubt that the conception of the opera had altered significantly.[3] Gone were the black/white flag and the jealousies of the rival Isoldes and nowhere was there mention of 'the beautiful dream of love'. What remained was a full-blooded musical conception, now saturated with an erotic hunger that could no longer be satisfied any more than it could be naively portrayed as a monument to a fulfilling erotic relationship permanently denied to its author. *Tristan* had changed from a relatively straightforward story of imagined love tragically compromised by jealousy into a desolate near-metaphysical exploration of the anguish of being-in-the-world brought about by the fatal intoxication of exquisite passion.

The *Tristan* factory

It has long been known, but seldom properly acknowledged, that Wagner's original intention was to turn *Tristan und Isolde* into an easily performable work that all opera houses would be eager to produce. As always Wagner urgently needed money. In 1856 when his negotiations with the firm of Breitkopf & Härtel about a contract to publish *Der Ring des Nibelungen* were about to fall through, he wrote to Liszt that if this were to happen (as indeed it did) he 'would have no alternative but to give up the *Nibelungen* and instead to start planning a simple work – like *Tristan* – that would give me the advantage of getting opera houses to produce it quickly and thereby earning myself some money'.[4] By September 1857, full of hope, but under the pressure of his ever-increasing financial worries that were only partly assuaged by the generosity of the Wesendoncks, he was able to announce to Breitkopf & Härtel:

> I am about to begin the musical composition of *Tristan and Isolde* – this will be the title of my new work – the libretto of which I have already finished. Among other things I have taken this subject to heart because it presents almost no difficulties for the scenery and the chorus. Practically the only demanding task will be to find a good pair of singers for the main parts, which means that I shall possibly easily get a good first performance and the chance of distributing it to the theatres very quickly, unimpeded by any obstacles.[5]

We know now that *Tristan und Isolde* later met with rejection because it was reputedly unperformable. Originally conceived as an opera that was to be relatively undemanding of its performers, it ended up being one of the most difficult works of the nineteenth century – a challenge to precisely the same circumstances of the opera business that had originally forced Wagner to conceive it as a 'simple work'.

On 4 January 1858, Wagner, who according to Hans von Bülow was in 'dire financial straits',[6] made the following offer to his publishers:

I propose a fee for the score of *Tristan* of six hundred Louis d'or, or twelve thousand francs. I must insist, however, that it be paid to me in full, and in cash, by the time the score is finished. I suggest that each time I deliver the full score of one of the three acts, I receive a third of the total fee, i.e., four thousand francs. For the production of the score we still have to decide the following. The score will be engraved, and the engraving is to begin immediately after I have sent in the manuscript. This can be arranged so that when I've finished the manuscript, the engraving will be finished shortly thereafter.[7]

Breitkopf & Härtel made a counter-offer of two hundred Louis d'or to be paid in two instalments on completion of the first and third acts. Wagner accepted without demur: it was still a not inconsiderable sum, and on top of it he eventually received, at his insistence, an advance payment of another hundred Louis d'or after finishing the second act on the strength of future royalties.[8]

Wagner's urgent need for cash led to a rigorous rationalization of the composition of *Tristan* that stood in stark contrast to the work's stubborn individualism and the almost flamboyant aura of erotic excess that surrounds it. To make sure he had a regular income, he suggested an arrangement rather like a factory assembly line that enabled him to work simultaneously on the opera's composition and its publication. As the dates of the genesis of *Tristan* make clear (see Table 1), the score was not put into print once the whole work was finished, but during work on the composition sketches, the detailed sketches of the orchestration, and the manuscript full score itself.[9] This meant that while Wagner was correcting the proofs of the first act, he was still busy composing the second; and similarly while correcting the proofs of the second act, he was still working on the third. Some of his instructions to his publisher are almost reminiscent of assembly-line conditions. He wrote to Härtel: 'Please be so good as to inform me exactly how much of my manuscript the engraver gets through daily or weekly; I'll then adapt accordingly and keep in step with him, though I'll always try to give him a bit extra as well'.[10] As a result, Wagner had to send off pages of the manuscript score of the third act before he had even finished writing down the rest of the act in his outline composition sketches, thereby denying himself the possibility of revising what he had already composed.

Table 1. *The genesis of the orchestral score of* Tristan und Isolde

		Composition sketch	Orchestral sketch (Particell)	Full score	Simultaneous production of the printed score
Act I	Beginning	1 October 1857	5 November 1857	6 February 1858	27 February 1858: contract sent to B 15 March 1858: B sends trial proof sheets to W
	End	31 December 1857	13 January 1858: W writes at the end 'never has anything been composed like *this*'	3 April 1858	5 May 1858: W receives forty pages to proof-read 20 November 1858: W receives final proof of Act I ending
Act II	Beginning	4 May 1858	5 July 1858	Towards the end of 1858	24 January 1859: W sends B 'a part of Act 2'
	End	1 July 1858	9 March 1859	18 March 1859	17 March 1859: W demands 100 Louis d'or from B 19 July 1859: B sends W proofs of first part of Act II
Act III	Beginning	9 April 1859	1 May 1859	April/May 1859	31 August 1859: W sends proofs of Act II to B 5 June 1859: W sends B first part of Act III 21 June 1859: B acknowledges receipt of pp. 255–74 of manuscript full score
	End	16 July 1859	19 July 1859	6 August 1859	7 August 1859: B receives the 'last instalment' of the manuscript full score, W receives the rest of his honorarium 14 December 1859: B receives final corrected proof of Act III 13 January 1860: B sends printed score to W

Abbreviations: B = Breitkopf & Härtel; W = Wagner

Anyone who wants to see the sketches and score of *Tristan* as 'gifts of heaven'[11] will probably take refuge in the idea that Wagner already had the entire work in his head before he wrote it down. But the composition sketches show that, although they are generally fluent, he was often not at all clear how the music should continue after sending what he had just finished off to the printer.[12] His sense of form was always one that groped its way forwards, in contrast to Beethoven who – in the sketches of the Sixth Symphony for instance – was in the habit of going back to music he thought he had finished and changing it significantly in order to create, retrospectively, the right balance in accordance with a long-range perspective of formal coherence.

What is exciting about the music of *Tristan* is that it presents a bold antithesis to the classical idea of sonata form. Apart from a few shorter passages, only Isolde's famous final scene in the opera could possibly qualify as a longer 'classically' inspired passage, as it is an obvious re-engagement with music previously heard in her passionate duet with Tristan in Act II. But the repetition of sections of the duet in the final scene is both too exact, in the sense that the passages have been lifted out of their original musical context and placed in new ones without significant change, and too radically different, because of large cuts in the original statement of the music and a halving of its note values. Isolde's *Liebestod* may count as a recapitulation of sorts, but hardly in the sense that Haydn, Mozart and Beethoven understood the process.[13] It seems more like a foreshortened memory of something that needs to be resolved, yet at the same time renounced, obliterated. In a sense, while writing *Tristan* Wagner resembled Orpheus in that he was not allowed to look back. The music constantly presses forward in search of formal possibilities that seem permanently open-ended – a radical aspect of the opera that had an even greater influence on modern music (Pierre Boulez's preoccupation with permanently evolving, non-repetitive forms, for instance) than its much-vaunted chromaticism.

In the midst of his *Tristan* factory, Wagner himself clearly suspected that the work was destined to change music history for ever: 'The process of correcting the proofs of the second act, while I was simultaneously in the throes of composing the ecstasies of the third act, had the strangest, even uncanny, effect on me; for it was in just those first scenes of this act [i.e. the third] that I realized with complete clarity that I had written the most audacious and original work of my life.'[14]

The ultimate private art

In apparent contrast to the purposeful rationality behind the genesis of *Tristan*, the *Wesendonck Lieder* were not composed in any particular order. Indeed, Wagner changed their order twice before settling on a final one for publication in 1862, and then only because he was practically forced to publish them to pay off yet more debts.[15] In other words, he neither conceived the lieder as a cycle nor at first did he want them printed and dragged into public view. This tends to support the generally accepted rationale for their existence as expressions of an adulterous passion that Wagner was at pains to keep private. Voss claims that Wagner wrote the *Wesendonck Lieder* as 'an artistic reaction against the apparent impossibility of consummating [his] love or, as far as Mathilde Wesendonck was concerned, as the symbolical expression of a mutual feeling which could not be displayed openly'.[16] But no conclusive evidence exists that Mathilde Wesendonck felt the same way about Wagner as he felt about her. Elsewhere Voss raises the perfectly legitimate question of why Otto Wesendonck, after the 'threat' to his marriage had come into the open, continued his support on such a lavish scale, qualifying him as one of Wagner's most generous patrons, second only to King Ludwig II.[17] The answer is surely that, as a successful businessman with a realistic perception of human relations, he knew the crucial difference between flirting and a deep-seated mutual erotic attraction that really would have endangered his marriage.

Wagner's own description of two of the songs – *Im Treibhaus* and *Träume* – each as a 'study for *Tristan and Isolde*'[18] suggests they had a wider purpose in relation to the composition of the opera than just his relationship with the author of their texts. (*Träume* formed the basis of the Act II love-duet's centrepiece 'O sink' hernieder' and *Im Treibhaus* was transformed into the bleak opening of Act III.) After all, Wagner was not in the habit of writing lieder at this stage in his career, which immediately suggests that there must have been a cogent artistic reason for his sudden decision to spend valuable time on them that could have been devoted to *Tristan*.

What I am suggesting is that all the *Wesendonck Lieder* had a wider creative connection with *Tristan* not limited to the two songs actually used in the larger work. In abstract terms the link is about style, expressive manner and gesture. But it is also about exploring an *idea* of the lied (almost by definition a diminutive art form on a private scale) that was just as central to the conception of *Tristan* as its larger symphonic ambition. Indeed, the work's many expressive subtleties are a result of this paradox.

Thoughts lavished on art song in Wagner's time also made it inseparable from the aesthetics of *Tristan*. As Liszt put it in 1855 in a seminal article on the lieder of Robert Franz in the *Neue Zeitschrift für Musik*: 'the lied is poetically and musically a product wedded exclusively to the Germanic muse like the words *Sehnsucht* ['intense longing'] and *Gemüth* [roughly: 'mind as a state of feeling'] . . . which belong only to the German language and remain untranslatable.'[19] Fortunately Liszt's slightly alarming nationalist sentiments pale before his reflections on the lied's aesthetic and psychological significance. As an avid reader of the *Neue Zeitschrift*, Wagner was almost certainly acquainted with them and – surely not entirely coincidentally – just before beginning in earnest with the composition of *Tristan* invited Robert Franz to the Wesendonck estate in Zurich in order to get to know his songs more intimately. His reaction was indifferent and (probably) not lacking in jealousy, which does not mean that he rejected Liszt's ideas, or lessened his ambition to write such lieder himself.[20]

According to Liszt, the lied with Robert Franz enters a 'new phase': he is a 'psychical colourist'; his lieder are mostly 'moods that are deeply self-absorbed' ('Stimmungen, die sich in sich vertiefen') and 'seldom strive dramatically beyond their limits'; his lyricism has 'much of a feminine sensitivity' about it; 'pain' ('Schmerz') is transformed in his lieder almost before our very eyes into 'a feeling of blissful dying away' ('ein Gefühl seligen Sichverlierens'); modulation determines feeling much more than melody; 'subsiduary modulations' ('Nebenmodulationen') surge into 'the smallest, most secret layers of feeling'; and finally, he is endlessly inventive in the way he avoids closing cadences in the vocal parts so that the music can press forward towards the end with a 'reverberating reinforcement' ('nachhallendes Bekräftigen') of the accompaniment.[21]

The litany of poetic and musical metaphor seems better suited now to the *Wesendonck Lieder*, and by extension to *Tristan*, than it does to the restricted expressive range of Franz's music. To put it another way: the serious exploration of the German lied and its expressive possibilities in the *Wesendonck Lieder* served as a vessel through which essential parts of *Tristan* had to pass. Alone, the tension between the private character of the lied and the public face of opera greatly helped to define the opera's sound-world – its static self-absorbed moods sharply contrasted with active high drama, the blissful dying-away of some of its music almost fiercely at odds with the symphonic momentum of its motifs, and last but certainly not least the intimate modulations of the most painful moments of confusion and self-examination brutally awakened by extrovert melody which show how the smallest, most secret layers of feeling are constantly vulnerable to public, often violent, action.

Perhaps most importantly, Wagner wanted to explore the nature of the lied to find exactly the right mood of quietist renunciation in *Tristan* – the wishing-to-be-apart-from-the-world inspired by Schopenhauer which found its equivalent in the famous romantic image, enshrined in the lied since the days of Goethe, of the poet accompanying himself on the lyre, losing himself in improvised song. 'His tender way of feeling', Liszt enthused about Robert Franz, 'and his fine, penetrating spirit (a spirit that nonetheless hates every noise, every pandemonium) hold him closed within himself, as if he were afraid of every exchange of opinion that could end in bitterness, as if to avoid every battle in which the strings of his lyre could be plucked too hastily and produce sounds that are less than pure, harmonically rich and tender'.[22]

Liszt thus defined the lied as the artistic expression of the (male) individual deeply absorbed in his own being, the ultimate private art. On one level, indeed, the genesis of the *Wesendonck Lieder* shows a similar disconcerting narcissism: Wagner gradually shrouded the lieder and his letters to Mathilde Wesendonck in total self-absorption to such an extent that he subtly began to erase all trace of her as the author of the poems. The title page of the first publication of the lieder – 'Five Poems for Woman's Voice Set to Music by Richard Wagner' ('Fünf Gedichte für Frauenstimme und Klavier') – omitted her name altogether, with the result that for most of the nineteenth century the texts were widely assumed to be by Wagner.[23] The lieder also reveal the saturnine state of mind that led to the unforgettable sound-world of *Tristan*: the lonely individual, talking on his own, searching for intimacy, and insisting on 'pure' love in the abstract, but discovering it only in music of striking melancholic intensity. Indeed, Wagner himself practically came to the same conclusion. Cosima Wagner reports in a memorable moment in her diaries that the arrival of an edition of the *Wesendonck Lieder* arranged for violin and piano prompted him to remark: 'With my so-called love affairs it was just as with my [first] marriage; Minna married me when I was in a very wretched position ... but at the same time I was quite without influence over her. And thus it was, too, with the other relationships; it all belonged somewhere else ... I just spoke in monologues.'[24]

The flight into the public realm

The view of *Tristan und Isolde* as both industrial product and isolationist experiment in musical intimacy says at least two things. First, only six months separated the completion of the manuscript score and the publication of the full score in January 1860, the fastest turn-around for any of Wagner's major works. Indeed, the speed with which Wagner and his publishers managed to get the opera into print is a sign that it was intended from the start as an emphatically public work. The fact that it was the first of Wagner's stage works to be properly engraved in full score – no mean undertaking for something so lengthy and complex – also strengthens the point. Forget the myth about the former revolutionary, now resigned, full of renunciation, wrestling with his inner demon, and suffering from a bad case of withdrawal from life. *Tristan* clearly represents a flight from the private into the public realm, not the reverse.

Second, Wagner's letters to his publisher about money and the flight into pure imagination that led him to distance himself from Mathilde Wesendonck hint at a desertion of feeling and collapse into abstract social relations which seem to be not only bizarrely at odds, but also more subtly in tune, with the hot-house aestheticism of *Tristan*. When Wagner wrote to Liszt on New Year's Eve in 1858, 'My Franz, when you see the second act of *Tristan* you will have to admit that I need a lot of money ... Send your Dante [Symphony] and your [Graner] Mass! But first money!',[25] he was consciously lifting the veil off a reality he knew was only superficially protected by fantasies of material and spiritual wealth. Indeed, the letter led to a serious rift between Wagner and Liszt, from which their relationship never completely recovered. Liszt wrote back sharply: 'As the Dante Symphony and the Mass do not count as bank shares, it will be superfluous to send them to Venice. I regard as no less superfluous the receipt from there of any more emergency telegrams and wounding letters. – In earnest, truest devotion, I remain your F. Liszt.'[26]

No wonder Liszt was disconcerted. He had received Act I of *Tristan* on 26 December and gushed to Wagner in an immediate letter of thanks about how the 'heavenly Christmas present' had put 'the entire children's world of Christmas trees decorated with golden fruits and gleaming presents' into the shade. 'Away with all the cares and toils of the real world', he continued, 'there [in *Tristan*] one can cry and let oneself go again'.[27] Wagner's answer to this particular piece of Lisztian wishful thinking was simple: 'You are replying', he wrote, 'with too much pathos',[28] almost as if he were snapping someone on a psychiatrist's couch out of a moment of tearful self-pity. The notion that his preoccupation with myth preempted many of Freud's insights into the human psyche is laid down in tablets of stone in modernist lore. His bracing remark to Liszt, however, suggests that he may well have dismissed modern psychoanalysis as so much humbug designed specifically to assuage essentially cold hearts protected by their wealth from life's realities. Certainly the stark contrast at the time between Wagner's impecunious circumstances and Liszt's socially and financially secure position seems to have sharpened the insight of the composer of *Tristan* into the bleak actuality of modern social relations. The sumptuous sounds of the work may act as a sop to the emotional discomforts of an outwardly comfortable life; but behind them, Wagner is suggesting, lies a bleak truth about human existence, which, from the safe, economically well-upholstered vantage-point of the successful bourgeois, no-one ever dares fully to acknowledge.

Paradoxically, the sheer intensity of feeling Wagner was putting into *Tristan* also demanded a less intimate audience: recipients at a safe distance unlikely to jeopardize further an emotional space already functioning at dangerous levels. Hence Wagner's eagerness to make it public as quickly as possible and with as many rational and neutral means as he could muster. Wagner's famous remarks to Mathilde Wesendonck about the supposed threat to the public's mental health posed by *Tristan* can therefore be read a bit differently:

> This *Tristan* is turning into something *terrible*! This last act!!! – I fear the opera will be banned – unless the whole thing is parodied by bad performances -: only mediocre performances can save me! Perfectly *good* ones are bound to drive people mad, – I can't imagine it otherwise. That's just how far I've had to go. Oh woe! I've just been in the thick of it! Adieu![29]

It is almost as if Wagner regarded his future *Tristan* audience as total strangers in whom he would find it easier to confide than in those closer to him – the audience as the 'big Other itself', the neutral receptacle for Wagner's secrets, as a post-Lacanian like Žižek might put it.[30] Indeed, the imagined rescue by mediocrity oddly expresses the hope that audiences will not react at all. Wagner is saying to Mathilde Wesendonck that he wants them to remain distant from *Tristan*, not only for their own safety and to rescue his public reputation, but also because he can only imagine their distance allowing those 'terrible' passages in the most fevered parts of *Tristan*'s Act III ever to come into being.

Enigmatic liaisons

Wagner gained some remarkable insights into himself and his work during his correspondence with Mathilde Wesendonck. By the time the letters were first published in 1904 their liaison was already the stuff of legend. Indeed, their appearance was a sign that the heirs of the Wesendoncks – Mathilde had died two years previously and Otto six years before that – were acutely conscious of publishing letters that, apart from providing valuable information about the composition of *Tristan*, would also confirm some unpalatable truths. The rapidly-collapsing barriers between public and private life in the nineteenth and early twentieth centuries, which allowed intimate details of human lives to become an inevitable part of public property, had already taken their toll. And to avoid embarrassment, those at the centre of public attention, similar to some celebrities now, increasingly found themselves compelled to half-censor or messily to reconstruct public perception. Perhaps sensing the inevitable, Mathilde Wesendonck had already gone out of her way in a short memoir published in 1896 to point out that 'money-matters were never discussed' between herself and Wagner.[31] It hardly takes a biographer of genius to detect in that statement a diversionary tactic. Wagner was heavily dependent on the patronage of the Wesendoncks at the time of *Tristan*; and he showed little restraint in upsetting household decorum, not only by expressing his feeling to Mathilde in private, but also by flirting openly with her in front of everyone. The situation eventually came to a head when Wagner serenaded Mathilde on the steps of the family villa on her birthday on 23 December 1857 with a chamber orchestration of *Träume* ('Dreams'), now the fifth song of the *Wesendonck Lieder*. And straining the good will of everyone to breaking point as usual he followed this up with a New Year's gift to her which consisted of the complete first act of *Tristan* in sketch form with a highly suggestive poem of dedication wrapped inside it.

Otto was not pleased. Wagner suddenly left for Paris to let things cool down and, sensing a serious threat to his income (not helped by the threat to Otto's fortune posed by economic turmoil in Europe at the time, which, however, like his displeasure with Wagner, soon blew over), immediately entered into the punishing contractual arrangement with the firm of Breitkopf & Härtel, guaranteeing him financial support until *Tristan* was finished and published. As we have seen, the circumstances of the contract had a significant role to play in the way *Tristan* came into being.

The supposed sexual shenanigans between Wagner and Mathilde Wesendonck have been so grossly exaggerated that it has become all the harder to trace the underlying seriousness of their relationship. Many biographers have implied that on Mathilde's part it was simply a craving for fame through association with a brilliant and powerful man. But as Dena Goodman points out in her work on Enlightenment salons, the trouble with this kind of argument is that it all too readily assumes the centrality of men in understanding the actions of women.[32] Wagner biographies have obviously played their part (most of them created by men) where the images of Wagner and the main characters in his life, even when treated salaciously, are still preserved in hardened nineteenth-century aspic. In their notorious book *The Truth About Wagner*, first published in 1930, Hurn and Root simply state with the school-boy enthusiasm of lip-smacking voyeurs that to the end of her life Mathilde Wesendonck 'never ceased to titillate at the lot that had been hers when she touched the fringe of greatness'.[33] Most biographers, too, have assumed that the compliant pretty face that blandly gazes into the wings of Johann Conrad Dorner's well-known portrait of her is an accurate reflection of her character.[34] Wagner's Victorian translator William Ashton Ellis fleetingly made her acquaintance in the last twenty years of her life and described her as a 'placid, sweet Madonna, the perfect emblem of a pearl, not opal, her eyes still dreaming of Nirvana, – no! emphatically no!' he spluttered on, '*she* could not have once been swayed by carnal passion'.[35] One wonders how Ellis – a medical doctor when not working on his time-consuming translations of Wagner's prose works – imagined she had conceived her five children!

Ellis is no less obtuse about her literary works, which include not only the five poems Wagner set to music as the *Wesendonck Lieder* (their modern, though as we have seen not their original title), but also several published plays, among them a reworking of the Alceste story, a drama on Frederick the Great, and a volume of folk-tales and legends. Ellis lists most of them in the 'Introductory' to his translation of the Wagner-Wesendonck correspondence. But his apparent generosity in alerting the reader to Mathilde Wesendonck's 'mental capacity' is full of problems. He claims that in her works Wagner's 'phraseology may be detected here and there' (in fact it is a surprise to see how unlike Wagner her writing is, belonging as it does to a 'classical' phase of romantic literature dominated by Goethe and Schiller, a characteristic that could be interpreted not just as conservatism plain and simple, but also as a conscious attempt to make her style distinct from Wagner's) and he also asserts that her five poems set to music by Wagner 'sprang from the depth of her heart', and have survived for that reason, implying of course that the rest of her oeuvre did not spring 'from the depth of her heart', and has therefore suffered eternal oblivion.

Mathilde Wesendonck's writings *in toto* are of greater biographical interest than Wagner scholars have claimed, though this is not the same thing as saying that they have great value as works of art. Ellis might not have mentioned her published works at all if Wolfgang Golther, whose edition of the Wagner-Wesendonck correspondence Ellis translated, had not been put under pressure by another woman to bring them to public attention – no less a person than Cosima Wagner. By the time the letters were about to be published, Cosima clearly sympathized with the recently deceased Mathilde's past attempts to find a role for herself in the public sphere of the nineteenth century more than she felt any jealousy toward her, thus overriding any qualms she may have had about the quality of the writings. Mathilde Wesendonck's works should be mentioned by Golther in his introduction to the edition, she insisted, because they reflect 'her own intellectual life'.[36] No more, no less.

As she may have admitted herself, Mathilde Wesendonck was no Madame Geoffrin or Mademoiselle de Lespinasse, two famous and illustrious salonnières of the Enlightenment. Still, in view of her organization of soirées, readings, concerts and major social events in her Zurich home and in the neighboring 'Asyl', she was, like them, a woman determined to shape the social and intellectual life around her according to her own needs.[37] The Enlightenment analogy can also help to explain why Wagner's letters to her were to a large extent far from casual, despite his later attempts to downplay their significance. 'To guard against any feeble mistakes,' he later told Cosima, with unconcealed disdain, 'I sent this lady her letters back and had mine burned, for I do not want anything to remain which might suggest it was ever a serious relationship'.[38]

In view of what Wagner had told her, Cosima was susprised to learn long after his death that many of the documents were still in Mathilde Wesendonck's estate. 'I am astonished that so many letters are there', she wrote to Golther, 'They should have been burnt a long time ago'.[39] What had Wagner been referring to? As good a guess as any (apart from the overly sceptical one that he may just have been inventing a story to placate Cosima) is that he was thinking of the aftermath of the crisis in the Wesendonck household in the first part of 1858 at a particularly sensitive moment during the genesis of *Tristan* when he was bracing himself for the musical composition of Act II. After his first wife Minna had threatened to collect evidence of an adulterous affair, destroying evidence susceptible to serious misunderstanding would have been prudent, to say the least. Indeed, the written communications surviving in print between Wagner and Mathilde Wesendonck up to the so-called Asyl catastrophe in the late spring and early summer of 1858 are almost all harmless short greetings, invitations to dinner, brief comments, expressions of thanks, and other things of that sort, which have few signs of the intellectual seriousness and sheer length of many of his later letters to her. The single exception is the long letter of 7 April 1858, headed factually (though for more lurid minds provocatively): 'Just out of bed.' It is in fact a serious attempt to interpret aspects of Goethe's *Faust*. An understandably jealous Minna intercepted it as it was being taken by a servant from Wagner's to Mathilde Wesendonck's quarters on the Wesendonck estate. It is hard to believe that there had not already been others like it or that it would have survived at all had not Minna decided to keep it as a memento of Richard's supposed unfaithfulness.[40] It was probably also a warning signal to her husband that she was now serious about obtaining real evidence: all the more reason to destroy whatever there was.

This possible scenario is only speculation; but it is notable that Wagner's extant letters to Mathilde after the 'affair' had died down continue with some of his most telling and succinct comments about art and philosophy. Despite its palpable gaps, including its unlikely one-sidedness in all probability caused by Mathilde's attempt to erase her part in it,[41] the correspondence has many of the hallmarks of an exchange of letters between late eighteenth-century figures: a serious formal engagement, a pact even, with responsibilities on each side, which could be broken after the relationship was over by the return and burning of letters, or their mutilation. One reason why the history of the correspondence is shrouded in mystery, lending it an air of perceived erotic tension that for the most part disguises its essentially formal qualities, is that no-one will ever know for certain how many letters the correspondents themselves destroyed. Nor will anyone ever be able to consult the originals that survived to the end of the nineteenth century. The letters were prepared for publication by Golther and Mathilde Wesendonck's heirs and returned to Bayreuth in 1904 after Cosima Wagner had reluctantly agreed to their appearance in print. Beyond sending strong hints to the editors, Cosima did not have final control over the publication (as is often assumed) and only when she got the letters back did she see it as her bounden duty to destroy them out of respect for Wagner's original wishes, suggesting somewhat acidly in an unpublished communication to Mathilde's son Karl von Wesendonck that it was something Mathilde herself should have done long ago: '[I] made the sacrifice, from which your mother shrank.'[42]

The golden age of private life

The trail of destruction that marks the fragmented survival of Wagner's and Mathilde Wesendonck's correspondence is a fitting sequel to the evolution of *Tristan und Isolde* from the tale of unrequited love it started out as being to the existential scrutiny of the annihilation of self it eventually became. Everyone has heard the cliché that *Tristan und Isolde* is 'the ultimate glorification of love'.[43] In a sense the work really is the love story to end all love stories: if one understands it well, no other pair of lovers, however star-crossed, can ever be quite the same again. Not even Shakespeare's *Romeo and Juliet*, at first sight perhaps the work *Tristan* most closely resembles, is as bleak. Far from a glorification of love, however, at the core of *Tristan* is the idea that the secret, all-else-excluding passion between two people is just as much an illusion as the public political sphere of human relations which threatens to invade it. They are martyrs in the name of freedom, not only from the public world that has caught them in its vice, but also from the torment of love itself, the dark allure of 'night' they both eventually reject as vehemently as they do the bright realm of 'day'.

The death-devoted rebellion against the public and the private in *Tristan* is undoubtedly one reason for its powerful effect on the nineteenth century, 'the golden age of private life',[44] during which the celebration of a realm of dreams and conflict served as the bulwark of reality and law. But the arc that stretched from the social engineering of the Jacobins in France in the 1790s – a time when the private was considered to have something conspiratorial about it at odds with the national good – to the cult of inwardness and aestheticism in *fin-de-siècle* Europe, when the influence of *Tristan* was at its height, also included in its range significant doubts about the equilibrium between the public and private spheres that liberal policy was meant to have achieved. In a sense it is precisely this 'equilibrium' that is under attack in *Tristan*. Already in Act I it is the pressure of a public event – Tristan's delivery of 'Ireland's daughter, loving and wild' (the sailor's apt description of Isolde at the start of the opera) as Cornwall's future queen – that practically encourages the lovers' fateful recognition of their hidden passion, after which the public and the private retain their tragic dependency on each other almost to the very end. To put it another way: Wagner's staging of the private in metaphysical, quasi-religious form takes on, before its final redemption, a drastic, almost tyrannical character that is not so much at odds with social authority as peculiarly reliant on it.

With its five moons – the five songs of the *Wesendonck Lieder* – *Tristan und Isolde* has therefore not become one of the most alluring planets in the operatic universe simply because it is a love story *in extremis*. The superficial image only disguises the deep trauma of desire in two individuals in the opera, whose fated relation to each other and the external events that condition it appear to be beyond their control. This existential predicament, which in turn affected the way Wagner misperceived, and subsequently denied, his serious relations with Mathilde Wesendonck, led him to write some of the most searing and emotionally disturbing music ever heard in the theatre. Indeed, since *Tristan und Isolde* was first put before its astonished audiences in 1865 nothing quite like it has ever been heard again. The strange tensions between the public and the private encoded in the drama, and even in the way its music unfolds, are doubtless one reason for the hold it still has on our imagination.

2 *Between memory and desire: Wagner's libretto and late Romantic subjectivity*

ARTHUR GROOS

It is frequently observed that *Tristan und Isolde* represents a turning-point, not only in the history of opera, but also in the history of music generally. Not surprisingly, scholarly interest in Wagner's music-drama has emphasized musical problems, starting in the late nineteenth century with leitmotifs and then moving to issues of tonality and structure (symphonic, then deep) – usually with only passing mention of the text being sung.[1] Indeed, Ernest Newman's claim that *Tristan und Isolde* would 'make an organic musical whole if played through by the orchestra without the voices' has frequently been seconded by other (mostly Anglo-American) scholars.[2] More recently, interest in the interplay and even disjunction of musical, verbal and stage systems in opera, and its inclusion in cultural studies of all kinds, has multiplied our perspectives on the genre, though this often still involves using the libretto as a means to identify musical contexts or fast-forward to philosophical, psychoanalytical or ideological decodings. The following chapter attempts to compensate for this neglect, suggesting some aspects of the verbal text of *Tristan und Isolde* and their contribution to the opera's extraordinary resonance in operatic history.

1

As scholars in recent decades have realized, Wagner publicized a variety of contradictory opinions about his music-dramas. To be sure, as a *composer* he encouraged a reception that privileged their 'symphonic' nature, placing him in a line of succession in German music that stretched back to Beethoven, Mozart, and Bach.[3] At the same time, however, as one of the first composers to be his own *librettist* as well, he also attempted to assure a reception of his texts that would place them in a tradition stretching from the German Middle Ages to Goethe, Schiller, and the Romantics and beyond, thus legitimizing them as serious literature. Indeed, in the early 1850s, Wagner asserted that with *Der fliegende Holländer* he had ceased making opera libretti and become a poet instead,[4] then underscored the claim by publishing his texts not only in conjunction with productions of his operas, but also allowing them to appear as independent works for the book trade. *Tristan und Isolde von Richard Wagner*, with no indication of its musical future, appeared in Leipzig in January 1859, a year before the score and six years before the Munich première.[5] The subtitle 'eine Handlung' ('an action'), a literal translation of the Greek δραμα (drama), was added later.

Scholarly assessments of Wagner's poetic 'dramas' in nineteenth-century German literary culture, however, seldom match the historical complexity of musicological analyses.[6] For one thing, nineteenth-century 'libretto language' represents a subdiscourse within the literary mainstream that has become unfamiliar even to literary scholars.[7] Twentieth-century musicologists are unaccustomed to the emotional and rhetorical excess of Romantic verse drama in general, not to mention the defamiliarization that comes with rhyming verse read independently of its musical context. In fact, *Tristan und Isolde* actually 'reads' better than attempts by well-regarded contemporary poets to realize the same subject. The eponymous hero and heroine's declaration of love after drinking the potion in Karl Immermann's unfinished verse narrative (1840), for example, while intending to express the inexpressible, seems underwhelming compared with Wagner's rhetorically virtuosic climax (see below, p. 43):[8]

Sie sagen nichts. Nur süßen Schalles	They say nothing. Now and then only the
Haucht: 'Du!' bisweilen – das ist Alles –	sweetly whispered 'Thou!' – that is all –
Von ihm zu ihr, von ihr an ihn,	from him to her, from her to him,
Wenn sie die Lippen dem Kuß entziehn.	when their lips withdraw from the kiss.
Urbestes woll'n sie offenbaren	They want to reveal what is most profound,
Und können sagen nichts als 'Du!'	and can say nothing other than: 'Thou!'

There are of course more interesting reminiscences of German poetry in the *Tristan* libretto,[9] which formerly – in a philological age that specialized in cataloguing 'influences' – were considered evidence of artistic dependence, but now seem, rather, to represent a deliberate engagement with mainstays of German cultural history. To start at the top: Wagner's use of the nonce-word 'Liebeslust' from Goethe's *Faust* as the final word in the Act I and II duets (see p. 41 below) suggests a considered intertextual strategy, making the climactic actions of *Tristan und Isolde* a corrective counterpoint to Goethe's drama, pointedly revealing his alternative to *the* central text of nineteenth-century German literature.[10] A second example: Isolde's Transfiguration (compare p. 50 below) clearly seems to gesture towards the poem 'Beethovens Büste' ('Beethoven's Bust') by Nikolaus Lenau (1802–1850):[11]

Sanftes Wogen, holdes Rieseln;	Gentle surging, lovely rippling;
Sind des Weltmeers kühle Wellen	Are the cool waves of the World-ocean
Süß beseelt zu Liebesstimmen?	Sweetly animated to voices of love?
Wie sie steigen, sinken, schwellen!	How they rise, sink, swell!

The intriguing complication here is that a poetic evocation of Beethoven's music lurks behind Isolde's description of the (symphonic) soundworld into which she expires, though of course in this case it seems to be Wagner's music recapitulated from the Act II love-duet that supplants Beethoven as the musical agent of her demise. On a more general level, the act-structures of the opera, with their penchant for extensive reminiscence and narrative, often praised as reflections of musical forms, also reflect a fashion for modern 'analytic' drama (for example, the work of Wagner's contemporary, Friedrich Hebbel), where events that precipitate the crisis occur before the action begins and are progressively revealed as events move towards their climax.

Wagner's appropriation of contemporary poetic motifs and dramatic structures is all the more important for understanding *Tristan und Isolde*, since his libretto can scarcely be considered an 'adaptation' of his medieval sources in the usual sense of the word. The incomplete Middle High German romance by Gottfried von Straßburg (*c.* 1210) and his Old French source by Thomas of Brittany (*c.* 1160), which also survives as a fragment (fortuitously containing most of the remaining scenes), comprise a rather sprawling narrative – some forty distinct episodes.[12] Wagner knew the medieval sources and contemporary scholarship extremely well.[13] But rather than telescoping episodes into a broad sequence of scenes, a common practice in nineteenth-century libretti,[14] his redaction concentrates on three brief moments, treating them with unusual freedom. In Act I, for example, the Irish hero Morold whom Tristan killed was not Isolde's uncle, as in the romance, but her betrothed instead, making the arresting gaze that stays her revenge, and her intended atonement through murder-suicide via the potion, a more intense and intimate psycho-drama. Different too is the stage action: instead of a pause to rest at an island in the middle of an exhausting sea voyage, during which an unnamed attendant confuses the potion with 'wine', Brangaene substitutes the love-potion for poison, precipitating a sudden release of long-repressed emotions by the hero and heroine just before landing in Cornwall.

The ensuing action also differs significantly. Act II takes place at night rather than during the day, focusing on the lovers' exalted meditation on love and death, which is suddenly interrupted by Marke; Gottfried, in contrast, narrates – not without irony – their hasty exit after discovering that the king has accidentally seen them making love in broad daylight and is rounding up witnesses. The introductory exchange between Brangaene and Isolde in Scene 1 (revealing the radical disjuncture between the day and night worlds) and Marke's anguished concluding monologue in Scene 3 (presenting the ethical claims of the day world as a counterpoint), have no equivalent in the medieval narrative. Act III follows the denouement of Thomas of Brittany's concluding fragment only insofar as it portrays Tristan's waiting for Isolde's arrival and her expiration over his corpse, though the details are radically different in the medieval romance, where a jealous rival, Isolde of the White Hands, falsely reports that the approaching ship has a black sail (i.e., that Isolde is not on board), and Tristan dies before she can land.

A summary of plot differences, of course, merely reveals the radical divergence of the libretto from the medieval romance. Wagner's discussion of Karl Ritter's plan for a dramatization of *Tristan* suggests some of the theoretical considerations involved:[15]

> At the time I had pulled no punches in pointing out to my young friend where the defects of his draft lay. He had confined himself to the adventurous incidents of the romance, while I had been immediately struck by its innate tragedy and was determined to cut away all the inessentials from this central theme. Returning from a walk one day, I jotted down the contents of the three acts in which I envisaged concentrating the material when I came to work it out at some future date.

Implicit in 'concentrating the material' is a fundamental transposition of genre from narrative to drama, with the corresponding shift from episodic breadth to tragic depth, a process that recapitulates the thesis of Wagner's main theoretical treatise, *Oper und Drama*, that modern drama evolved out of medieval romance by reducing episodic narrative to an internal unity grounded in the subjectivity of the characters. It is not surprising that Wagner's disparaging remarks about Gottfried's narrative in the famous letter to Mathilde Wesendonck of 30 May 1859 refer to its 'immaturity' and 'incompleteness', thus intimating the myth's fruition and completion only in his definitive modern dramatization.[16]

The shift in genre from medieval narrative to modern drama leads us to a central concern of *Tristan und Isolde*: the hero and heroine's subjectivity. According to the simultaneously opaque and partisan formulation in *Oper und Drama*, narrative proceeds 'from without inwards . . . from complex surroundings intelligible only with difficulty . . . and sinks exhausted before a portrait of the individual', whereas drama proceeds 'from within outwards . . . from a simple, universally intelligible surrounding to an ever richer unfolding of individuality'.[17] As a result of this focus on 'individuality', drama condenses the multiplicity of moments in narrative 'to a particular illustration of the participants' character'.[18] Put in more concrete terms: many episodes of the medieval romance other than the moments chosen by Wagner for the basis of his three acts nonetheless appear in the opera – as reminiscences of characters attempting to understand or justify past experience. Thus, although drinking the potion, on which the climactic event of Act I is based, occurs well after the mid-point of Gottfried's romance,[19] many preceding narrative episodes pervade the operatic hero and heroine's arguments over the conflicted past that culminate in their drink of 'reconciliation'. Act III traces an even wider loop: Tristan's monologue after his return from the brink of death regresses to the beginning of his consciousness, the birth that simultaneously caused the death of his mother in the opening episodes of the medieval romance.

If narrative represents one major component of the drama's emphasis on subjectivity, continually attempting to ground the principals' consciousness through recollections of their history, there is a complementary process that looks forward: the striving of Tristan and Isolde to define and realize their evolving love, which culminates in the dissolution of their sense of self, i.e., in death.[20] This dialectic between memory and desire has a common mode of articulation, emphasizing the *process* of recollection and longing, a process that consumes the majority of the text and supports the constant distension of narrative and dialogue, providing the textual basis for the constant deferral of cadential resolution in 'endless melody'. Such structures are prominent in Wagner's late music-dramas, to be sure, but no more so than here.

Given this centrality of Romantic subjectivity, it is surely no coincidence that the dramatic climaxes in each act of *Tristan und Isolde* have remarkably similar endings involving a heady mixture of bliss, self-consciousness, and desire. These climaxes occur in the duet at the end of the potion scene (Act I, Scene 5),[21]

Du mir einzig bewußt,	Of you alone I am conscious,
höchste Liebes-Lust!	highest love-bliss/desire!

at the conclusion of the *Liebesnacht* or 'love-night' (Act II, Scene 2),

ein-bewußt:	one-conscious:
heiß erglühter Brust	of ardently glowing breast
höchste Liebes-lust!	the highest love-bliss/desire!

and in the last moment of Isolde's *Verklärung* or Transfiguration (Act III, Scene 3),

unbewußt –	unconscious –
höchste Lust!	highest bliss/desire!

Commentators usually translate the exclamations 'Liebes-Lust!' and 'Lust!' with something like 'supreme joy of love' or 'highest bliss', imposing an explicitness on the original that it does not actually express. The German word *Lust* has two sets of meanings: joy (bliss, delight, pleasure, etc.) and the anticipation of that emotion (wish, desire, longing, etc.). This ambiguity also characterizes the unusual compound *Liebeslust* (with the further complication, alluded to above, that the word had appeared previously only in Goethe's *Faust*).[22] For our purposes, it is important to emphasize that the ambiguity of *Liebeslust* and *Lust* at the climactic moments of *Tristan und Isolde* articulates a particularly intense tension between desire and fulfilment that the arrival of King Marke interrupts in Acts I and II, suddenly transforming joy to longing, and perhaps even leaving ambiguous the apparent resolution of their deaths at the end of Act III.

While the ambiguity of the *Lust* in these three climactic passages establishes the centrality of longing throughout the work, the phrase or word with which it rhymes has a precise meaning in each instance that tracks the developing consciousness of the hero and heroine. All three rhyme words derive from the root *bewußt* (aware, conscious):

'Du mir einzig bewußt' (Act I), 'ein-bewußt' (Act II), and 'unbewußt' (Act III) respectively. The exclamation at the end of Act I, 'Du mir einzig bewußt' ('Of you alone I am aware'), characterizes the effect of the love-potion, which makes Tristan and Isolde aware of their previously unconscious attraction for each other at the same time that it makes them aware of nothing else. The ecstatic 'ein-bewußt', which climaxes their exploration of the brave new world of love and death in Act II, evokes the transcendent union of 'one-consciousness', which they can realize only by casting off the shackles of individuation that separate them. Finally, Isolde's Transfiguration calls upon the heroine quite literally to expire 'unbewußt' into the surrounding universe, thus becoming 'un-conscious'. These simple variations – 'conscious', 'one-conscious' and 'unconscious' – epitomize in telegraph style the trajectory of consciousness and desire that begins with Tristan and Isolde's new-found love and ends only with its realization in death.

2

The action leading to this chain of climaxes begins in each act with diegetic or stage music that sets the scene and makes us aware of the stage as a locus for the drama's conflicting epistemologies: the unaccompanied sailor's song in Act I, with its antithetical evocation of 'eastward' and 'westward', emerging eerily from outside the audience's frame of vision, '*aus der Höhe, wie vom Mast her*' ('*from above, as if from the mast*'); the hunting music of Act II, which precipitates the argument between Brangaene and Isolde over its interpretation and the motivations of the hunters; the shepherd's 'alte Weise' ('ancient tune') in Act III, which temporarily brings Tristan back from the brink of death. At the same time, the larger structure of each act traces a different dramatic development: the interior journey traced by Tristan and Isolde towards awareness of their love while their ship races towards its destination; the lovers' heedless rejection of the day world in pursuing their union in night and death; and the double focus on their separate deaths. These differing actions invite a more detailed analysis.

In Act I, Wagner suggests a bipartite division of the visible stage by means of directions for moving the curtains that separate Isolde's chamber from the rest of the ship: At the beginning of Scene 1, the curtains are '*nach dem Hintergrunde zu gänzlich geschlossen*' ('*completely closed off towards the background*'), separating Isolde and Brangaene from Tristan, Kurwenal, and the crew, visually confirming the principals' self-imposed silence that has lasted since their departure from Ireland. Isolde's frustrated outburst forces open the curtain, revealing Tristan as the object of her obsession, and 'opening' the way in Scene 2 for the initial attempt at communication. Tristan's unwillingness to respond to Brangaene's three variations of Isolde's order culminates in Kurwenal's retort – the 'Tristan'-ballad delivered '*mit höchster Stärke*' ('*at greatest volume*'). Kurwenal's blustery, diagetic musical 'number' forecloses any possibility of real dialogue, and Brangaene retreats, closing the curtain behind her. Scene 3 returns again to Isolde and Brangaene, '*allein, bei vollkommen wieder geschlossenen Vorhängen*' ('*alone, with the curtains completely closed again*'), at which point a second attempt at rapprochement begins.

Appropriately enough, the curtains remain closed until they are '*weit auseinander gerissen*' ('*torn wide apart*') at the climax of the lovers' duet in Scene 5, reinforcing the verbal ambiguity of this climax with a visual one. Verbally, the growing consciousness of Tristan and Isolde proceeds from a virtuoso display of rhetorical parallelisms to one of increasing unison:

Jach in der Brust	Suddenly in the breast
jauchzende Lust!	exulting joy!
Isolde! Tristan!	Isolde! Tristan!
Tristan! Isolde!	Tristan! Isolde!
Welten-entronnen	From worlds escaped
du mir gewonnen!	You won for me!
Du mir einzig bewußt,	Of you alone I am aware,
höchste Liebes-Lust!	highest love-bliss/desire!

Rhymed couplets underscore the congruence of the lovers' desire, the past participles in particular suggesting the completion of an irreversible process: Tristan and Isolde have escaped from the feudal world and won each other, moving from the public sphere to the exclusive realm of their new-found private consciousness. The only unrhymed lines in the passage, the chiastic exchange of lovers' names, emphasize that they now comprise a separate unity, 'consonant' only with each other. The sudden re-opening of the curtain at this moment once more provides visual counterpoint: at the precise instant that the psychological barriers to their love are removed and they become conscious of it, Tristan and Isolde are also revealed to the approaching members of the crew and Marke's court in all their vulnerability, establishing the double theme of their ever-deepening love and its conflict with the external feudal world.

The discussion that leads to this climactic development, unlike the one-sided and closed discursive forms in which their stories are initially presented, i.e., the myth of Tristan in Kurwenal's ballad (Scene 2) and the self-conscious narration of Isolde (Scene 3), forces Tristan and Isolde to confront the past together, beginning with the public reconciliation in Ireland that began their private silence, moving backward in time to the events involving Tantris and Morold, and then proceeding forward again. Both characters close their journey into the past by relating it to the present: Tristan by offering his sword, Isolde by rejecting it in favour of a drink of atonement. This crucial moment seems to relate this highly 'analytical' act, with its convergence of external and internal action, to the 'circular journey' frequently implied by Romantic literature.[23] The ship arrives at the linear goal towards which it has relentlessly progressed at the same time that the lovers reach the end of their circular journey of the mind, arriving at the threshold of understanding their hitherto repressed affinity, for which the effects of the potion and the opening curtains are but the outward and visible signs.

If the resolution of a contested past during the last moments of a symbolic narrative journey forms the basic structure of Act I, the central episode of Act II, the *Liebesnacht* or 'love-night' in Scene 2, uses as its basis a comparatively simple, though highly appropriate lyric genre, that of the dawn-song or *Tagelied*.[24] One of the principal genres of medieval German love poetry, it typically focuses on the parting at dawn of illicit lovers, who frequently lament the ineluctability of day, sometimes with interruptions by a 'watchman' who warns them of impending danger. Wagner's dramatization of this medieval song type reinforces the point of the scene: Tristan and Isolde's preoccupation with themselves in the 'lyric timelessness' of their self-involvement, heedless of Brangaene's warnings, cannot prevent the arrival of day – or the relentless progress of the drama towards discovery and death. Indeed, their metaphysical explorations at the end of the *Liebesnacht* proceed by ignoring the present and fixating on an extended binary opposition of past and future, day and night. Tristan and Isolde long to negate the frustrations of the feudal day-world, suggested by the preposition 'ohne' (without), and replace them with a future state that realizes their longing, validated by affirmative adjectives in alternate lines:

Ohne Wähnen	Without deluding –
sanftes Sehnen,	gentle longing,
ohne Bangen	without fearing –
süß Verlangen;	sweet yearning;
ohne Wehen	without woes –
hehr Vergehen,	sublime dying.
ohne Schmachten	Without languishing –
hold Umnachten;	lovely darkening;
ohne Scheiden	without separating,
ohne Meiden,	without avoiding –
traut allein,	intimately alone,
ewig heim,	forever home,
in ungemess'nen Räumen	in unmeasured spaces
übersel'ges Träumen.	most happy dreaming.

The actual transition from the medieval world, which both would like to do 'without', to a future realm beyond time and space (already hypothesized in Novalis's *Hymnen an die Nacht*)[25] requires a further narrowing and intensification of their already isolated subjectivity. Wagner leads his hero and heroine from the self-conscious deliberations on the conjunction '*und*' that reminds them of their conjoined fates (Tristan *and* Isolde) to a heightened form of chiastic relationship.[26] In affirming death as a way of destroying the separation of individuation – 'Doch dies Wörtlein: und – / wär' es zerstört' ('But this little word 'and' – if it were destroyed') – the lovers again move to a rhetorical climax, progressing from the conjunction 'and' (philologists also call conjunctions 'copulatives') to chiasmus as the vehicle for realizing a union beyond consciousness.

The libretto's increasingly elaborate chiasmus suggests a continuing process of intensification between the duet in Act I (see p. 43) and here:

ISOLDE:	Du Isolde,	You Isolde,
	Tristan ich,	Tristan I,
	nicht mehr Isolde!	no longer Isolde!
TRISTAN:	Tristan du,	Tristan you,
	ich Isolde,	I Isolde,
	nicht mehr Tristan!	no longer Tristan!

On the surface, Isolde and Tristan yearn to become 'nicht mehr Isolde' and 'nicht mehr Tristan' respectively; they seem to long for death, the state that according to Schopenhauer affords the opportunity to be 'nicht mehr Ich' ('no longer I').[27] But a Schopenhauerian conception of death merely as the negation of consciousness does not adequately characterize Wagner's lovers, since they also desire to merge personalities with each other. Isolde expresses this wish in the form of a chiasmus (Du : Isolde = Tristan : ich), as does Tristan (Tristan : du = ich : Isolde); both exchanges of the speaker's personality, through a reversal of the sequence in Isolde's chiasmus and Tristan's, also combine in the duet to establish a meta-chiastic relationship between the two in which – by denying *self*-consciousness – they become *one*-conscious, 'einbewußt'.[28]

As they strive towards this disembodied relationship, where each will exchange consciousness with the other and be subsumed into a metaphysical singularity, first and second person pronouns – the characteristic expression of the Romantic consciousness's division of the world into *Ich* and *Nicht Ich* – disappear from their discourse. In their place, Tristan and Isolde invoke a metaphysical journey beyond the division of individuation into a brave new world of night beyond the limits of space and time:

ohne Nennen,	Without naming,
ohne Trennen,	without parting,
neu Erkennen,	new knowing,
neu Entbrennen;	new enflaming,
endlos ewig	forever endless
ein-bewußt:	one-conscious:
heiß erglühter Brust	of ardently glowing breast
höchste Liebes-Lust!	the highest love-bliss/desire!

Brangaene's sudden cry and the entry of Kurwenal, followed by Marke and Melot, interrupt this journey, but we witness its continuation and conclusion in Isolde's Transfiguration at the end of the opera.

3

Tristan features prominently in several highly acclaimed interpretations of Act III that place him at the centre of the tragedy. Joseph Kerman's analysis of the double trajectory of Tristan's extended opening monologue underpins his assertion that the hero increasingly claims our interest in the course of the drama, his *agon* becoming its central, transcendent religious experience.[29] Tristan was also staged as the focus of a highly acclaimed production at Bayreuth by Jean-Pierre Ponnelle in 1981, which presented Isolde's Transfiguration as a projection of the dying hero, and which in turn stimulated several suggestive Lacanian-influenced analyses.[30] These are, to be sure, readings of Ponnelle's staging rather than Wagner's score, which explicitly states that the dying Tristan looks up and speaks her name, then dies ('*sterbend zu ihr hinaufblickend.* Isolde! [*er stirbt*]'), after which Isolde sinks down unconscious on what the stage direction explicitly calls Tristan's corpse ('*sie sinkt bewußtlos über die Leiche zusammen*'). But such misreadings of the text seem driven in part by an important concern: that although the opera seems to elevate Tristan and Isolde's 'shared death into its explicit ideological goal, this is precisely *not* what effectively happens – . . . they die one after the other, each immersed in his or her solipsistic dream'.[31]

Of course, an interpretation centred on operatic rather than ideological concerns can pursue other explanations, such as the traditionally greater interest of 'dissimilar' love-duets (and, by extension, love-deaths), with their additional potential for gender differentiation. From the perspective of the entire drama, the apparently disconnected death scenes could also be viewed as the working out of complementary forces of memory and desire, regression and progression, that have motivated the action, beginning with the opposing directions of 'westwards' and 'eastwards' evoked by the Sailor's song in the first lines of the opera.[32] If Tristan's monologue is regressive, moving backwards in time to a state of undifferentiated desire at birth, Isolde's is progressive, moving towards the ultimate dissolution of self in the world, accomplishing this by completing the music of the Act II love-duet interrupted more than an hour previously.

Moreover, Isolde's death scene – both the term Transfiguration (*Verklärung*) and Love-Death (*Liebestod*) are legitimate[33] – also seems to be a realization of her initial desire, expressed in the outburst 'Entartet Geschlecht!' ('Degenerate race!') in the first scene of Act I, to raise wind and waves to destroy the ship and every living, breathing thing around it.[34] Of course, that impotent 'rage aria' wished to conjure up external forces of nature as instruments of her revenge, while here the heroine 'drowns' in a synaesthetic ocean of perceptions that only she experiences. Indeed, the nature and intensity of that experience are so singular that it is difficult to find sources or analogues, and even these are partial at best. It may be helpful, therefore, to survey the possibilities, beginning with the mad scenes made popular by the operas of Donizetti and Bellini,[35] which Wagner knew and even conducted early in his career. In both cases, the bystanders remain detached and passive, enabling them to witness the heroine's altered behaviour and diagnose it as aberrant, become an audience for her performance of that difference, and finally mourn her death.

But whereas mad scenes stage and confirm a heroine's lapse into insanity, the last scene of *Tristan und Isolde* seems instead to recapitulate the disparate perceptions separating the day and night worlds that have dominated the opera since the end of Act I. To be sure, what Isolde experiences isolates her from the other figures, and them from her. Brangaene inquires, 'Hörst du uns nicht?' ('Don't you hear us?'), which Isolde, '*die nichts um sie her vernommen*' ('*who has perceived nothing around her*'), counters by repeatedly asking whether they see what is happening, 'Freunde, seht ihr's nicht?' ('Friends, don't you see it?'), finally suspecting that she alone hears the melody to which she expires ('Höre ich nur diese Weise?'). In Wagner's prose draft [see p. 18], that melody is identified as an 'alte Liebesweise' ('ancient love melody'); in the finished score, however, the 'melody' of Isolde's *Liebestod* is unmarked, and seems to be the orchestra's recapitulation of the Act II love-duet. In any case, the bystanders on stage neither see the 'action' nor hear the 'melody' whose sensual impact Isolde so graphically describes, and they do not return the action to 'normality' by singing a horrified response to her death, as is the case with many mad scenes. Isolde's rapturous demise is thus not aberrant, but validated as the 'last word' of the opera.

Two other forms of terminal ecstasy provide possible analogues for comparison. One could, for example, relate this scene to German Romanticism's interest in the Otherworld, in particular its fascination with the relationship between the natural and supernatural, the direct ancestors of Wagner's day and night worlds. There is in fact a well-known operatic precedent: E. T. A. Hoffmann's *Undine* (1816), in which a fairy heroine lures her unfaithful lover back to her supernatural aquatic kingdom, her tears penetrating his eyes and breast in a watery 'Liebes-Tod'.[36] In *Tristan*, of course, the gender roles are reversed, and there is no revenge. The most commonly cited analogue is religious. Wagner on several occasions compared Titian's *Assunta*, which he had first seen in Venice in 1859, with Isolde, and scholars frequently associate Isolde's Transfiguration with the Assumption of the Virgin Mary.[37] The chorale-like beginning of the *Liebestod* certainly imputes some kind of religious dimension to the scene, as does the final stage direction prescribing the bystanders' reaction to the 'miracle' and Marke's concluding benediction: '(*Isolde sinks in Brangaene's arms, as if transfigured* ['*verklärt*'], *onto Tristan's corpse.*

Catharsis and reverie among the bystanders. Marke blesses the corpses. The curtain falls slowly.)' Again, however, there is a significant difference: Isolde does not ascend, but sinks down. Both the motion she imagines and the one we see are transcendent, but of this world.

Isolde's Transfiguration thus resembles other forms of ecstatic death only partially, remaining, as with so many things in this opera, *sui generis*. Indeed, it is difficult to describe it with any objective certainty, other than the fact that she sinks down lifeless on Tristan's corpse. We witness most of Isolde's demise indirectly, through her subjective description and the ocean of orchestral sound in which she gradually 'drowns' as pure vocality.[38] This singularly performative act of will and imagination involves a progression: Isolde first experiences the exodus of Tristan's spirit from his corpse as both radiant *pneuma* and music, forces that simultaneously seduce and engulf her. Indeed, it seems characteristic of Wagner's androcentric approach to myth, which so often uses women to redeem men (what Nietzsche mocked as 'Senta-sentimentality'), that Isolde must follow Tristan's expiration into the world-breath in order to exhaust their passion, and that this seductive action is displaced to her imagination and desire. It will surprise no-one familiar with post-modern theory that the redemptive action begins with the originary 'gaze' with which Tristan first enthralled her. Taking up the three missing vital signs from her dirge in the previous scene, 'Gebrochen der Blick! – / Still das Herz! – . . . / Nicht eines Atems / flücht'ges Wehn!' ('His gaze broken! His heart quiet! No fleeting rustling of a breath!'), Isolde sees (and calls upon the bystanders – or an imagined audience – to see) each of these return to life, proceeding from the gaze and its extension as numinous radiance to the heartbeat and a gentle breath:

Mild und leise	Gently and softly,
wie er lächelt,	how he smiles,
wie das Auge	how he nobly
hold er öffnet:	opens his eye –
seht ihr, Freunde,	Do you see it, friends,
seht ihr's nicht?	don't you see it?
Immer lichter	Ever brighter
wie er leuchtet,	how he shines,
wie er minnig	how he lovingly,
immer mächt'ger,	ever more powerfully,
Stern-umstrahlet	radiant with stars,
hoch sich hebt:	raises himself up:
seht ihr, Freunde	do you see it, friends,

seht ihr's nicht?	don't you see it?
Wie das Herz ihm	How his heart
mutig schwillt,	bravely swells,
voll und hehr	fully and nobly
im Busen quillt;	beats in his breast?
wie den Lippen,	How from his lips
wonnig mild	delightfully soft
süßer Atem	sweet breath
sanft entweht: –	gently wafts –
Freunde, seht –	Friends, look!
fühlt und seht ihr's nicht?	Don't you see and feel it?

Her third and final question to the bystanders unanswered, Isolde turns inward, asking more tentative questions of herself. Tristan's *pneuma* or 'süßer Atem' ('sweet breath') now becomes an enticing melody – a process that she will soon echo with her own 'sweet' expiration:

Höre ich nur	Do only I hear
diese Weise,	this melody,
die so wunder-	which so wonder-
voll and leise,	fully and softly,
Wonne klagend,	delight lamenting,
alles sagend,	everything saying,
mild versöhnend	gently reconciling,
aus ihm tönend,	from him resounding,
auf sich schwingt,	soars up,
in mich dringt,	penetrates me,
hold erhallend	sweetly sounding,
um mich klingt?	rings around me?
Heller schallend,	Sounding clearer,
mich umwallend,	flowing around me,
sind es Wellen	are they waves
sanfter Lüfte?	of gentle breezes?
Sind es Wogen	Are they billows
wonniger Düfte?	of delightful fragrances?
Wie sie schwellen,	As they swirl,
mich umrauschen,	roar around me,
soll ich atmen,	shall I breathe,
soll ich lauschen?	shall I listen?
Soll ich schlürfen,	Shall I sip,
untertauchen,	submerge?
süß in Düften	in their fragrances
mich verhauchen?	sweetly expire?

The passage renders – to use a musical analogy – one extended transition: the heroine's perception begins as an enticing melody that grows increasingly louder and more tactile, forcing itself on her ('*in* mich dringt'), enveloping her ('*um* mich klingt', 'mich *um*wallend', 'mich *um*rauschen'), finally pervading her respiratory system ('Lüfte', 'Düfte') and becoming tangible as waves ('Wellen', 'Wogen'). Several responses to this increasingly insistent synaesthetic force seem possible: listening ('lauschen'), tasting and touching in a hesitant and then total form ('schlürfen', 'untertauchen'), and – finally – expiring ('verhauchen'), which, as the last of her questions, constitutes the hesitant rough draft for the act that follows. As if in response to this juggernaut of questions – some twelve in less than fifty lines – Isolde affirms the submerging of her entire being in this totality of sensation:

In des Wonnemeeres	In the surging swell
wogendem Schwall,	of an ocean of delight,
in der Duft-Wellen	in the ringing sound
tönendem Schall,	of waves of fragrance,
in des Welt-Atems	in the World-breath's
wehendem All –	wafting universe –
ertrinken –	to drown,
versinken –	sink down,
unbewußt, –	unconscious –
höchste Lust!	highest bliss/desire!

Appropriately enough, the process is represented as an ecstatic sentence fragment, beginning with a three-fold motion towards ('in') this enveloping flood of sound and sense, whose fluidity the participles underscore ('wogend', 'tönend', 'wehend'). Its magnitude is expressed not only by the overriding concept of the world-breath, but by the word 'Welt-Atem' itself, whose two stressed accents give it unusual emphasis, and whose lack of rhyme draws attention to its singularity as a universal force engulfing everything else – the long deferred resolution to Isolde's attempt to conjure up an engulfing 'storm' at the beginning of Act I. What subsequently happens is unclear, since there is no longer a first-person pronoun to create a sense of self and direct the action of a verb. Rather, the 'subject' of the fragment is the process of Isolde's ecstatic submersion into the unseen universe impinging upon her, represented by the infinitives 'ertrinken' and 'versinken'.

It would be difficult for any purely literary analysis to suggest how the text and music of these final lines create such a tremendous sense of release, a sense that according to some even transcends pleasure.[39]

One obvious answer has to do with the proleptic effect of the music's finally reaching a conclusion anticipated more than an hour previously during the 'Love-night' in Act II, Scene 2, a process also traced verbally by the final rhymes on *bewußt/Lust* discussed above. A more tangible, small-scale resolution is the remarkable concluding transition, emphasized in the reversal of metrical accent in those final two lines (from 'er**trink**en' to '**un**be**wußt**'). Moreover, as the *Tristan*-analysts observe, Isolde expires into the world-breath, not as the character Isolde (who has ceased to exist), but as disembodied voice, wonderfully suggested by sibilants in the words 'unbe*wußt*' and 'hö*chste* Lu*st*'. The power of this onomatopoeic conclusion lies not only in resolving the drama and its conflict between subject and world, but in adumbrating the resolution of a more deep-seated tension within the systems of opera itself, enabling persona to become voice, and words to become music. The rest is not silence, but the orchestra.

3 *The Prelude and the play*

JOSEPH KERMAN

1

In the days of his ascendancy, Wagner was a figure to reckon with on the concert stage as well as in the opera house; his fame and his appeal arose from orchestral excerpts from his operas, as well as from the operas themselves. Today such excerpts are less popular on concert programmes and recordings. A hardy survivor is the combination of the Prelude to *Tristan und Isolde* and Isolde's Transfiguration (the so-called *Liebestod*), the opera's final scene, sometimes performed with a singer, sometimes without.[1] 'Bleeding chunks', Tovey exasperatedly called such concert items carved from the operas' capacious cadavers, and it must be granted that the Prelude and the Transfiguration one after another make a peculiar mixed grill.[2] The opening pit music, before the curtain rises, joined to a (sometimes) wordless version of the concluding cantilena sung by Isolde after all of the action (conventionally considered) is over: this makes for a drastic short-circuit of Wagner's intricate music-drama.

Indeed, the perennial success of the Prelude and Transfiguration must seem startling, even ominous to lovers of *Tristan und Isolde: The Opera*. They can understand Wagner's promotion of this composite concert number in the 1860s, to broadcast excerpts of a work that had repeatedly defied efforts at production; and they must acknowledge the superior appeal of the gloomy Prelude joined to the rapturous Transfiguration as compared to the gloomy Prelude alone. But they also know that to appreciate the Transfiguration truly, one must have lived through the great love scene in Act II of the opera, whose music it resumes in a spiritualized form. And the Prelude, as they know, is just that: the initiation into a much greater experience in the course of which, among other things, the music of the Prelude achieves its full development and hence its true meaning, beauty, and force.

For concert-goers, there are clearly satisfactions to the Prelude and Transfiguration apart from such truths – apart from the opera at all. Similar satisfactions also seem to be available to music theorists. They have theorized so extensively about the Prelude (in particular) and the Transfiguration that it was possible for a leading Wagner authority, Robert Bailey, to issue a whole book of writings about these items. Included are essays or excerpts running to some 170 pages by no fewer than seventeen authors.[3] What is startling, once again, is how little they find to say, or were allowed by the excerpting editor to say, about the opera itself.

Perhaps, though, it is not so startling. For even as regards the Prelude and Transfiguration, one observes that these writings limit themselves almost entirely to matters of melody and harmony, broadly defined. The present essay will address aspects of this music besides melody and harmony, and also seek to place the Prelude in the context of the total music-drama. This line is not taken in a polemic spirit, to redress what can only be seen as the anti-operatic bias of Bailey's collection. The larger point is that the music of the Prelude is essential to the music of the opera itself, more profoundly so than in the case of any earlier opera (or, at a guess, any later one). Wagner's dramatic vision hinges on the way the opera emerges from the Prelude, on the way the Prelude plays in to the opera. Arguably, an examination of this topic can provide the most effective short route to grasping the musical dramaturgy of *Tristan und Isolde*.

2

Much has been written about the linear and harmonic aspects of bars 1–17 of *Tristan und Isolde*, much more than can be summarized here. Let us bite the bullet and summarize none of it at all, for there are other important points to make about this music – points about rhythm, dynamics, and affect. A single-staff reproduction as in Ex. 3.1 should suffice for illustration, even though this defangs the famous 'Tristan' chords at the points where the equally famous chromatic motifs converge.

To speak first about rhythm: the phrases or cells formed as the two motifs converge are disjoined by silences which feel, at this slow tempo, unmeasured, though only the last of them is literally so (that is, marked with a fermata). The Prelude's first downbeat, too, is placed in time somewhat enigmatically; the five slow quaver beats

Ex. 3.1

of crescendo on the cello F in bar 1 are hard to count and construe. So are the rests in bars 3–4 and 7–8 (different rests in each case). After bar 11 the music falters, as one fermata follows another. Only with the cello melody that emerges in bar 18 after the big deceptive cadence does Wagner establish some kind of normal motion (see Ex. 3.1).

The dark, mysterious yearning quality of this opening passage is due not only to its chromatic lines and harmony, and to its orchestration, but also to its disjointed rhythm; this seems obvious. And however apt or inept it may seem to describe this opening as 'dark, mysterious, and yearning', there can be little doubt that things begin to change in and around the fermatas in bars 11 and 13. The repetition of the naked appoggiatura E♯–F♯, grasping for resolution, grows intense and breathy to the point of harshness. This effect is heightened by the carefully differentiated dynamics at each of the appoggiatura's appearances. Then – when the bass E is supplied and resolves deceptively to F – the dynamic flares up to a momentary *fortissimo* as the music takes on its first explicitly sexual tinge. A spasm of desire, reinforced by vaulting French horns, cedes to a withdrawal exquisitely calculated in the anticipation of passionate renewal. It is the forward-moving cello melody that validates that anticipation.

Since the Prelude has interested theorists mainly on account of its chromaticism, they have not had a great deal to say about this cello melody. There is undeniably a sense of let-down when the involuted harmonies of the opening give way to a rather Lohengrinish march around standard secondary dominants and diminished sevenths skirting C major. Yet in the broadest sense, the cello melody – a genuinely 'endless melody' – coheres with bars 1–17 as an essential part of Wagner's idea. The linear connection in the middle of bar 17 (from A to A) is broken registrally, but this break is softened inasmuch as the same instrument that began the Prelude, the cello, resumes the pitch and the tessitura of the opening. And the diatonic cello melody seems in some deep sense to 'resolve' the chromaticism of the opening bars (of course, this is only an interim resolution). Though itself open-ended, the cello melody provisionally closes the chromatic drama of the opening.

For the purposes of analysis, bars 1–17 of the Prelude are usually isolated. Bailey calls them the 'opening unit'. It is never easy to find the right terminology for music's unique structures, and in the present case 'unit' suggests a fixity that seems unfortunate, even apart from the desirability of stretching the reference to cover the open-ended diatonic response from the cello. The term that will be adopted here – for we do need a term to carry on the discussion – is 'complex'.

3

The end of the Prelude returns to the same 'complex' as at the beginning: the chromatic motifs converging on the 'Tristan' chord, the three-fold upward sequence, the deceptive cadence and the diatonic cello melody. But there are big differences. So far from emerging as a tentative *pianissimo*, the first motif rides the surge of a powerful climax and is blared out three times in succession by the French horns. On the first 'Tristan' chord, the Prelude reaches its loudest *fortissimo*, only to back down again to *piano* in just a few seconds.

Then at the end of the passage, the cello melody is reharmonized. The chord change is simple, the effect wonderfully bleak (see Ex. 3.2).

Ex. 3.2

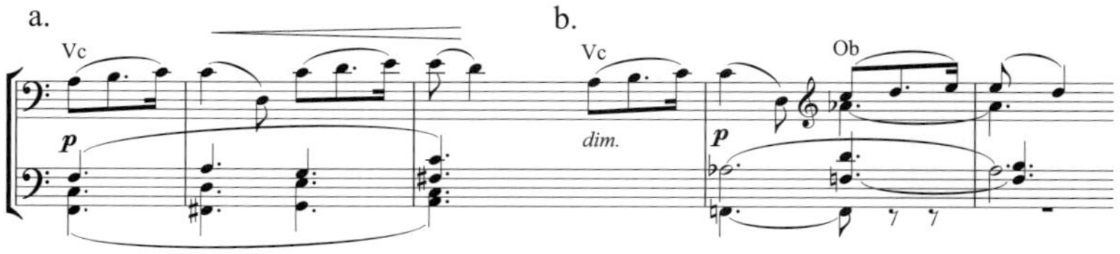

Wagner himself described the Prelude as 'one long-articulated impulse' in which insatiable longing swell[s] up from the timidest avowal of the most delicate attraction, through anxious sighs, hopes and fears, laments and wishes, raptures and torments, to the mightiest onset and to the most powerful effort to find the breach that will reveal to the infinitely craving heart the path into the sea of love's endless rapture. In vain! Its power spent, the heart sinks back ...

and on another occasion as the progression 'from the timidest lament in inappeasable longing, the tenderest shudder, to the most terrible outpouring of an avowal of hopeless love'.[4] He said nothing about the technical tour de force whereby the most terrible outpouring of hopeless love is set to the same music as the timidest avowal. (As is often observed, Wagner the *Vielschreiber* wrote little about his specific compositional procedures and actions.)

The same music – except for differences especially in dynamics, affect, and also rhythm. For the halting quality that was so striking at the beginning disappears in the return. The gaps between the cells are equalized and filled in by a new motif (actually, the retrograde of an old one) played by the violins. This violin motif sounds rhetorical, recitative-like; in any case, looking ahead to the opera itself, at later appearances of this music the pregnant gaps tend to be filled by declamatory singing, Wagner's equivalent of recitative. And with the benefit of hindsight, we can recognize that the music was composed with all those halts precisely so that they could be filled in in this way later. Put differently, the opening of the Prelude was designed not only to lay out the opera's unique musical language, but also to provide an elastic framework for recitatives, for actual verbal language.

Indeed, it is hard to see how Wagner could have proceeded differently if he meant to use the Prelude complex as a recurring element in the course of the drama. The point can be made most sharply by a comparison with the opera's other large recurring musical element, namely the music of Isolde's Transfiguration. As is well known, the Transfiguration music begins life as a 24-bar rounded melody ('So stürben wir, um ungetrennt') introduced by Tristan within the Act II love-duet, repeated by Isolde and Tristan, and then developed by the two of them in the duet's rapturous ending section. All of this music returns at length in the orchestra at the end of Act III, substantially unchanged up to some added cadential pages at the end; Isolde sings her new words ('Mild und leise') to new counterpoint set against what is now the orchestral melody. But whereas the Transfiguration music is lyrical in origin and vocal in concept, the Prelude complex is quintessentially orchestral. It is not music to be sung through, to one set of words or another. If the aggregate of orchestral ideas in the Prelude is to recur *en bloc*, it needs to accommodate words in the interstices. Through those words the recurring music interacts with and controls the developing dramatic action.

Themes with pregnant rhythmic halts in them are a well-known Beethovenian speciality. That great Romantic favourite the Sonata in D minor, Op. 31, No. 2, has fermatas in its opening theme which are unexpectedly filled by long, explicitly recitative-like passages when the theme returns at the recapitulation. Wagner prized another famous place of the same kind, the brief oboe cadenza in the first movement of the Fifth Symphony. After experiencing 'the inspired delivery of the great Schroeder-Devrient', wrote Wagner in his essay 'On Conducting',[5]

> I could no longer bear hearing that passage thrown away as it invariably was. Furthermore, my handling of it made me realize the importance of the first violins' fermata in the corresponding passage in the exposition; and the powerful impression from those two apparently insignificant details let to a fresh understanding of the movement as a whole.

Fresh understanding – and, it may be, fresh inspiration for work of his own.

Indeed, the tremendous return of the opening music at the climax of the *Tristan* Prelude, discussed above, can be seen as Wagner's inspired misreading, as the American critic Harold Bloom would say, of the triumphant recapitulations so typical of Beethoven, exemplified by the Fifth Symphony. The insistent A♭–F'–E'–D♯' in the horns chromaticizes the even more insistent A♭'–A♭'–A♭'–F' in the horns, etc., just before Beethoven's recapitulation. If it seems strange to think of Beethoven's Fifth as a model for certain aspects of the *Tristan* Prelude, consider (for certain other aspects) this passage from Act I, Scene 3 of *Don Giovanni* (Ex. 3.3).

Ex. 3.3

4

Each of the two versions of the Prelude complex heard within the Prelude is drawn upon in the course of the opera – the 'timidest avowal' and the 'terrible outpouring'. Whereas the long melody comprising 'So stürben wir' and its developments returns in the opera just once, at length, and substantially unchanged, the Prelude complex returns many times in many varied forms: varied in metre, rhythm, tempo, dynamics, orchestration, with the addition of counterpoints, and so on. These variations supply new meanings to each of the dramatic situations they articulate, while at the same time drawing them all together. Interestingly, the Prelude complex usually remains unvaried in pitch and harmony. In theoretical parlance, pitch (pitch-class) and harmony serve here as the basic referential parameters.

A final word about 'So stürben wir': Wagner used the one return of this music to make a major dramatic point in *Tristan und Isolde* – indeed, *the* major point. Isolde's Transfiguration is the action (or passion) that complements and fulfils Tristan's death in her arms a few minutes earlier. Likewise, returns of the Prelude complex in what we may call its 'strong' form – a form in which all its components are emphatically present – articulate other important dramatic junctures. Put more accurately, returns of the Prelude complex in its strong form allowed Wagner to define certain points in the drama as the principal ones.

One principal point is singled out in each act (the drama of *Tristan und Isolde* consists largely of psychological action that precipitates one momentous event in each of the three acts).[6] In Act I and Act III, the points in question are obvious enough: the drinking of the love-potion in Act I and the death of Tristan in Act III. In Act II, the point chosen is less obvious, and will bear some discussion later in this chapter: the return comes not at the interruption of Tristan and Isolde's tryst by Marke and his hunting party, nor at the stabbing of Tristan by Melot, but rather at Tristan's response to Marke's extended reproach.

In Act I, what is recalled is the 'terrible outpouring' from the end of the Prelude. The harmonic preparation is the same, the dynamic is *fortissimo*, and Wagner contrives a *slancio* for the beginning that tops even the blaring horns of the Prelude ... by the simple expedient of having Isolde actually sing the opening motif ('Ich trink' sie dir!'). There follows, after the quick *diminuendo*, Wagner's most extreme

Ex. 3.4

distention of the gaps built in to the Prelude complex at its opening, 'timidest avowal' appearance. After a new fermata on the first 'Tristan' chord, the original rest of bars 3–4 (see Ex. 3.1) expands to ten bars full of slow orchestral music with stage directions:

> Then [Isolde] throws away the goblet. They both shudder, and gaze into one another's eyes with the utmost emotion ... their death-defiant expression changes to the glow of passion.

Shuddering is registered by a *pianissimo* tremolo slide in the cellos, death-defiance by a portion of the impressive 'Todgeweihtes Haupt! Todgeweihtes Herz!' motif (sung by Isolde in Act I, Scene 2), and the growing passion by the second sequential appearance of the opening motif. Trembling and tight heart-clutching, prescribed at a point corresponding to the rest in bars 7–8 of the Prelude, receive similar musical representations. The sequel includes the fermatas of bars 11 and 13 (heard here for the last time in the opera), the deceptive cadence, and the cello melody, the latter now doubled by dissociated gasps from the embracees – 'Tristan!', 'Isolde!', and so on (see Ex. 3.4).

The shenanigans in this scene, perhaps, have always been an embarrassment to Wagnerians. Ernest Newman, for one, averted his eyes while taking a mean swipe at the singers of *Tristan*, rather than the composer:[7] 'There follows the episode – generally an awkward one on the stage – that makes heavier demands on the singers as actors than any other situation in Wagner's works, demands which not one Tristan or Isolde in a hundred can meet.'

Or perhaps Wagner's musical semaphoring of onstage gestures is accepted by today's unembarrassable opera-goers as a matter of course, in much the same way they savour the dramatic values of accompanied recitatives in Handel. Let us hope so: for the drinking of the love-potion must be understood and, if possible, experienced as a crucial moment in Act I. As the climactic resolution of fifty-odd minutes of psychological action, it stands out as the most grandiose of the many returns of the Prelude complex that Wagner planned for the opera as a whole.

So potent is this return that it produces a sort of aftershock a minute later, when a headlong version of the Prelude complex underpins the lovers' hasty little duet. We must call this a 'weak' return, in as much as the opening motif – the one Isolde had sung to the words 'Ich trink' sie dir!' – gets lost in all the excitement.

5

In Act III, at Tristan's death, the return of the Prelude complex in its 'strong' form has clear points of contact with the Act I return discussed above. Again the opening rides the surge of a climax, and again the 'Todgeweihtes Haupt' motif is present. Played by the trumpets *fortissimo*, this motif serves to introduce the return, overlapping with it in a violent (and barely grammatical) fashion. While in a sense Wagner wanted to project the nexus of love and death at every moment in *Tristan und Isolde*, first and foremost he needed to draw the connection both at and between the climax points of Acts I and III, the drinking of the love-potion and the death of Tristan (see Ex. 3.5).

Ex. 3.5

After its crashing entrance, the music of the Prelude complex is compressed as never before; this is admirably matched to the urgency and agony of the dramatic situation. (Contrast this with the slow-motion effect in Act I.) But the passage is marked with a long *allargando* and *diminuendo*, so that by the time the deceptive cadence arrives, it has completely lost its typical sexually-tinged surge to a *fortissimo*. Delayed by long extensions of the cadential melody-notes B" and A" – in effect, written-out fermatas – the cello melody that promised the continuation of the passion comes exceptionally late. It is also exceptionally slow ('Sehr langsam'). Again recalling Act I, Tristan gasps the one word 'Isolde!' against the cello melody, which breaks off graphically, only-too-graphically at the precise moment of his decease. 'Isolde!' is sung to the notes E' and D' marked with actual fermatas, echoing the written out fermatas on B" and A" just beforehand.

It's been a long evening for Tristan, but he must try to extend those fermatas as long as he can:[8]

> Hold that fermata of mine! Cling to it . . . as though you were wringing the last drop of life out of it. I was dividing the seas in order to behold the abyss below. I was parting the clouds in order to behold the shining sun and the blue sky.

Also sprach Richard Wagner: though not, it is true, in connection with any of the fermatas in his opera. He was speaking in Beethoven's name about the fermata at the beginning of the Fifth Symphony.

Over the full course of *Tristan und Isolde*, the rhythmic dynamic of the Prelude complex has been almost exactly inverted. Originally this music moves haltingly, with cryptic gaps and fermatas. It achieves its true stride only with the deceptive cadence and the cello melody, which surges forward confidently as if the emotion it portrays will never cease. When Isolde enters in Act III, the music flows with painful rapidity, gradually braking into the drawn-out deceptive cadence and the very slow, late-entering, fermata-studded cello melody. With Isolde's 'Ha!' the music ceases entirely – and is sealed off from the sequel by one more fermata. Isolde should cling to that one, too.

6

Act II of *Tristan und Isolde* has largely a different thematic vocabulary from Act I. Act II is about Night and Day, the latter representing everything the lovers must reject, and while there is still much talk about love and death, these ideas have acquired new meanings and new music. Death is now seen as transcendence and release, not as something ominous and to be feared – the clear message of 'Todgeweihtes Haupt! Todgeweihtes Herz!', a motif seldom heard in Act II. Nor is any of the Prelude music much in evidence. Therefore the Prelude complex makes a particularly strong effect when it returns towards the end of the act.

This happens after the ten-minute reproach by King Marke, when Tristan speaks only cursorily to Marke before turning to Isolde: 'O König, das / kann ich dir nicht sagen; / und was du frägst, / das kannst du nie erfahren' ('O King, this I cannot tell you, and what you would ask, you can never experience'). On one level – the level of everyday morality and etiquette – these words administer an intolerable snub, and no doubt that is how Melot takes them.[9] The audience, however, witnesses more than a breakdown of normal human relations. We experience a rupture of the opera's basic dramaturgical fabric. In Wagner, everybody *always* responds when they are addressed, usually at length. Tristan even finds the time to frame a rejoinder to Melot's challenge at the end of the present act; and in the next one he mumbles a response to Kurwenal's chatter when he is barely out of his coma. His refusal to engage with Marke articulates a moment of major importance to the drama. For although the lovers have talked a good deal about rejecting the world of Day, this is the moment when talk gives way to action.

The breach of the dramaturgical norm is enforced by the regressive music. It is as though Wagner has directed the conductor to close the score and turn back to page one. What returns is – for the first time – the 'timidest avowal': the dynamic is *pianissimo*, once again, and the spare scoring is very similar (with the Prelude's unaccompanied cellos replaced by an unaccompanied English horn). The original rests in the model are filled by declamatory recitative. They still sound or can sound relatively unmetred because Tristan stumbles through the 6/8 music in 4/8 time, his words dazed and faltering (see Ex. 3.6).

Tristan is experiencing a trauma here that prefigures the plunge into *Urvergessen* that ensues when he falls upon Melot's sword. What occupies Tristan at this moment – and surely Isolde too – is not Marke's reproach, not the memory of love acknowledged with the drinking of the love-potion, but rather an acceptance of that death-dedicated passion which existed between them long before the action of the opera began. Only on some such grounds can we rationalize the

Ex. 3.6

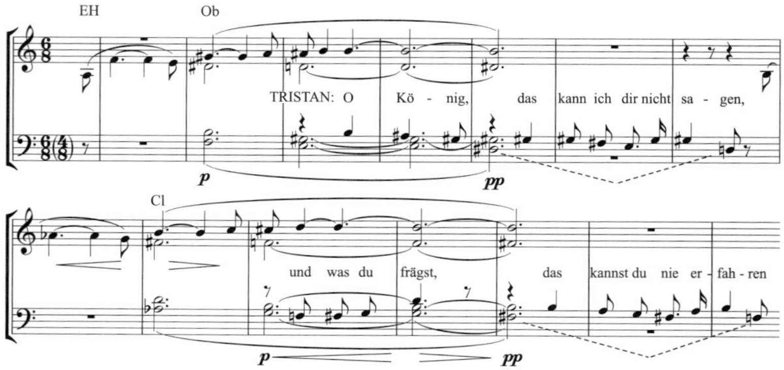

shock caused by the seeming inhumanity of Tristan's extraordinary snub. Tristan has dropped out of Act II; though his larynx may be on stage, his musical presence is back in the inchoate psychic well-spring of the drama before the curtain has even lifted.

As a rule, the Prelude complex in its returns remains unvaried in pitch and harmony; but the Act II return is an exception that proves the rule. It does so with a little demonstration of Wagnerian harmonic virtuosity. Nineteenth-century composers learned that dissonances can be made to resolve not only to consonances, but also, and with interesting results, to weaker dissonances. Here Wagner offers a two-stage resolution from a 'Tristan' chord (dissonant) to a dominant-seventh chord (dissonant, but less dissonant) to a six-four chord (still less dissonant). The effect of the extra chord added to the first two sequential cells is twice to transmute the gloomy yearning of the original model into numb desolation. The catatonic way in which Tristan cancels these two extra harmonies before proceeding with the sequence (as shown in Ex. 3.6 by dotted lines) is another symptom of his breakdown.

This harmonic variation, however, is as nothing compared to the harmonic variation which overcomes this version of the Prelude complex at its destination. This is now radically and luminously transformed. The deceptive cadence that prepares the destination changes, and opens not upon the expected diatonic cello melody, but upon another diatonic melody in another key.[10] The key, A♭, is the key of the love-duet, and what Tristan turns to here as he turns to Isolde (he has momentarily recouped from his trauma) is music first

Ex. 3.7

Ex. 3.8

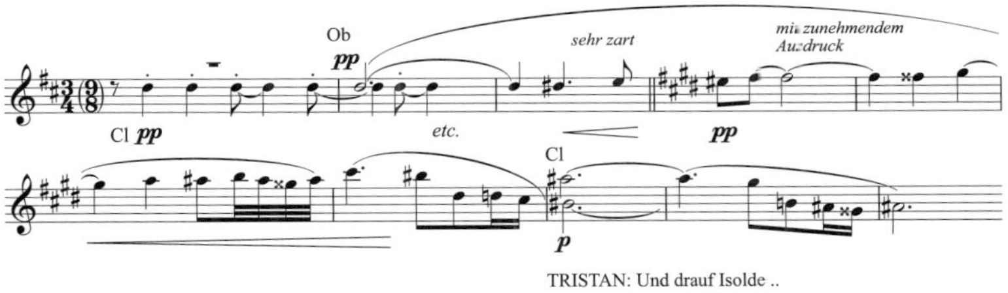

heard on that occasion. Dubbed 'Felicity' by Lavignac – one of his egregiously Victorian labels – this music coming here and now registers irony and pathos.[11] Its meaning deepens as 'Felicity' turns to 'Death the Liberator' (see Ex. 3.7).

There is a beautiful remote echo of this new destination early in Act III. At the next appearance of the Prelude complex a 'weak' return is heard when Tristan swoons and Kurwenal, fearing for his life, listens anxiously for his heartbeat. As a forecast of Tristan's actual death, this 'weak' return obviously serves as a forecast of the 'strong' return on that occasion. In technical terms, however, it has more in common with the Act II return: the opening is very quiet; the basic cell receives another new harmonic resolution; recitative (no fewer than ten lines of it, on this occasion) fills the gaps between the cells; and once again the destination is neither the original diatonic cello melody nor the original key. The destination is, in fact, not even diatonic. Oboe and overlapping clarinet play a sweetly attenuated variant of Tristan's most recent chromatic motif, first sung at his greatest epiphany about the love-potion ('Ich selbst, ich hab' ihn gebraut!'). This materializes over an excruciatingly prolonged bass F♯ (see Ex. 3.8).

Ex. 3.9

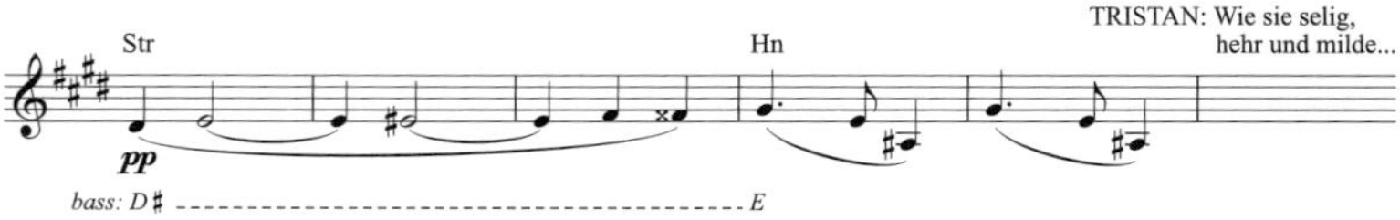

But the true, stable destination of the Prelude complex comes a phrase or two later, after a new deceptive cadence: a recall of the 'Felicity' music which was heard at the analogous point in Act II. Tristan is about to begin one of his most moving solos (see Ex. 3.9).

This is admittedly to stretch the term 'Prelude complex' and the concept behind it rather far. And indeed, all technical and quasi-technical terms have to be stretched hard to keep up with Wagner's mature practice: one thinks of terms such as 'leitmotif', 'period', and 'tonality'.

7

The 'art of transition', Wagner wrote in a much cited letter of 29 October 1859 to Mathilde Wesendonck, was the secret behind his musical form. This essay has attempted to analyse the art of variation that Wagner also developed at that time, in the course of composing the opera so closely bound up with Mathilde.

Variation is meant here in the most compendious sense, to cover changes in all possible parameters: melody, harmony, texture, dynamics, rhythm, pace, affect and others. For flexibility, range, ingenuity and sheer imaginativeness, it would be hard to cite a richer example of Wagner's art of variation than that applied to the complex train of musical ideas at the beginning of the *Tristan* Prelude. There is nothing quite like it elsewhere in his work, nor, perhaps in anybody else's. What is special about these variations is that the 'theme' consists of so many different elements in a directed series, and that in the variations, while the elements are generally all in place, their *affect* and that of their series is so richly varied.

On a less technical level, analysis can also point to the way these variations contribute to Wagner's musical dramaturgy. When in the Prelude the 'timidest avowal' of love moves in short order to love's 'terrible outpouring', one phase of the opera's action is forecast or epitomized (one thinks, as maybe Wagner did, of the trumpet call in the Overture to *Leonore* No. 3). At our first sighting of Tristan soon after the curtain rises, when Brangaene draws the inner curtain on the marquee, a 'weak' return of the Prelude complex accompanies Isolde's first oblique reference to her love ('Mir erkoren . . .'). In this compressed, understated return, the third sequential cell is replaced by Isolde's singing of 'Todgeweihtes Haupt! Todgeweihtes Herz!' Then the cello melody comes with its death-tinged minor-mode inflection (Ex. 3.2b). The association with death established in this way resonates at several other returns, among them another 'weak' one in Act I when the women discuss the casket of philtres. Here the recitatives 'Kennst du der Mutter Künste nicht', etc., fill the gaps in the original complex.

The 'terrible outpouring' version of the Prelude complex – but without its fateful minor-tinged conclusion – resonates hugely during the drinking of the love-potion in Act I and at Tristan's death in Act III. In the first case, Wagner also labours to project the lovers' confusion and excitement by means of multiple musical gestures tucked in between the components of the Prelude complex. In the second case, the pathetic reversal of the rhythmic dynamic terminates in the cut-off at Isolde's 'Ha!' (Ex. 3.5), which depicts the literal death of Tristan, yet also makes clear that this can be no final conclusion. It is only Tristan who expires in the grip of 'the most terrible outpouring of an avowal of hopeless love': Isolde's Transfiguration is required to complete Wagner's scheme.

The Act II return is perhaps the most interesting, registering as it does not an immediate emotional reaction but an emotional state that has had time to sink in. Things have been registering on Tristan for ten minutes. Hence the dryness of the recitative and of the 'extra' chords, and hence also the freedom to resolve not in the familiar cello melody but in another, more recent and poignant one. And the reflection of all this in Act III, where Tristan swoons, is at once the quietest and most subtle of all the returns.

What analysis of this or any other kind cannot do, of course, is direct the way the listener will respond to these returns, to the blunt ones as well as to the subtle. Such responses – of acceptance, submission, enchantment, indifference, rejection – will determine how far we are able to enter into the world-view of *Tristan und Isolde*. Things are safe enough with the first return, the variation within the Prelude itself. If one may judge, as seems fair enough, from the perennial success of the Prelude and Transfiguration in the concert hall, this maintains its canonic status as one of the most unshakably convincing strokes in Wagner. And once the listener-spectators have submitted so far to the famous Wagnerian magic, it is hard to see how they can fail to thrill at the return of this music when Tristan is first discovered, standing silently at the ship's stern, Isolde meanwhile pronouncing her cryptic omens. They may find the magic wearing perilously thin at the kiss at the end of Act I; and the spell may snap completely for a moment at Tristan's death – only to return in full force, it must be hoped, during the Transfiguration.

Most problematic is the crux in Act II: most problematic, and also most critical for our acquiescence to the world-view of *Tristan und Isolde*. Wagner's use of the Prelude complex confirms Tristan's non-response to Marke as a dramatic turning-point second to none in the opera. To be sure, no one drinks, dies, extinguishes torches, or suffers discovery, but Tristan by mentally rejecting the world of Day takes an active, positive step of the first importance. This positivity is crucial, for while it is all very well to say (and, as Wagner does, to show) that Tristan and Isolde have been caught in a permanent and permanently doomed love from before the action started, *Tristan* is a drama and a drama has to hinge on nodes of immediate action. Music which, at the start of the Prelude, had haltingly represented that love returns in an extraordinary variation to clarify the turning-point. It is not too much to say that ultimately our response to this variation will determine our belief in Wagner's dramatic vision.

4 *In the realm of the senses: sight, sound and the music of desire in* Tristan und Isolde

THOMAS GREY

In a brief disquisition 'On the Term "Music Drama"' from 1872, Wagner makes a contemptuous reference to one of his many outspoken critics, Wilhelm Heinrich Riehl, 'who somewhere has complained that his faculties of seeing and hearing fail him' when confronted with the works of this composer.[1] The essay is a response to the neologism *Musikdrama* as a designation for Wagner's 'post-operatic' musical stage works, already in common use despite its lack of a pedigree in his theoretical writings and its absence from the title pages of his libretti or scores. 'But then what', he asks, 'should we name such an inaudible and invisible thing? I am almost inclined to commit myself to the visible quality alone and stay with the term *Schauspiel*' – that is, the standard German word for a spoken drama, one that conjoins two nouns commonly used in English to denote stage spectacle or drama: 'show' and 'play'. Alluding to his etymology of drama, earlier in the essay, as deriving from the Greek root signifying the representation of human deeds or actions, he concludes: 'I would gladly think of my dramas as "deeds of music made visible"'.[2]

The phrase is both unwieldy and more than a little pretentious, as even Wagner realizes when he goes on to dismiss it, half-deprecatingly, as 'a regular art-philosophical title to grace the catalogue of some future Polonius at one of our artistically inclined courts'.[3] He also registers the irony of suggesting a *visually* articulated conception of drama in the case of a work such as *Tristan und Isolde*, where the subconscious, invisible workings of the Schopenhauerian Will seem to override any sort of concern for theatrical spectacle or conventional stage action. Wagner underlines this incongruity at the end of his essay 'On the term "Music Drama"' when he ironically re-imagines the climactic centre of *Tristan* in terms of standard grand-operatic dramaturgy. It would have been a simple matter, he suggests, to set Act II against a brilliant court ball, 'during which the illicit lovers could lose themselves in some convenient little arbour or shrubbery at the appropriate moment, where their discovery would generate a suitably scandalous impression and the whole apparatus that goes with that'. The 'apparatus' he alludes to is the grand operatic ensemble of shock and indignation, followed by a thrilling *stretta* in which the lovers, their confidants, the villain (here Melot), and the victim (here King Marke), would simultaneously express their contrasting emotions in parallel strophes over a series of raucously extended cadences. 'Yet instead', Wagner concludes, 'almost nothing but music occurs in this act, and unfortunately, so much of it and of such a kind as to incapacitate the aural faculties of Herr Riehl – and more's the pity, considering that there is so little to look at'.[4]

Tristan und Isolde is indeed notorious for the obsessively 'inward' character of its drama, and the overwhelming paucity of traditional dramatic intrigue, action or spectacle – the premise of Wagner's ironizing comments at the end of the essay just cited. The roots of the work go back to Wagner's first immersion in the philosophy of Schopenhauer in 1854, at a time when he had largely removed himself from contact with the theatre for over five years and had recently renounced the whole aesthetic foundation of contemporary opera at great length in the treatise *Opera and Drama* (1851–2). Even before drafting the libretto, Wagner began developing *Tristan* in the form of musical motifs and a general musical mood, as testified by several well-known letters and sketches.[5] Drama as articulated by words and visual action would seem to be entirely subordinated here to a drama of ideas and emotions, embodied in a tremendous network of enigmatic musical motifs, complex harmonic progressions, shifting instrumental timbres, and impassioned singing. As Wagner himself put it: the very core of the work consists of 'almost nothing but music'.

And yet, despite the signal absence of traditional action or spectacle in *Tristan*, the drama is structured to a significant degree by a dialectic of vision and hearing, the very faculties its performance had so severely tried in Wagner's critic W. H. Riehl. It might seem merely tautological, of course, to say that a drama (whether spoken or sung) is articulated by sight and sound. My point is rather that *Tristan und Isolde* deploys the senses of sight and sound in a distinctively *thematic* way, complementing to some extent the lack of conventional dramatic interest, but also relating to fundamental themes of the drama itself. In what follows I want to suggest some ways in which *Tristan* might be interpreted through the structural oppositions it presents between the visible and invisible, and between what is heard and what is silent. Further, I will suggest that a process of conflating or synthesizing sight, sound and the other modes of sensory perception is initiated in the course of the central love scene of Act II, though only completed in Isolde's final 'Transfiguration' (the so-called *Liebestod*), just as this final episode of the opera completes the musical process initiated, but drastically interrupted, in that epic 'love-duet'.

Invisible voices and the 'veil of *Maya*'

Each of the three acts of *Tristan und Isolde* begins with an 'acousmatic' effect, in the language of film theory: an unaccompanied voice or solo instrument issuing from some real, phenomenal presence within the broader fictional world of the drama, but a presence that remains invisible to the audience, as it does to the characters on stage.[6] In each case, this music directs our attention beyond the visible frame of the stage and proscenium-arch towards some higher, deeper or wider dimension of the imaginary space of the drama. It is as if Wagner is, among other things, teaching us a fundamental lesson about his music-drama: behind the world of appearances, the visible mimesis of the drama, there is another dimension of sounds, of music we should attend to, and more closely. But, as we also learn from the example of the opera's three act-beginnings, interpreting the true meaning of this hidden sound-world can be a challenge. There is no simple dichotomy of 'lying' appearances (the visible world), on one hand, and a musical or sonorous 'truth' behind them, on the other, despite what Wagner says to this effect in his Schopenhauerian 'Beethoven' essay.[7] The world of sounds may not 'lie' outright, as the daylight world is accused of doing, but its signs and meanings are still far from transparent or unambiguous.

When the curtain rises on Act I of *Tristan und Isolde* we hear the unaccompanied voice of a young sailor aloft in the rigging of Tristan's ship, singing to a strange, disjointed series of chromatically inflected phrases of the 'wild Irish maid' left at home, and of her sighs which he imagines wafting across the waters to fill the sails of the ship, driving it eastwards to Cornwall. Act II begins with the antiphonal echoes of hunting horns behind the scenes: the aural trace of King Marke's nocturnal hunting party gradually receding into the distance. At the outset of Act III we hear another melancholic folk-like improvisation, even more weirdly distorted and distended than the sailor's song of Act I: the 'old, sad tune' ('alte, ernste Weise') of the piping shepherd, played by an offstage English horn.[8] Like the horn calls of Act II, the 'alte Weise' functions as a crucial acoustic sign within the drama. The horn calls warn Isolde of the proximity of Marke and his company, hence the necessity of deferring the *visual* sign for Tristan to appear (extinguishing the torch that burns outside her chamber). Like the sailor's song in Act I, the shepherd's 'sad tune' of Act III signifies not a presence, but an absence: in this case the continued absence of Isolde's ship from the horizon where the mortally wounded Tristan desperately longs for it to appear.

All three of these 'acousmatic' musical effects are subsequently woven into the leitmotivic orchestral fabric of the respectively ensuing scenes with increasing musical and psychological complexity. At the same time, each of these examples emerges from and/or interacts with the music of the respective instrumental preludes in significant ways, significant among other things for how we might perceive the relation of the audible and the visible dimensions of the drama. In each case, the 'natural' though as yet invisible music heard as the curtain rises functions as a kind of transition from the wholly non-visual, 'noumenal' expressive realm of orchestral music (the orchestral preludes) into the visible, phenomenal world of the drama. In Schopenhauerian terms, these passages of unaccompanied, unseen music, attributable to specific dramatic agents, lead us from the immediate representation of passions or feelings (the inchoate workings of the Will) in the orchestra to their indirect representation in the drama, i.e., the Will as embodied in individuated physical appearances. As the material of aesthetic artifice, the settings, props and characters of the drama represent the contingency of the material world of appearances altogether, in the Platonic-Kantian metaphysical tradition adopted by Schopenhauer. Those 'shadows' we see on stage, despite their corporeal reality, bear the same relation to the noumenal reality of the music sounding behind or beneath them as do the perceptible 'shadows' of the physical world to the Platonic 'ideas'.

In *Tristan und Isolde* the stage curtain thus acts something like the 'veil of *Maya*', the figure Schopenhauer borrows from the Hindu *Vedas* and *Puranas* to signify the illusory world of phenomenal appearances vis-à-vis the fundamental energies of the Will that generate all phenomena and govern them at every level. But the resemblance is an inverted one. While the curtain is drawn, during the orchestral preludes, we experience a brief aural 'glimpse' into the noumenal world behind appearances. Then when the curtain rises, the 'veil of *Maya*' descends: the world of visible phenomena is superimposed on the sounding representation of the Will, the dimension of inner urges and feelings embodied by the orchestra. Here too, Wagner's game with 'acousmatic' voices or melodies serves a transitional function. At the juncture between orchestral prelude and musical drama, the audience as well as the characters on stage are momentarily caught up in a liminal dimension between sound and sight, between the Will itself and its external manifestations.

The sailor's song in Act I is a calculated provocation. Isolde is correct in identifying it as such, even though she misinterprets it, mistakenly believing that it is addressed to her: 'Wer wagt mich zu höhnen?' ('Who dares to mock me?'). For generations, operas had almost invariably opened with lusty, full-voiced choruses, backed up by all the orchestral resources at hand, wooing the audience with a vivid scenic-musical impression. *Tristan* begins instead with this single invisible, unaccompanied voice, chanting a strange song without a clear key (equivocating between C minor, E♭ major, G minor, and B♭ major), metrically indeterminate (with its fermatas and internal shift from 3/4 to 4/4) and irregularly phrased (see Ex. 4.1).

Ex. 4.1 Sailor's song

Granted, the Prelude to Act I hardly leads us to expect a chorus of jolly peasants or carousing courtiers to set things in motion. But even within the radically unique context created by the Prelude, the attenuated aural gesture of the song is a surprise, a provocation, a jarring contrast to the intensely lush, passionate orchestral outpouring that has preceded it.

Within Wagner's oeuvre itself the Prelude to Act I is also *sui generis*, not only because of its famous tonal indeterminacy, intensive motivic integration and formal distension, but also because of what we might call its resistance to imagery. From *Der fliegende Holländer* down to *Parsifal*, most of the overtures and preludes are intimately engaged with visual attributes of the dramas, adumbrating these by a whole range of timbral, gestural and dynamic means that are subsequently confirmed and further developed in the course of the drama. In *Tristan*, however, the Prelude to Act I remains resolutely 'invisible', unsusceptible to visual exegesis, even from the perspective of the opera as a whole. In this regard it is perhaps the definitive demonstration of that 'dimming of vision' ('Depotenzierung des Gesichts') Wagner identified as characteristic of the most intense mode of musical listening in his Schopenhauerian 'Beethoven' essay of 1870.[9]

The voice of the young sailor thus effects a shift of register, rather like the baritone recitative in the finale of Beethoven's Ninth Symphony following the gradated instrumental intonation of the hymn-like 'Joy' theme. In this case it is a transition not only from the orchestra to human voice, but also from the direct musical representation of the Will in the Prelude to the world of objectified, visible representations in the drama, as already suggested. As Beethoven does in his finale, Wagner links orchestra to voice by first reducing the former to a single, unison line: here a brief six-bar unison coda in cellos and basses (see Ex. 4.2) that subtly previews the pitch contours of the sailor's song as well as its distorted echo in the motif of Isolde's 'anger' enunciated by the strings almost immediately following.

Ex. 4.2

After the conclusion of the sailor's song, its theme is then briefly bodied out in the lower strings, sequentially developed and harmonized over a dominant B♭ as Brangaene scans the horizon and predicts an imminent landfall ('Blaue Streifen / steigen im Osten auf . . . vor Abend / erreichen wir sicher das Land'). Isolde seizes the theme from Brangaene and tears it asunder, as it were, in a sort of compact recitative and 'rage aria' ('Entartet Geschlecht!' . . . 'Hört meinen Willen, / zagende Winde'), as she recalls her abject situation. Significantly, this angry response entwines shreds of the sailor's song with seething iterations of the rising four-note chromatic cell from the opening measures of the prelude (see Ex. 4.3), traditionally labelled as the 'Desire' motif – a figure that, together with the celebrated 'Tristan' chord that launches it in the Prelude, will remain a fundamental component of the entire score.[10]

The ambiguity of its dramatic associations – with the alchemy of magic potions on one hand, and that of genuine psychological and

Ex. 4.3

erotic desire on the other – is already operative here, as Isolde rails against the ineffectual sorcery of her maternal line and struggles to master her conflicted feelings towards Tristan. When the sailor, still invisible in the rigging, reprises the central phrases of his song at the beginning of Scene 2, this is answered by a more explicit and extensive reprise of the Prelude's fateful opening, welling up in tremolo strings, *pianissimo*, from the same bass and cello unison that introduced the song earlier.

From this point on the motif of the sailor's song will recur only intermittently, mainly to remind Isolde – and the audience – of the presence of the outer world of phenomenal reality that she wishes to forget, even obliterate. When the theme is briefly taken up by Tristan's crew it remains at first a disembodied, acousmatic effect (the crew singing from the wings). Not until the very end of the act, after the metaphysical crisis represented by the drinking of the love (-death)-potion, does an accelerated version of the theme become attached to visible bodies, as the crew finally materializes in anticipation of landing ('Heil König Marke, Heil!'). Swept up in a confusion of those secret, invisible motives of death, desire, and the magical arts of psychic transformation, Tristan and Isolde are at the same time inundated by the brilliant C-major glare of the outer world. Thus, the theme that tentatively lifted the curtain on the visible world of the drama now celebrates an apotheosis of 'presence', both aural and visual, while the dialectic of inner Will and external appearances likewise achieves its most pointed musical articulation in these final, hectic moments of the act.

Throughout Act I, starting with the sailor's song, attention has been frequently focused on the offstage horizon, until Tristan's ship finally reaches the shores of Cornwall and the end of the act; the offstage trumpets and trombones that greet this landfall with repeated C-major fanfares create a kind of aural bridge between the ship's deck on stage and the *terra firma* just beyond. Later, Act III will be characterized by a still more intense scopic fixation with the horizon, as Kurwenal and the young shepherd watch for the arrival of Isolde's ship at Kareol, the thread on which the life of the mortally wounded Tristan remains hanging. At the opening of Act II, the antiphonal echoes of offstage hunting horns (over an extended pedal-point in the orchestral timpani) create a vivid impression of the forest depths that surround Isolde and Brangaene, similarly drawing attention to what lies beyond the visible frame of the stage. In the nocturnal setting of

Act II, however, Isolde and Brangaene must rely on their ears: when will King Marke's hunting party recede from earshot and the coast be clear for the lovers' rendezvous? Even their signal to Tristan is a matter of *extinguishing* the visible sign (the torch guarding Isolde's chamber), in keeping with the intense desire of both Tristan and Isolde to flee the visible world of 'day' in favour of darkness and interiority (the world of sound, and music). Tristan and Isolde are driven by a desire to escape into invisibility, one might say, to cast off their existence as individuated bodies, forced on them by the 'daylight' world of appearance, and to become indissolubly merged in a nocturnal realm of pure sound.

Whatever may be the greater 'truth' of the world of sound or musical tones, its signs are no more secure. If anything, musical signs are even more prone to subjective distortion or misreading (at least those occurring within the frame of the drama, as opposed to the orchestral leitmotifs). While Brangaene clearly hears the echoing horns, as we do, Isolde does not – she will not. And while the warning torch must be extinguished, Isolde can wilfully transform the horn calls into the rustling of leaves and the splashing waters of the spring (see Ex. 4.4). Isolde accuses Brangaene of hearing falsely, but Brangaene points, more persuasively, to the distorting power of subjectivity, more powerful precisely because sound, rather than sight, is the natural domain of subjective interiority: 'Dich täuscht des Wunsches / Ungestüm, / zu vernehmen, was du wähnst' ('Your impatient desire deceives you into hearing what you wish to hear'). Indeed, the only reliable, unambiguous musical sign here is the surging chromaticism of Isolde's desire, alternately rising and falling, that spills over from the orchestral Prelude.[11]

Unlike the sailor's song in Act I, the offstage horn calls of Act II do not continue to figure in the musical texture of the act after the opening moments. For that brief time, however, the horn calls engage in a more intense, subtler, more dramatically charged dialogue with the characters' perceptions and their own 'internal' music than anything that had been effected by the sailor's song in Act I. As a sign, this 'natural' music is more closely interrogated by its listeners (Isolde and Brangaene), and their listening further underlines the fact that aural signs, no less than visual ones, are equivocal, open to subjective reading and misreading.

The role of the shepherd's 'old, sad tune' ('alte, ernste Weise') in Act III presents something of a synthesis of the acousmatic effects in

Ex. 4.4 'Nicht Hörnerschall tönt so hold . . .'

the previous acts. Like the sailor's song in Act I, it is a long, drawn-out solo line intoned at length (though wordlessly, by an offstage English horn) before it starts to be worked into the dialogic texture of the scene. Like the sailor's song, too, it involves a strange mixture of folk-like stylistic markers: in this case, a fragment of the traditional Alpine *ranz des vaches* calls, well-known to nineteenth-century audiences as a pastoral topos, inflected with a queasy chromaticism that bridges the artificial *naïveté* of the folk-like material with the highly modern, 'sentimental' artifice of the *Tristan* idiom itself.[12] The role of an associative instrumental timbre (pastoral-melancholic English horn) recalls the function of French horns, as 'hunting horns', in Act II, likewise acting as an aural signal, though the quasi-vocal character of the tortuous, lamenting solo line here recalls (and intensifies) these qualities shared by the earlier sailor's song. The 'alte Weise' continues to function throughout the act as a natural, sounding sign, while it also seeps into the orchestral texture as a psychological-musical sign, or leitmotif, subject to dramatic-musical development. (In this way it again resembles the sailor's song.) The intense and subtle dialogic interaction between acoustic sign, characters and orchestra briefly modelled at the opening of Act II is carried on at much greater length: throughout Tristan's protracted 'delirium' and up through the alternate signal, the shepherd's 'merry tune' or 'lustige Weise', when that finally announces the sighting of Isolde's ship.

Altogether, the tension between seeing and hearing is wrought to an exquisite pitch in Act III. The magnificently attenuated gestures of the orchestral prelude convey the impression of a vast and desolate horizon, the steel-grey surface of the sea that symbolizes the bleak, empty day in contrast to the lush depths of night in the previous act ('Öd' und leer das Meer', the shepherd announces, 'The sea is desolate and empty'). Neither Tristan, prostrate throughout most of the act, nor the audience (in most productions) can see this horizon from the perspective of the vigilant shepherd. We are all dependent on the shepherd's musical signals as he reads the horizon for signs of Isolde's approach.

In this way attention remains focused – excruciatingly so – on the anticipated *sighting* of Isolde's ship during much of the act. 'Kurwenal, siehst du es nicht?' ('Kurwenal, do you not see it yet?') asks Tristan, desperately, at the first climax of his feverish delirium (answered in the negative by the shepherd's 'alte Weise' offstage). And then with redoubled desperation, after regaining consciousness for the last time: 'Das Schiff? Das Schiff? / Isoldens Schiff? / Du mußt es sehen! / Mußt es sehen! / Das Schiff? Sähst du's noch nicht?' ('The ship, the ship!? Isolde's ship? You must see it! You must! The ship? Don't you see it yet?') – at which emotional and musical breaking point the shepherd finally changes his tune, quite literally, to the quick triple-time 'lustige Weise'. Before each of these climaxes Tristan even imagines the sight of Isolde's ship for himself, too impatient for the actual event: at first in a brief frenzy ('Sie weht, sie weht, / die Flagge am Mast') and the second time in a calm, wholly internal vision that echoes music from the centre of the Act II love scene, now creating an isolated moment of tonal serenity in E major ('Wie sie selig, / hehr und milde / wandelt durch / des Meers Gefilde').

At the act's climax Wagner stretches out the tension of Isolde's arrival through a play of offstage appearance and disappearance. When Isolde finally does appear, Tristan recalls their ecstatic meeting in the previous act (as does the orchestra). But the intensity with which he has been *listening* for her arrival confuses his recollection. Referring to the visual signal for that earlier tryst (the extinguishing of the torch outside Isolde's chamber), he cries: 'Wie, hör' ich das Licht? / Die Leuchte, ha! / Die Leuchte verlischt. / Zu ihr! Zu ihr!' ('What, do I hear the light? The torch, ha! The torch goes out. To her! to her!') Sight and sound are confounded in Tristan's final moment, a synaesthetic confusion that heralds his ultimate physical collapse.[13] For of course, it is Tristan's own life, not the distant torch of Act II, that is about to be extinguished. The chaotic welter of orchestral motifs greeting Isolde's arrival quickly subsides to reveal those musical signs of the 'invisible' Will that opened the opera (see Ex. 4.5): the tentative figures of 'Suffering' (horns at bar 3 of system 2) and 'Desire' (woodwinds at bar 1 of system 3), followed by the final iteration in the opera of the upward-striving cello line (at its original pitch) associated with the fatally sympathetic 'Glance' (cellos at bar 1 of system 7) exchanged by the two lovers long before the opera began.

The history of a glance

Out of the roughly half-dozen important leitmotifs presented in the Act I Prelude this so-called 'Glance' motif is given the most explicit semantic 'exposition' in the opera, in the manner of the principal leitmotifs of the *Ring* operas.[14] The 'scopic' association indicated by the motif's traditional label ('Glance' or 'Look', or perhaps better, 'Gaze') derives from its rhetorically prominent statement near the centre of Isolde's expository narrative to Brangaene in Act I, explaining the troubled history between herself and Tristan.[15] Within that narrative, the motif is embedded inside what we could call a 'poetic-musical period' (to invoke the unit of musical-dramatic measure proposed by Wagner in *Opera and Drama*): a passage of thirty bars, closed at one end in E minor, in which the 'Glance' motif (played '*sehr*

Ex. 4.5 The 'Blick' ('Glance') motifs heard at Tristan's death

zurückhaltend' and '*ausdrucksvoll*' by a solo viola) is framed by the refrain-like material that begins and dominates the entire narration. The motif returns to round out this 'period', leading into its concluding cadence, where it also clinches its dramatic association by underscoring the accented word *Blick* itself: 'mit dem Blick mich nicht mehr beschwere' ('and trouble me no more with his gaze').

Ex. 4.5 (cont.)

In the text of this 'period' Isolde explains how she failed to wreak her intended vengeance on Tristan – the killer of her betrothed Morold – when the wounded, vulnerable Tristan looked pitifully into her eyes (the two statements of the 'Glance' motif within this passage are shown in Exx. 4.6a and 4.6b):

Ex. 4.6a

Ex. 4.6b

Von seinem Lager
blickt' er her, –
nicht auf das Schwert,
nicht auf die Hand, –
er sah mir in die Augen.
Seines Elendes
jammerte mich; –
das Schwert – ich ließ es fallen!
Die Morold schlug, die Wunde,
sie heilt' ich, daß er gesunde
und heim nach Hause kehre, –
mit dem Blick mich nicht mehr beschwere!

From his sickbed
he looked up –
not at the sword,
not at my hand –
he looked into my eyes.
His suffering
made me wretched;
the sword – I let it fall.
The wound Morold inflicted,
I healed it, that hale again
he could return home,
and trouble me no more with his gaze.

Paradoxically, this moment of intense, mutual scopic engagement – the drama's whole point of origin, in a sense – is a moment the audience never *sees* at all, but only hears about (in this narration). It is surely significant for the broader meaning of Wagner's drama, with its layering of Schopenhauerian resignation or renunciation of the Will over the plot motifs of the original legend, that the love of Isolde for Tristan is born not of desire, but of profound sympathy for his suffering. And while we will never see for ourselves this originary 'gaze', the attention commanded by Isolde's telling of it might alert us to the predominant role of 'looking' throughout Act I of the opera.

While there is indeed very little to look *at* in Act I of *Tristan*, as Wagner himself noted in his ironic response to his critic W. H. Riehl (in the 'Music Drama' essay), the *act* of looking plays a surprisingly significant role. Isolde's story about pardoning the wounded Tristan, after looking him in the eyes, immediately alerts Brangaene to her previous *failure* to see: 'O Wunder! Wo hatt' ich die Augen?' ('How strange! And where were my eyes?'). The action of Act I as a whole is articulated, as Arthur Groos points out (see pp. 42–4), by the shifting position of the tapestry or curtain that isolates Isolde and Brangaene from the view of others, or, when drawn, permits visual communication with Tristan and the rest of the ship. As the act opens, the invisible young sailor sings of his westward 'gaze' ('Blick') back towards Ireland, and the word *Blick* itself remains a kind of verbal leitmotif throughout the act – in the stage directions as much as in the verses of the libretto. Our first glimpse of Tristan finds him 'gazing pensively at the sea' (presumably in the direction of Cornwall, his destination); at the same time, at the beginning of Scene 2, Isolde's 'gaze' ('Blick') is trained on Tristan as she intones the ominous, oracular lines 'Mir erkoren, / mir verloren, / hehr und heil, / kühn und feig! / Todgeweihtes Haupt! / Todgeweihtes Herz!' ('Chosen for me, lost to me, great and glorious, bold and cowardly! Head consecrated to death! Heart consecrated to death!') to the opening motifs of the Prelude. And so on throughout the act: Isolde and Tristan remain intensely aware of each other's presence, at first mutually occluded from view, until they finally come face to face in the lengthy final scene (Scene 5). Throughout most of Act I, one might say, the intensity of their outward-directed gazing mirrors their determination *not* to look within themselves, *not* to scrutinize their internal motives and feelings.[16]

The turn, of course, comes with the drinking of the potion, after which Tristan and Isolde become and remain wholly preoccupied with 'inwardness', the true inner feelings at last disclosed to themselves and

Ex. 4.7

each other, although these feelings remain largely invisible and inscrutable to the others around them. Upon drinking to Tristan's *Sühne-eid* or oath of atonement ('Tristans Ehre – / höchste Treu! / Tristans Elend – / kühnster Trotz! . . . Vergessens güt'ger Trank, / dich trink' ich sonder Wank!')[17] – and in the process thoroughly confounding the motives of love and death, in both psychological and musical terms – Tristan and Isolde commit themselves to an almost exclusively inner-directed sense of vision for the rest of the drama. Yet it is also at this moment, or rather in the immediate aftermath of this moment, that for the first time the audience itself *sees* Tristan and Isolde exchange a version of that fateful glance of sympathy, love and mutual identification narrated by Isolde in the earlier scene to the significant accompaniment of the 'Glance' motif. The sight of their mutual gaze is at last accompanied, and confirmed, by that motif, which here (see Ex. 4.7) caps the protracted, fragmented and now gesturally accompanied reprise of the Prelude's motivic exposition (bars 1–17).[18] Throughout this musical reprise and dramatic 'realization' (in the terms of *Opera and Drama*) of the Prelude's tentative, foreboding, emotionally pregnant opening, the two figures – according to Wagner's stage directions – remain '*in the greatest state of excitement, though without moving, while gazing fixedly into each other's eyes, in which the expression of mortal defiance* ['*Todestrotz*'] *soon yields to one of fiery passion*'.

Of course, it is really the music that must show us this transformation of the lovers' mutual gaze, which could hardly be conveyed visually in the opera house by even the subtlest of singer-actors. And this occurs at the moment the 'Glance' motif spills over into an ecstatic *fantasia* on the whole set of Prelude motifs, now '*Lebhaft, mit Steigerung*' ('lively, and building') that forms the coda or stretta to the final scene of the act (from Tristan's line, 'Seligste Frau!'). This climactic re-enactment of their mutual gaze is thus a two-fold 'realization': not only does it define for us – make dramatically present – the meaning of the Prelude's mysterious, emotionally charged motifs; it also represents the moment at which Tristan and Isolde themselves finally realize, or admit to, their own hitherto suppressed desires.

After those climactic psychological-musical-dramatic 'realizations' at the end of Act I, the 'Glance' motif apparently ceases to be relevant to the drama. In fact, the motif almost disappears from the score altogether, apart from the moment of Tristan's death, mentioned above (at the last return of the original Prelude material). At this final juncture, where Tristan literally 'looks his last', two key moments from the history of the lovers – and of this motif – are recalled and superimposed, with a poignant irony. That original, unseen 'glance' or gaze of the sick Tristan searching the eyes and soul of Isolde is re-enacted here while Tristan, now dying in Isolde's arms, looks up to her a last time ('*sterbend zu Isolde aufblickend*'). And, while the original motivic sequence of the Act I Prelude is now condensed rather than protracted, as it had been after the drinking of the potion at the end of Act I, the frantic musical energy that ushers in Isolde here in Act III, the forceful eruption of the Prelude motifs in the orchestra and the halting, desperate 'Glance' itself all recall the climax of Act I, as well. Musically and dramatically, Tristan's death is an inversion, of sorts, of that earlier moment. Where the arching, drawn-out 'Glance' motif issued in a passionate avowal of love over a surging flow of 'endless melody' (a transformation of the Prelude motifs) toward the end of Act I, here the 'Glance' motif breaks off in silence (at Isolde's 'Ha!'), followed by a fragmentation of the musical discourse. Only with Isolde's Transfiguration is the full flow of the music finally re-established. The inversion is thematic, too. In Act I, there is an explosion of love where death was expected; in Act III, death interposes itself just as the two lovers are re-united. The invertible or complementary relation of the two terms, love and death, is of course a lesson Tristan and Isolde have learned in the meantime, and one on which they expatiate at length in the course of Act II.

Night vision

In Act II of *Tristan und Isolde* the lovers and the action as a whole recede from the visible world, at least until day breaks and their tryst is discovered by Marke and his hunting party. The long, rhetorically and musically abstruse episode following the lovers' reunion at the opening of Act II, Scene 2 (the so-called *Tagesgespräch* or 'discourse on day') attempts to stage a quasi-metaphysical flight from 'day', as symbol of the external world of individuated phenomena, into 'night', the realm of subjectivity and the symbol of a unified world of essences beyond the pale of mortal existence. The metaphorics of day and night so extensively developed here also articulate a rejection of the visible, through the emphatically reiterated dismissals of daylight in favour of darkness, and of illusory appearance in favour of a truth that can only be experienced and confirmed subjectively. It is in these terms, for example, that Tristan celebrates his and Isolde's conversion to being 'votaries of the night' ('Nachtgeweihte') in the final phase of their *Tagesgespräch* (the word 'Nachtgeweihte' here underscored by a sustained, full orchestral statement of the 'Tristan' chord):

O! nun waren wir	Oh, then we became
Nachtgeweihte!	votaries of the night!
Der tückische Tag,	The devious day,
der Neidbereite,	so prone to envy,
trennen konnt' uns sein Trug,	might seek to divide us with tricks,
doch nicht mehr täuschen sein Lug!	but could not deceive us with lies!
Seine eitle Pracht,	Its vainglory
seinen prahlenden Schein	and pompous show
verlacht, wem die Nacht	are derided by him whose sight
den Blick geweiht.	is dedicated to the night.[19]

The last two lines echo an idea expressed in Tristan's preceding speech (beginning 'O Heil dem Tranke!') in which he praises the potion for having opened to him the gates of death and therein a glimpse of the 'wondrous realm of night' ('Wunderreich der Nacht'), a glimpse afforded him by a metaphorical faculty of 'night vision':

Von dem Bild in des Herzens	From the picture held
bergenden Schrein	in my heart's safe-keeping
scheucht' er des Tages	[the draught] dispelled day's
täuschenden Schein,	illusory light,
daß nachtsichtig mein Auge	so that my eye's night vision
wahr es zu sehen tauge.	served to see it truly.

(The music again signals the fundamental affinity between 'night' and the developing sensibilities of Tristan and Isolde: the last two lines call up both the 'Tristan' chord and the sequenced 'Desire' motif from the Prelude, at original pitch.) Following the common mythical trope, Tristan renounces the sight of ordinary things to become truly 'visionary' – clairvoyant at a different, interior or transcendent level.

By the time they reach the languorous central phase of the scene, 'O sink' hernieder, Nacht der Liebe' (the expressive core of the opera), Isolde has followed Tristan's example. 'Bricht mein Blick sich / wonn'-erblindet, / erbleicht die Welt / mit ihrem Blenden' ('When my sight ceases, blinded by delight, the world's brightness pales'), they sing together. A further, climactic iteration of the 'Tristan' chord and a near-resolution of the 'Desire' motif articulate the end of the first large paragraph of this slow phase, as Tristan and Isolde anticipate a 'oneness' with each other and within the realm of undifferentiated being on the other side of existence: 'die uns der Tag / trügend erhellt, / zu täuschendem Wahn / entgegengestellt, / selbst dann / bin ich die Welt' ('Poised against [the world], with its lies and tricks, which day has falsely illumined, I myself become the world').

If Tristan and Isolde reject the outer, visible world of appearances in favour of an 'interior' subjective vision (Tristan's 'night vision') in Act II, we might ask whether their other senses – their hearing in particular – experience some kind of compensatory amplification. Do these characters, in other words, experience that 'debilitation of vision' ('Depotenzierung des Gesichts') of which Wagner speaks in the 'Beethoven' essay, the condition that allowed him to hear strange intimations of another world in the invisible nocturnal song of the Venetian gondoliers or the distant antiphony of Alpine shepherds?[20]

The answer might be an equivocal 'yes'. Above all, we can hear (and 'sense') in the music of their extended love scene that Tristan and Isolde have entered a realm in heightened sensory experience – that they experience the proximity of each other and of their immediate environment with a preternatural intensity. Their condition here, I would argue, is an approach to the condition ultimately achieved by Isolde in her Transfiguration at the end of the opera. On a strictly musical level, Wagner makes that point very clearly: the climactic phase of the whole love scene (beginning from 'So stürben wir, / um ungetrennt, / ewig einig / ohne End'') is, of course, interrupted, only to be 'recollected in tranquility' by Isolde in the Transfiguration and there brought to a final resolution.

This condition of transcendent oblivion – of oneness within the realm of pure Will beyond (or preceding) its phenomenal representation – is also figured as a collapsing of the individual senses into a sort of meta-sensory wholeness, a *Gesamtkunstwerk* of sensation.[21] Such a condition is only intimated in the love scene, anticipating its fuller realization in the Transfiguration. Moreover, the anticipation-realization model is also reflected in the motivic and harmonic relation of the respective episodes: in each case the motivic sequences of the 'Love-Death' or Transfiguration work their way by chromatic semitones from A♭ to B natural. But the key of B is only firmly established in the Transfiguration (from 'Höre ich nur diese Weise?'); and as a proper cadential goal, of course, it is only reached at the end of the opera. Still, this tonal goal *is* first suggested in the love scene, when, moving into the final ecstatic phase of the scene, Tristan and Isolde invoke the 'longed-for love-death' ('sehnend verlangter Liebestod') that will perfect their union. Their text here seems to be willingly submerged in the sequential swelling of the Transfiguration motifs (as we may interpret them, in hindsight), thickly scored and restlessly modulating.[22] Abandoning any kind of complete, autonomous syntax, the short four-syllable lines merely accumulate in a reckless pile of rhymes, semantically gesturing in the direction of a release – at once physical and metaphysical – of the mounting passion. Music and language alike become briefly unanchored in the frenzied intensity of the moment.

Another and perhaps better illustration of the lovers' liminal, strangely confused sensory condition in Act II is the episode of Brangaene's 'Watch Song' that gently punctuates their blissful communion. Brangaene's song, a version of the medieval *aubade* or *alba* warning illicit lovers of dawn's approach, is yet another 'acousmatic' effect, her voice drifting down to Tristan and Isolde from her invisible perch on the watchtower. Unlike the acousmatic song and signal in Acts I and III, however, this instance is not subject to misinterpretation, but instead to a wilful deafness, similar to Isolde's response to the distant horn calls at the opening of Act II. Also like the beginning of Act II, the deafness is to the *sense* of the signal, not to the sound *per se*. In each case the sound is filtered through the listener's consciousness, its foreboding message erased by means of a sonic transformation. We know that Brangaene's warning about the imminent approach of day has been heard, since Isolde afterwards dismisses the 'envious watcher', just as Tristan dismisses the day itself. But apart from several minor-mode inflections appropriate to the admonitory tenor of Brangaene's text, the vocal line is drawn out in a wholly beguiling manner, cloaked in some of the lushest, most seductive orchestral sonorities of the entire score (see below, p. 116). In contrast to the text, the music seems calculated to lure the two lovers into a state of blissful unconsciousness of the world rather than to warn them of impending dangers.

To judge by the seductive character of the vocal line and the orchestration, we are hearing this song from the perspective of Tristan and Isolde. The delicate harp arpeggios, the soaring line of *divisi* violins cushioned by undulating chordal figuration in violas and cellos, the oboes' gentle sounding of the 'Slumber' ('Liebesruh') motif that forms the subject of the lovers' discourse before and after this episode: none of these timbres or melodic ideas serves the message of Brangaene's words. Once again, desire has transmuted external sounds to suit the temperament of the listener. As Brangaene chided Isolde at the opening of the act: 'Your desire deceives you into hearing what you wish to hear'. To judge by what *we* hear, it is not that Tristan and Isolde's hearing is impaired, any more than the darkness has entirely shrouded their vision. Rather, in this 'wondrous realm of night' they hear, see, and feel only according to the new dimension of hyper-reality towards which they are striving, and which they (or at least Isolde) will reach at the conclusion of the drama. Brangaene's warnings are thus transformed by the altered sensory perception of her listeners into an ecstatic nocturnal reverie that merely draws them, and us, closer to the ultimate breach between phenomenal reality and that oceanic void Isolde finally discovers, or imagines, at the end.

Isolde's Transfiguration and the conflation of sensory experience

When Isolde brings about her own demise at the end of the opera, seemingly by sheer force of will, she also achieves the conflation of sensory experience into a higher, unified mode of perception that is anticipated, as suggested above, in the love scene of Act II. As also suggested, this deferred realization of a unified sensory perception accompanies the structural (melodic-harmonic) completion of a musical trajectory initiated in the duet, from 'So stürben wir, um ungetrennt' up to the catastrophic interruption. The synaesthetic unity that Isolde seems to experience and that she describes (or at least intimates) in her closing monologue is apparently a kind of threshold experience pointing the way to the ultimate state of harmonious resolution and 'oneness' that awaits her beyond, upon concluding her mortal existence and achieving the long-desired quiescence of the Will.[23]

The text of Isolde's Transfiguration is addressed to a handful of auditors around her: the drama's few survivors, whom she at this point, however, neither sees nor hears. The text is structured as a series of rhetorical questions. At first the questions are posed to this oddly 'absent' audience, but then (at 'Höre ich nur diese Weise?') they become reflexive. In the first two rhetorical 'periods' of the speech Isolde asks whether anyone else sees or hears what she does, describing sights and sounds that clearly do exist for her alone, emanating from some transcendental realm beyond the world of her audience. First she fantasizes a vision of Tristan's dead body:

Mild und leise	Mild and soft,
wie er lächelt,	how he smiles,
wie das Auge	how his eyes
hold er öffnet –	are fair and open –
seht ihr's, Freunde?	Do you see this, friends?
Seht ihr's nicht?	Don't you see it?
Immer lichter	Ever brighter,
wie er leuchtet,	how he shines,
sternumstrahlet,	ringed by starlight,
hoch sich hebt?	rising up –
Seht ihr's nicht?	do you not see this?
Wie das Herz ihm	How his heart
mutig schwillt,	bravely swells,
voll und hehr	full and regal
im Busen ihm quillt?	in his breast?
Wie den Lippen,	How from his lips,
wonnig mild,	blissfully mild,
süßer Atem	his sweet breath
sanft entweht: –	gently exudes –
Freunde! Seht!	Friends, look!
Fühlt und seht ihr's nicht?	Do you not feel and see this?

Isolde's vision of Tristan here moves from phenomenal reality (his peaceful smile in death, his eyes) to things she apparently imagines (his body 'glowing' and rising to a starry apotheosis, the swelling or heaving of his heart/breast, his expiring breath). As if correcting herself – realizing that no one, herself included, can really 'see' his breath – she adds, 'Do you not *feel* and see this?'

The subsequent 'period' of her text then addresses the *auditory* dimension of her 'vision' of Tristan's death and transfiguration:

Höre ich nur	Do I alone hear
diese Weise,	this melody,
die so wunder-	that so wonderfully
voll und leise,	and softly
Wonne klagend,	cries of bliss,
alles sagend,	saying all,
mild versöhnend	gently reconciling,
aus ihm tönend,	sounding from him
in mich dringet,	and within me,
auf sich schwinget,	rising up
hold erhallend	and echoing
um mich klinget?	all about me?

The rhetoric, to begin with, follows that of the preceding period: 'Do you not hear what *I* can hear?' But now Isolde becomes carried away by her own heightened perceptions, and in the course of this one extended rhetorical question she apparently loses any interest in her nominal audience, wholly enraptured by the mysterious 'music' that envelops her ('diese Weise, die so wundervoll und leise . . . um mich klinget'). We might fairly infer that Isolde becomes conscious of the 'noumenal' orchestral music surging beneath her, music that in theory exists only on the other side of the invisible theatrical 'fourth wall', the soundtrack that speaks to the audience but not ordinarily to the characters on stage.[24] As she begins her Transfiguration, leaving the ordinary phenomenal world for what lies beyond, Isolde suddenly hears the entire orchestra as a kind of 'acousmatic' musical effect. Surrounded and penetrated by these sounds, she abandons herself to their agency. Indeed, it seems to be this *music* that effects her Transfiguration.[25]

In the final 'period' of the text – the questions now apparently addressed to herself alone, in a state of ecstatic bemusement – Isolde completes the synthesis of sensory experience:

Heller schallend,	Brightly ringing
mich umwallend,	all about me,
sind es Wellen	are these the billowing
sanfter Lüfte?	of soft breezes?
Sind es Wogen	Are they waves
wonniger Düfte?	of blissful scents?
Wie sie schwellen,	How they grow
mich umrauschen,	and intoxicate me –

soll ich atmen, — should I breathe in,
soll ich lauschen? — should I listen?
Soll ich schlürfen, — Should I drink them in
untertauchen? — or dive beneath them,
Süß in düften — and sweetly
mich verhauchen? — expire in them?

The musical sounds (the mysterious 'melody' emanating from Tristan) are also breezes brushing her cheeks, sweetly perfumed (i.e., the senses of touch and smell), which she 'drinks in' (i.e., tastes?) before abandoning herself, body and soul, to this metaphysical ocean that exists beyond the realm of individuated appearances and beyond the pressures of the individual desiring Will:

In dem wogenden Schwall, — In the surging flood,
in dem tönenden Schall, — in the ringing sound,
in des Welt-Atems — in the world-breath's
wehendem All, – — infinite gasp –
ertrinken, — to drown,
versinken, – — to sink –
unbewußt, – — unconscious –
höchste Lust![26] — highest bliss!

Still situated as we are in the world she leaves behind, we cannot say for sure whether the collapsing of the individual senses in the synthetic experience of her Transfiguration adumbrates the condition of the world beyond, or merely characterizes the passage into it. Considering the famous, and emblematic, stilling of 'desire' figured in the final resolution of the 'Tristan' chord and of the rising chromatic oboe line ('Desire') in the opera's final bars (see Ex. 4.8), it is

Ex. 4.8

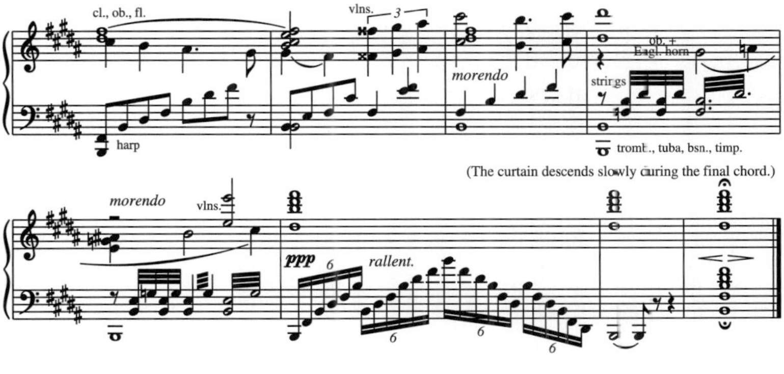

reasonable to suppose that the Nirvana achieved here involves leaving behind the world of sense-perception altogether ('unbewußt – höchste Lust!').

The senses are, after all, primary vehicles of the Will that constrains us at every turn in this life. At the same time, this intensified, quasi-metaphysical and pan-sensory communion with the deceased Tristan appears to be a necessary – and pleasurable – threshold state for Isolde. (We might recall that Wagner wished to teach Schopenhauer that sexual consummation, rather than being a sign of our enslavement to the Will, could actually figure our redemption from it.[27]) It is this brief moment of sensual clairvoyance that enables Isolde to achieve the ultimate bliss ('höchste Lust') of a realm *beyond* desire, and *beyond* the senses. Those of us left behind in this sublunar world can at least console ourselves in the meantime with the vicarious experience of that process in the music of Isolde's Transfiguration.

5 *A mantle of sound for the night: timbre in Wagner's* Tristan und Isolde

JÜRGEN MAEHDER

Two lovers, not knowing that each is beloved, believing rather that each is deeply wounded and despised, desire each other to drink the Death potion, on the pretext of being reconciled over their mutual injuries, but driven in truth by an unconscious motive: they wish for release by death from all further separation and pretence. The belief that death is near sets free their soul and brings them into a brief, terrible happiness, as if they really had escaped from day, from deception, even from life itself.

Nietzsche, 'Richard Wagner in Bayreuth', *Untimely Meditations*

1

Two attempts were made at the turn of the last century to capture the intoxicating effect of Wagner's *Tristan und Isolde* by rendering highpoints of the opera in hymnic prose. In Gabriele d'Annunzio's *Trionfo della Morte* (1894), the protagonists Giorgio Aurispa and Ippolita Sanzio read *Tristan* at the piano as a preparation for death;[1] Thomas Mann's *Tristan* (1903) – possibly a conscious and not unironical response to the aestheticism of d'Annunzio's heroes – also situates a couple at the piano, absorbed in playing *Tristan*.[2] Both texts reflect a literature whose longing for death, aestheticism and decadent eroticism has its roots in two seminal works written almost simultaneously in the mid-nineteenth century: Wagner's *Tristan und Isolde*, and – additionally – Baudelaire's *Les Fleurs du mal* (1857).[3]

In their feverish expectation of merging art and life, the lovers immersed in *Tristan und Isolde* at the piano nonetheless neglect the means by which Wagner's music casts its spell: the medium of orchestral sound. The flooding of Isolde's voice in waves of orchestral sound ('In des Wonnemeeres / wogendem Schwall, – / in der Duft-Wellen / tönendem Schall, / in des Welt-Atems / wehendem All – / ertrinken – / versinken – / unbewußt – / höchste Lust'[4]) also suggests the musical effect of this passage: the obliteration of subjectivity, completely enveloping the listener in a sonic continuum that paralyses all reflection. The first line of Baudelaire's poem *La Musique*, written at the same time, suggests this effect of Wagner's orchestral language: 'La musique parfois me prend comme une mer!' ('Music will often take me like the sea!')[5] In the essay 'Richard Wagner and *Tannhäuser*', Baudelaire described his reaction to the Prelude to *Lohengrin* in terms of an ethereal vision of light. It is introduced by a quotation from his sonnet 'Correspondances' from *Les Fleurs du mal*, the second quatrain of which could also stand as a motto at the beginning of Act II of *Tristan und Isolde*:[6]

Comme de longs échos qui de loin se confondent	As the long echoes, shadowy, profound,
Dans une ténébreuse et profonde unité,	Heard from afar, blend in a unity,
Vaste comme la nuit et comme la clarté,	Vast as the night, as sunlight's clarity,
Les parfums, les couleurs et les sons se répondent.	So perfumes, colours, sounds may correspond.

French symbolism reacted much more consciously to the sounds that rise from what d'Annunzio calls the 'Mystic Gulf'[7] than, for instance, contemporary manuals on instrumentation, whose terminology had already been rendered obsolete by the orchestral technique of *Lohengrin*. An interpretation of orchestration in *Tristan und Isolde*, accordingly, cannot be made without recourse to the most advanced European poetry of the time. Indeed, the rigorous phonetic structure of French symbolist language could even exemplify the novelty of sound structures in Wagner's score – the force that holds it together as a unit – and suggest some reasons for the impact of Wagner's orchestral idiom.[8]

This increased musical complexity (and not just the dissolution of traditional chordal structures and relationships presupposed by a musicology fixated on pitch relationships) provoked Ernst Bloch's observation regarding *Tristan und Isolde* as a 'transcendent opera'. Taking the love-potion as a point of departure, Bloch formulated the following interpretation of its sonic world:[9]

> What happens because of or beyond the Irish potion, however, is never action; it is not even a key, not even a catalyst, not even the sort of accident which is really not one and which tragic necessity involves as its accomplice; instead, just as a place one has never been can nonetheless be called home, it is only a temporal glimpse, a temporal derivate of what happens within eternity,

within the supratemporality, mythicality of love. Here two human beings advance into the night; they go from one world over into another, and otherwise nothing happens, as one should be able to recognize from the first act and certainly the last two acts, and nothing sounds but the music of their advance and their ultimate disappearance.

In approaching *Tristan und Isolde*, therefore, it may be useful to draw attention to the absence of traditional conflicts between characters. Rather, the orchestra emerges as the medium through which the protagonists' emotions are expressed, providing a subtext or psychological commentary on an action that withdraws largely into the inner life of the lovers. In the great fantasies on love and death in Acts II and III, when the syntax of the sung text disintegrates under the intensity of emotion, and the real dramatic action – the union of the two lovers – transcends what is possible to represent on stage, the primary expressive role passes to the orchestra, whose greater knowledge transforms action into musical episodes of a novelty that astonished even their creator.[10]

The dramaturgical peculiarities of this opera – e.g., the relegation of outer stage action to the periphery of each act, the almost complete lack of 'local colour', and the transposition of other incidents of the action to the psychic 'interior' of the characters[11] – all contribute to the absolute domination of the score, transforming personal constellations almost into an emanation, as it were, of the orchestral flow. This musical commentary, with which the 'knowing orchestra' ('wissendes Orchester') elucidates the inner life of the protagonists, required new compositional techniques in order to communicate complex forms of discourse with speech-like logical structure. Each act of *Tristan und Isolde* moves from 'Day', the desolate reality of existence, towards its transcendence in a gradual loss of reality. This process is interrupted in each act by an intervention from outside, which almost renders absurd the contrast between the dream world conjured up by the music, which the lovers regard as the only true and desirable reality, and the reality of the ship, Marke's court, and the castle at Kareol. The resulting inversion of perspective, which magnifies the emotions and experiences of the protagonists and reduces those of the 'co-actors'– there are no antagonists in the traditional sense, except perhaps for Melot – is in effect due solely to Wagner's poetic and musical language.[12]

The isolation of the individual as a result of the 'loss of the world' is one of the dominant themes of later nineteenth-century art.

Wagner's *Tristan* played a large part in helping it to its pre-eminence. The realm of aesthetic experiences accessible to the creative artist shrank under the conditions of life in the early modern industrial age. The effects that industrialization had on the quality of the environment could not but appear brutal, and the submersion of creative individuality in the new mass society repugnant. To find his own image and reflection, the artist had recourse to a hermetic realm that made it possible to forget the banality of the everyday world. Like the poet's role in Baudelaire's 'The Albatross', the 'loneliness together' ('Einsamkeit zu zweit') of the lovers in *Tristan* belongs to an early phase of the aesthetic isolation of art, for although the action on stage represents the disintegration of inter-human communication, the score has complete confidence in the communicability of this situation. The audience witnesses the lovers' state of being 'lost to the world', which, in collision with reality, almost reaches the point of absurd theatre – as for instance, Tristan asks 'Which king?' when King Marke's arrival on board is announced at the end of Act I.

The mystical fusion of love and death in *Tristan* also created an inherently musical problem that – with the possible exception of the Venusberg scenes in *Tannhäuser* – had never arisen before: the need to find a musical language to express pervasive ambivalence and ambiguity. Seeking to illustrate this aspect of late Wagnerian drama, Theodor Adorno chose an example from *Die Meistersinger* (probably because he would have had to cite the score of *Tristan* in its entirety), describing the phenomenon as a result of the interdependence between the psychological use made of the musical language and the differentiation of its harmonic structure:[13]

> To illustrate, we may think of the characteristic chord with the allegorical rubric 'Spring's command, sweet necessity' ['Lenzes Gebot, die süße Not'] in *The Mastersingers*, which represents the element of erotic passion and hence summarizes the whole action. It tells both of the poignant pain of non-fulfillment and of the pleasure that lies in the tension: it is both sweet and necessary. This intermediate stratum of expression, which is indeed the epitome of the musical modernity of the nineteenth century, did not exist before Wagner. That suffering can be sweet, and that the poles of pleasure and pain are not rigidly opposed to one another, but are mediated, is something that both composers and audience learned uniquely from him, and it is this experience alone that made it possible for dissonance to extend its range over the whole language of music.

This refinement of psychological characterization required a musical language in which a hierarchy of dissonant chords could function as analogues of complex emotions. Such chords were already part of the mid-nineteenth century's compositional stock-in-trade; but Wagner invested them with so much individuality that they became quasi-thematic. For reasons of motivic significance the opera's principal configuration of pitches, associated with the so-called 'Yearning' motif and known as the 'Tristan' chord, is strongly dissonant and has extremely complex harmonic properties. Heard together, the notes F / B / D♯' / G♯' produce a specific sound difficult to classify with the categories of traditional harmonic theory;[14] even the intervallic sequence tritone/major third/perfect fourth differs from the normal structure of chords – traditionally built from superimposed thirds – within the framework of major/minor harmony. The 'Tristan' chord is more dissonant than an ordinary seventh chord, so that its resolution onto the seventh chord on E at the beginning of the Prelude is registered as a relaxation of tension; and the resolution, perceived as immanent, of the seventh chord to a pure triad – which in fact does not happen – would have created a third, and more basic, degree of harmonic tension. Diminished, augmented and altered chords add further tension, which can scarcely be perceived distinctly because the sliding, chromatic part-writing of the chordal connections veils the sound properties of individual chords.

Only within a harmonic language of such complexity was it possible for a chord to assume the structural function of a motif, and conceivable for a dissonance to be individualized and made sufficiently distinct from the sounds acceptable at the time. Calling the 'Tristan' chord a 'leitmotif', however, does not adequately define its function, as this smacks too much of traditional Wagner analysis, in which belaboured 'bar form' (AAB) schemes were imposed on large structures within the operas, and musical semantics was thought to be explained adequately by catalogues of leitmotifs.[15] Anything not assigned to either category was further referred to a harmonic theory that only succeeded in distorting the harmonic language of *Tristan* by discussing even the most significant chords in traditional terms.[16] Later developments of *fin-de-siècle* music history – it is perfectly reasonable to talk about 'music after *Tristan*'[17] – provide more appropriate theoretical models for explaining *Tristan* than traditional harmonic theory. If one needed a

Ex. 5.1

convenient expression for characterizing these models, one might refer to 'intervallic thinking', as distinct from thinking within the system of major/minor tonality.[18]

The four-note configuration F / B / D♯' / G♯' – it has become part of the history of Romantic harmony – possesses an importance in *Tristan* that has little in common with a distinctive harmonic combination that can be transposed at will. Time and again one encounters passages where these four notes – and only these – assert a quasi-thematic importance coupled with their absolute pitch levels. The musical fabric is determined not by key relationships (as in the music of Haydn, Mozart and Beethoven, for whom the concept of a key – e.g., E♭ major – implied a quite specific range of meaning),[19] but by the presence of these four notes. This process, which could be described as a rudimentary precursor of Olivier Messiaen's technique of pre-serial modal composition,[20] can be illustrated by a few examples tracing some intervallic transformations of the first three bars of *Tristan und Isolde*.

The Prelude begins with the sighing motif generally known as the 'Yearning' motif, starting with a rising and chromatically descending sigh on the cellos, which serves as anacrusis to a four-note woodwind chord, followed by a chromatically rising sigh in the first oboe (see Ex. 5.1).

The following bars, which repeat this shape sequentially with some variation in orchestration, offer one possible means of developing the motif. Another, theoretically more interesting one, is shown in the following example from the end of the Prelude: the melodic line of the cellos and double basses can be seen as derived from the four notes of the 'Tristan' chord, if those notes (enharmonically changed: A♭ = G♯, E♭ = D♯) are read from top to bottom, with the interpolation of one other note (G) (see Ex. 5.2).[21]

Ex. 5.2

Ex. 5.3

The most familiar example of a transformation of the 'Yearning' motif is the so-called 'Tantris' motif. According to the medieval romance, Tristan cast himself adrift in a boat in order to be found and taken to Isolde, the only person who could cure the wound inflicted by Morold, disguising his identity by transposing the two syllables of his real name: Tan-tris. When this incident is narrated in Acts I and III, the music traces a chromatically descending motif that exactly reverses the four-note sigh on the first oboe at the beginning of the Prelude, preceded by an anacrusis and followed by the next step in the chromatic descent (see Ex. 5.3).

It seems reasonable to suggest that 'Tantris' reverses the 'Yearning' motif in order to express the logical associations of the action in an autonomous musical semantics. That the relationship is intentional can be confirmed by several passages where Wagner's setting of the words, even down to individual names, is equal to the task of constructing a semantics that, while conceived in the logic of the text, is musically autonomous.[22] When Isolde reveals her emotional conflict to Brangaene at the beginning of Act I, she initially refers to Tristan without naming him:

ISOLDE: Was hältst du von dem Knechte?	What do you think of that vassal?
BRANGAENE: Wen meinst du?	Whom do you mean?

To a listener familiar with the motivic relationships of Act I, the falling fifth from E to A reveals the identity of the 'vassal', for as the dialogue proceeds the same two notes occur twice again in association with Tristan's name, each consciously contrasting the two-note phrase with its inversion (see Ex. 5.4).

Ex. 5.4a

Ex. 5.4b

Ex. 5.4c

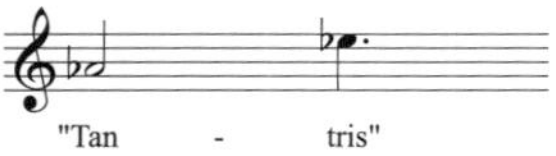

Ex. 5.5

Lowering the two notes by a semitone when inverted for 'Tantris' also locates Isolde's emotional response to the falsehood within a musical structure; the image of the text mirrored in the music is thus refracted by the emotional 'subtext' of the dialogue. Analysis of these linear pitch transformations can also be applied to the profound ambivalence – central to the action of *Tristan* – between the lovers' yearning and its fulfilment. The vocal line heard for the first time in Act II at the words 'O sink' hernieder, Nacht der Liebe' reveals a remarkable characteristic: the notes marked in Ex. 5.5 are those of the 'Tristan' chord enharmonically altered.

Simply by renaming the notes, the 'Tristan' chord, which in its original version (with tritone and fourth as pivotal intervals) appears related to the key of A minor, is enharmonically transformed into a traditional 9–7 chord with missing root, obviously belonging to the tonal sphere of G♭ major as its dominant chord (Fig. 5.1).

The score of the entire opera reveals that its ambivalent musical material results from the ambiguity of these two forms of the

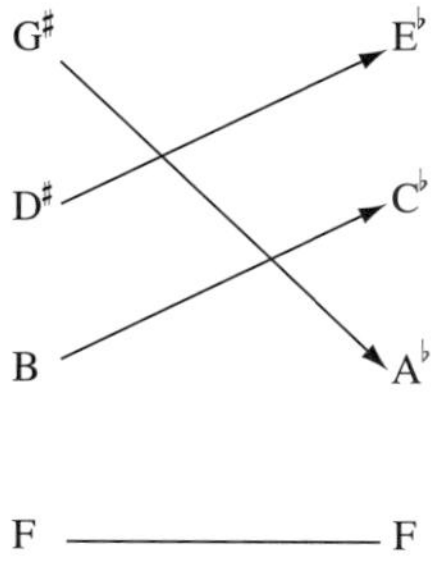

Fig. 5.1

'Tristan' chord, used both vertically and horizontally. The ambivalence, however, is achieved by assigning the two forms (differences in their respective degrees of tension are determined each time by the harmonic context) to different areas of association within the dramatic structure, areas that can be associated, broadly speaking, with 'Yearning' and 'Fulfillment'. Although the substance of the two pitch configurations is identical, their different sonorities are clearly audible. Each occurrence is further enhanced by a specific orchestral timbre: Wagner uses the bright purity of unmixed woodwinds for the more dissonant A-minor form, while the G♭-major form is usually heard with divided strings supporting soft woodwind chords. In those instances where the chord is used as a pivot between remote tonalities and dramatic contexts, the orchestration is so close to that of the chord's twin that little more is needed to effect the transition.

This particular pitch structure, perhaps the high-point of constructive complexity in nineteenth-century harmony, can be interpreted as the musical substratum of a fundamental antagonism between pleasure and pain, love and death, yearning and fulfilment that pervades *Tristan und Isolde*. In Wagner's score, for the first time in the history of music, mediation between qualitatively different sound-worlds is brought about not by the opposition of 'positive' and 'negative' sound-areas, as in German Romantic opera (where the negative area was normally the place for dissonance),[23] but by an ambivalent sound-aggregate that contains its own negation within itself: its precise semantic significance at any point in the score is realized through the interplay between its specific harmonic ambience and the individual timbre connected with its occurrence.

2

The emergence of an orchestral palette capable of accompanying the entire range of psychic states, including madness and intoxication, developed in Romantic opera out of the practice of associating instrumental timbres with semantic meanings.[24] Compared with Wagner's own Romantic operas, the orchestral technique of *Tristan und Isolde* advanced considerably, and the aesthetic foundation of Wagner's use of orchestral timbres also underwent a profound change. To understand the aesthetic basis of the opera's orchestral sound, it may be helpful to look briefly at the technique of orchestration in German Romantic opera during the first half of the nineteenth century. This will not only make it easier to discern the particular characteristics of orchestral sonority in Wagner's mature works, but will also demonstrate what *Tristan* owes to developments initiated by the German Romantics.

The demand for an unmistakable and coherent orchestral texture for individual works, which had become common in Viennese classical music, also spread to opera during the first half of the nineteenth century, where a certain amount of formalism had been tolerated as typical of the genre. The need for originality produced a progressive attitude towards orchestration, which aimed on the one hand at increasing the available timbres by introducing new instruments,[25] and on the other hand at synthesizing new timbres through increased mastery of scoring techniques. Dispositions of timbres – whose reference to constellations of the action seemed natural in an age demanding dramatic truth – are created most easily by a succession of pure instrumental timbres. But in as much as each instrument could be assigned to only one person, one action or one motif, the orchestra's sphere of expression would thus be severely limited and it would be impossible to achieve an individual orchestral sound. Greater complexity can be attained by a method of orchestration that attaches either a pure sound or a blend of timbres to individual concepts. The ever increasing supply of combinations made available by continuous innovation can be redistributed anew for each work; each instrument can contribute its timbre to various combinations and at the same time function with its individual timbre in connection with one particular concept.

This brief overview of composition with a stable disposition of timbres corresponds to the orchestration in Carl Maria von Weber's

Freischütz (1821). The horns in the overture, the sombre mixture of clarinets in low registers, timpani and pizzicato double basses to depict Samiel, the soft blend that envelops Agathe's prayer: all these timbres belonged to the basic Romantic orchestral palette and presented a distinct profile to the listener.[26] Being unchangeable, however, these timbres could not suggest character development in inherently musical terms. Moreover, a more complex musical character located somewhere between the forces of good and evil was inconceivable at this stage of development, and the only way in which musical ambivalence could be realized was to make a character – Max, for instance – vacillate between the two opposing sides. The result was the curious musical passivity of ambivalent heroes in German Romantic opera.

After depicting the ambivalent nature of temptation and sin in the bewitching Venusberg music of *Tannhäuser*, Wagner created in *Lohengrin* the first opera in which a homogeneous orchestral sound adapts itself to every facet of the drama by constantly transforming the timbral combinations that had previously been used only according to the static system sketched above. The innovations in the orchestra that made this development possible by around 1848 are too numerous to list here, but they include the enlargement of the body of stringed instruments, the incorporation of the cor anglais and bass clarinet into the standard orchestral texture, the introduction of the valved horn as the only horn instrument (instead of the hybrid horn group still used in *Der fliegende Holländer* and *Tannhäuser*) and its integration into the orchestra as an intermediate between woodwind and brass – and a general raising of playing standards. Wagner proceeded to turn these developments to aesthetic advantage in *Lohengrin*, creating an almost dematerialized orchestral sound, the transformations of which took place without perceptible caesuras, as if the whole texture of orchestral sound were developing organically. In his fragment 'Elements of the Romantic', Novalis had already envisaged this virtual immediacy: 'The phenomena must be there, like the notes on an Aeolian harp, all at once, without origin – without revealing their instrument.'[27]

After Wagner's *Der fliegende Holländer*, the world of individual sound combinations that comments on the scene, as in *Freischütz*, gradually expanded and made room for variations in timbre that provided a whole gamut of differing degrees of volume and presence. The tradition of French Grand Opéra had already created the necessity for organizing musical sound both within and beyond the real space of the stage.[28] The frequent offstage fanfares in Wagner's Romantic operas, the stereophonic disposition of the hunting horns in Act I of *Tannhäuser*, and the sounds of an offstage battle in Act III of *Rienzi* confirm Wagner's early mastery in creating virtual musical spatiality.[29] The composer's subsequent innovations in sound transformation are closely associated with the necessity, inherent in the leitmotif technique, for an adequate musical expression of presentiment and recollection.[30] Especially in *Der Ring des Nibelungen*, which is dependent on narration and recapitulation, the musical narrative causes the history of the characters to crystallize as musical structure: differing degrees of presence of one and the same motif make it possible to represent distance not only in space but also in time.[31]

Moreover, even Wagner's earliest scores contain moments in which a further technique of tonal differentiation can be observed: alienation of timbres by consciously distorting the natural sound of instruments or by an orchestration that, through its intentional deficiencies, 'impairs' the texture.[32] In addition to the possibility of modifying the volume of a given sound in accordance with dramaturgical requirements, the composer thus had at his command a wide range of tonal 'positivity' or 'negativity': the normal timbre of a wind instrument could be modified by making it play in an unfavourable register, or a high-pitched chord in the woodwind group could be given a piercing or hollow character according to the choice of instruments and the use of a more or less favourable register. Obviously, a conscious alienation of timbre became only perceptible as such when the background of normal orchestral sound featured an adequate degree of perfection as to distinguish itself from the intended distortion.

While Viennese classical music had aimed at a non-homogeneous sound characterized by the audibility of a multitude of distinct orchestral layers, a feature which originated as the result of the limitations of many eighteenth-century instruments, a new and homogeneous ideal of orchestral sound evolved during the first half of the nineteenth century. Numerous improvements to the structure and playing technique of the instruments of the orchestra gradually brought a partial solution to the imperfections which, at the beginning of the nineteenth century, had still been responsible for the relative heterogeneity of the orchestra.[33] In *Lohengrin*, Wagner developed a form of orchestration in which the shortcomings of the individual instruments could be corrected by perfection in scoring. Thanks to his absolute mastery of orchestration, Wagner achieved an orchestral idiom in his later works whose guiding principle was no longer individual instrumental timbre but a synthetically conceived disposition of sound structures according to 'families' of instruments, whose relation to the phonetic structure of speech he discussed in *Opera and Drama*:[34]

In its determinant influence on the quality of the tone entrusted to it, one might term a musical instrument the consonantal *onset of the Root*, displaying itself as a *Stabreim* [alliteration] *binding together* all the tones executable upon it. The kinship of the instruments to one another might thus be easily decided by the likeness of this initial sound, according as it shewed itself as a softer or harsher delivery, so to say, of the consonant they originally shared in common. As a matter of fact, we possess families of instruments that own an originally like initial, which merely shades off according to the respective character of the offspring, in a similar way to e.g. the consonants P, B and W in word-speech; and just as with W we stumble across a resemblance to F, so the pedigree of the instrumental families might easily be discovered to embrace a very complex ramification, whose exact tracing, and a characteristic employment of its members in groups according to their likeness or diversity, could not but present us with an Orchestra endowed with far more individual powers of speech than have even yet appeared, – seeing that the Orchestra is at present a long way from being known enough in its interpreting capacity.

Under the influence of this new concept of orchestral sound, the French poet René Ghil attempted in his *Traité du verbe* (1886) to classify the sounds of speech in reference to the physics experiments of Hermann von Helmholtz, and deduce a symbolist theory of language and poetry from it. Stéphane Mallarmé, who wrote his 'Avant-dire au *Traité du verbe*' as a foreword to Ghil's book, called the result a 'spirituelle instrumentation parlée'.[35] In 'Richard Wagner. Rêverie d'un poëte français' (1885), Mallarmé provided a more detailed description of the role of timbre in Wagner's music-dramas:[36]

Now at last we have music which is obedient only to its own most complex laws, above all to the vague and the intuitive. First it mingles the colours and forms of the actor with its own timbres and motifs, thereby creating a richer atmosphere of Revery than would be possible for any earthbound melody, creating a deity draped in the invisible folds of a musical texture. And then it sweeps him away in a wave of Passion which is too furiously unleashed to be borne by one alone; hurls him down, twists him about, and even robs him of his senses (they are lost in this superhuman rush), only to give them back again, so that he may be all-victorious in a song which bursts through the agony of creative thought. The hero, living as much in the clouds as on the earth, always appears in a distance which is filled with the mist of lamentations, victories, and joy breathed forth by the instruments. Thus he goes back to the world's beginnings.

...

Here, then, on the stage, Legend is enthroned.

For the second time in history, the people (first Greek and now German) can borrow sacred feelings from the past and look upon the secret of their origins, even as that secret is being acted out. Some strange new primitive happiness keeps them seated there before that mobile veil of orchestral delicacy, before that magnificence which adorns their genesis.

The consequences of an orchestration that derives from an overriding idea of sound rather than from the collaboration of a given number of instruments can be clearly discerned in *Tristan und Isolde*. In contrast to the 'alienated sound' that characterizes many German Romantic operas of the generation of Louis Spohr and Heinrich Marschner as well as the works of Hector Berlioz, there are moments in *Tristan und Isolde* of a beauty hitherto undreamed of. One of the most important consequences of this new form of composition was the extraordinary expansion of the orchestral palette, which Wagner enriched with previously unimagined extremes of tonal beauty and distortion. A notable innovation was Wagner's new approach to mass scoring, which even took into account the possible shortcomings of individual performers and the resulting vagueness of tone production. In his famous discussion of Wagner's technique of 'al fresco' orchestration in the last act of *Walküre*, Richard Strauss gave a convincing interpretation of the composer's novel imagination of timbres:[37]

This style, whose principal characteristic is the absolute clarity and performability of every phrase by every instrument, can be contrasted with another style with an 'al fresco' treatment of the orchestra, which was actually introduced by Wagner and relates to the earlier style in the way that the style developed by the Florentine masters out of the miniature illumination of the fourteenth and fifteenth centuries relates to the 'broad painting style' of Velasquez, Rembrandt, Franz Hals and Turner with their wonderfully shaded colour mixtures and differentiated light effects. The most striking example is the treatment of violins in the 'Magic Fire Music' in Act III of *Walküre*. To reproduce the flaming and licking tongues of fire, Wagner composed a phrase whose elements can scarcely be performed throughout by an outstanding soloist or be repeated perfectly. When performed by sixteen to thirty-two violins the ensemble passage creates such a wonderful, striking effect that one simply cannot imagine a better rendering of a blazing fire flickering with a thousand blended hues.

Finally, the special acoustics of the Bayreuth Festspielhaus, with its covered orchestra pit, had been designed by the composer for the creation of a homogeneous orchestral sound.[38] Not only is the blending of individual timbres enhanced by the elimination of their upper partials, but the resultant sound is also subject to a perspectival 'filtering' dependent on the different positions of the instrumental groups in relation to the pit's opening. The general reduction in the intensity of sound from the covered orchestra resulted in a 'stopping down' of the overall sound volume and allowed a 'close-up' of the unfiltered voices on stage. Furthermore, the differentiated manner of dampening the louder instruments according to their position rebalances the orchestral sound and produces a 'synthetic' overall sound in which the 'de-individualized' instruments are merged. The covered orchestra in the Bayreuth theatre represents the final abandonment of the classical ideal of a community of instruments conversing with one another.[39] The 'Bayreuth sound' thereby reinforces an inherent tendency of Wagner's orchestration technique; the technological perfection of the product, i.e., the orchestral sound, aims at the virtual disappearance of the producing agent in order to achieve its maximum effect: 'The occultation of production by means of the outward appearance of the product – that is the formal law governing the works of Richard Wagner.'[40]

3

In as much as the basic material for orchestral sound in *Tristan und Isolde* no longer consists of separate instrumental timbres, but of various aggregates of those timbres (products of the sonic imagination of their creator), sounds can no longer be described only by naming the instruments producing them. Every description must also rely on the reader's memory. Because of the necessity to distinguish relationships between numerous composite sounds, the description of orchestral timbres for a score such as *Tristan und Isolde* relies mostly on an abstract system of coordinates that might be characterized as 'sonority' and 'brightness'. Only a few instruments – those with the most distinctive use in the history of orchestral sound – have a precise function in addition to their participation in the creation of composite timbres. Heard against the overall background of composite timbres, the timbre of a solo instrument assumes the character of a special effect.[41] The cor anglais solo in Act III, where Wagner intuitively succeeded in discovering expressive possibilities that had not yet been exploited, became the paradigm for subsequent use of the instrument.[42] A symbol of mourning throughout the score, the cor anglais replaces the cellos in the rising leap of the sixth (the sighing motif of the love-potion) when Tristan is forced to answer Marke at the end of Act II: 'O König, das kann ich dir nicht sagen; und was du frägst, das kannst du nie erfahren' ('O King, that I cannot tell you; and what you ask, you can never learn').

The necessity of developing new and unfamiliar orchestral timbres for the 'realm of night' in *Tristan* resulted in a series of innovations based partly on assigning new functions to familiar timbres and partly on the development of completely new types of orchestral writing. Starting from the level of orchestration achieved in *Rheingold* and *Walküre*, Wagner developed for *Tristan und Isolde* a constantly changing ecstatic sound whose constituent orchestral colours could be deployed independently of the leitmotifs originally associated with them. Richard Strauss especially recommended that beginning composers study the particular use of French horns in the score of *Tristan*.[43] Indeed, the sound of the French horn not only provides a cohesive element in sound mixtures but also appears subject to a particular logic of use. The French horn was necessarily the only instrument that could be used for suggesting the nocturnal hunt in Act II. Although seemingly propitious for the lovers, the hunt later represents a hostile threat, creating negative implications for the sound of the horn and preventing use of the instrument's ethereal quality that makes it ideal for representing exceptional psychic states. By means of ingenious orchestration, however, Wagner succeeded in splitting up the components of the brassy tone of the hunting horns – ambivalent as symbols of the hunt – and reintegrating them into a larger, dramaturgically coherent system of timbres.

At the beginning of Act II, when Isolde and Brangaene are anxiously listening for the sound of the hunting horns to fade away, sounds of the hunt and nature gradually merge. The distant blaring of the horns on stage, sounding soft on account of their distance,[44] is taken up by a chord for the four horns in the orchestra, which are muted to make their sound agree with the noisier but distant – and thus softer – sounds on stage. The resulting composite is both near and far, tranquil and yet wavering as a result of the movement in the calls of the stage horns, which are gradually faded out. This movement passes seamlessly on to clarinets with oscillating sextuplets that are then joined by the semiquaver-figurations of the second violins and violas. Almost imperceptibly a transformation of the horn sound

Ex. 5.6

takes place, over a stationary chord in the first violins, into the sonic image of a murmuring brook (see Ex. 5.6):

Isolde:	Nicht Hörnerschall tönt so hold, des Quelles sanft rieselnde Welle rauscht so wonnig daher.	The sound of horns is not so fair; the gentle trickling of the stream rustles so delightfully to me.

We are unaware of the detailed organization of this miracle when listening to the seamless transitions in the sounds of nature. The hunting horns become absorbed into the sonic world of the nocturnal love scene, which at first barely uses unblended horn sounds alone. Only in the soft suspension chords in the woodwinds, on which Tristan and Isolde's love-duet is based ('O sink' hernieder'), does the tone colour of the horn ensemble return by stages to its main function. The horns' new sphere of signification was hesitantly announced at Tristan's words 'was dort in keuscher Nacht dunkel verschlossen wacht'. After the relative harshness of the distant hunting horns, their sound splits into two different timbres with distinct functions: the pressed, brassy sound of stopped notes, which at the end of Act II retrospectively symbolize Melot's treachery (and thus refer to the four-part chord on stopped horns at Brangaene's words 'Ein einz'ger war's, ich achtet' es wohl', introducing Melot to the listener) and the soft, ethereal sound of softly played notes on the horn. Almost as a reminiscence, four horns introduce Tristan's words at the end of the night of love ('Dem Land, das Tristan meint, der Sonne Licht nicht scheint'). In Act III a longer solo passage on four horns to Tristan's 'Wie sie selig, hehr und milde' evokes the vision of his beloved. Further passages would have to be quoted to suggest all the manifold combinations of this sound with related timbres, but one should at least note that Tristan's 'dunkel nächt'ges Land' (Act II) and 'weites Reich der Weltennacht' (Act III) are characterized by a darkening of the sound of the horns, which Wagner effected with a chordal base in the trombones – a feature used for entire sections in Act III of *Walküre* ('Der Augen leuchtendes Paar, das oft ich lächelnd gekost').[45]

The compositional technique employed here might be described as a 'logic of timbres': not only characters but also instrumental sounds have a history of their own, and their status at any given point in the score is no longer interchangeable with that at any other point. The overall disposition of orchestral timbres in *Tristan* can be most clearly seen from the fact that after the Prelude, which precedes the action as its external quintessence, so to speak, the full richness of orchestral sound is unleashed only towards the end of Act I, immediately after the drinking of the love-potion. The orchestral structure, which in Act I is somewhat block-like compared to the following acts, with its long held notes, tremolo passages, and unison runs in the strings, gives way to a complete dissolution of the orchestral fabric into

Ex. 5.7

choppy figurations of individual parts at the words 'Sehnender Minne schwellendes Blühen' (see Ex. 5.7).

One of the basic achievements of the *Tristan* score is this swelling orchestral sound with intense movement in the inner voices; by means of a constantly changing distribution of functions in frequently divided instrumental parts, no particular timbre predominates, even though it is not tutti composition. In a slow tempo, this type of scoring consists of an extensive framework of wind parts filled out and enlivened by arpeggios in the strings and harp; the violins often play the upper melody in a high register. The constant inner movement of this sound results from the considerable independence of the secondary voices as well as the acceleration of their motion relative to the tempo of the principal orchestral texture. In these passages individual parts and the musical sense of the whole diverge so markedly that the compositional legitimation of an instrumental line increasingly relies on the sonic result it produces. The gradual transformation of timbre that follows the words 'Frau Minne kenntest Du nicht? Nicht ihres Zaubers Macht?' is representative of Wagner's careful blending of woodwind and brass chords, which subconsciously influences the perception of the main melody in the first and second violins (see Ex. 5.8).

Pseudo-polyphonic figuration, arpeggios and repetitions in irregular rhythms are features of an exceptionally differentiated musical stratum in Wagner's later works. One of the finest examples of this technique is Brangaene's song from the watchtower in the middle of Act II, which dresses the medieval convention of the *Tagelied* or dawn-song in the sound-fabric of a *fin-de-siècle* phantasmagoria.[46] Surrounded by an unusual number of orchestral parts that work against the metric pattern of the vocal line,[47] Brangaene's song runs through the passage, so to speak, like a sustained note. The distortion of the regularly structured melody dictated by the tempo marking – and the superimposition of a highly differentiated orchestration full of inner movement – obscure the melodic contours and give the impression of time standing still.

Against a ground of harmonic filling-in parts – woodwinds, horns, and tutti strings – which is enlivened by arpeggios from the harp and half the violas and cellos, there arises a motivically individualized layer of eight solo violins and one solo viola, which surround the sustained notes of Brangaene's vocal line with a five-part web of sound (see Ex. 5.9). In the third bar of the example, the role of leading melodic instrument is taken over by an oboe solo; two bars later it is replaced again by the solo strings. No distribution of roles seems permanent throughout this passage; constant changes in the functions of the different instruments within a very small space and a system of continually new division of the strings create a fluctuating sound with a luminosity that is the result of the ceaseless inner motion.[48]

Ex. 5.8

The ‘knowing orchestra’ does not comment on the singer’s warning but suspends the course of time in order to lend permanence to the ‘fulfilled moment’ of love. The suspension of musical time in Wagner’s later works has a clear range of applications. Passages in which the listener’s attention is directed to the unfolding of static

Ex. 5.9

sound by arresting cadential progress together with dense inner motion in the instrumentation first occur in *Rheingold* (the Prelude, the thunderstorm, the rainbow) and belong to the category of 'nature scenes'.[49] In *Tristan*, however, Wagner employed a similar compositional technique to create the musical symbol of enchantment: at the peak of textural complexity, fifteen independent strings produce a band of sound that completely envelops the voice of Brangaene resounding from the back of the stage, while Tristan and Isolde are silent. The orchestra lends them its eloquence (see Ex. 5.9).

Gabriele d'Annunzio chose precisely this moment of the enchantment of love for the basic idea of the poem *Isolda* in his cycle *Le Adultere* (1883):[50]

ISOLDA

Tristan mourut pur su amour
E la belle Iseult pur tendrur.

'Notte d'oblio, d'amore e di mistero,
Notte soave augusta eterna, o Morte
invincibile e pura, apri le porte
a noi del tuo meraviglioso impero!

Fuga per sempre il giorno! Occulto
è il vero
sol nel cor profondo ed è sì forte
che crea pur fiori da gli abissi.
O Morte
fuga per sempre il Giorno menzognero!...'

Ma scendea de la torre un'altra voce:
'Vigilate! La notte è breve; è vano
il sogno.' Mute su l'antico parco

le stelle impallidivano. La voce
ripetea: 'Vigilate!' E nel lontano
risonava la caccia di Re Marco.

'Night of oblivion, of love and mystery,
gentle Night, august, eternal, O Death
invincible and pure, open the gates
of your marvellous realm to us!

Flee the day forever! The true sun is
hidden
deep in the heart and is so strong
that it even creates flowers from abysses.
O Death,
flee deceitful Day forever!'

But from the tower came another voice:
'Be on guard! Night is brief; dreaming
is in vain.' In the ancient park the mute

stars grew pale. The voice repeated:
'Be on guard!' And in the distance
resounded the hunt of King Marke.

It was not until the 1880s that *Tristan*'s tonal aesthetic and its compositional technique began to be fully appreciated by other composers, few of whom were able to escape the influence of their model, and who – almost as if Brangaene's warning 'Habet acht!' ('Beware!') were addressed not only to Tristan and Isolde, but also to a later generation of *Tristan*-addicts – sought to create new and personal music by transcending Wagner's technical means and intensifying his timbral complexity.[51] In particular, Act III of *Tristan* abounds in episodes where the continual transformation of a pleasing sonority into timbral negativity expresses a musico-dramatic meaning; in others the unreality of Tristan's hallucinations is reflected by islands of consonance floating amidst intentionally distorted sonorities. This was perhaps the first time that a new kind of 'alienated orchestral sound' was heard: prominently exposed lines, standing out against the

Ex. 5.10

accompaniment, are deliberately assigned to instruments that are forced to use awkward registers. Ex. 5.10 shows one of the most audacious passages in *Tristan*. What makes the passage appear in advance of its time – parallels would not be found before Gustav

Mahler – is not the complexity of the orchestration but the intentional honing of the sound by requiring some extreme feat or other from the instruments.

This was the passage selected by Adorno at the end of his monograph on Wagner to invoke the modernity of *Tristan*:

The feverish passages in Act III of *Tristan* contain that black, abrupt, jagged music which instead of underlining the vision unmasks it. Music, the most magical of all the arts, learns how to break the spell it casts over the characters. . . . It is not for nothing that those phrases in the *Tristan* score which follow the words 'Der furchtbare Trank' ['that potion so dread'] stand on the threshold of modern music in whose first canonic work, Schoenberg's F♯ minor quartet, we find the words, 'Nimm mir die Liebe, gib mir dein Glück!' ['Take love from me, give me your happiness!'][52]

(translated by Arthur Groos)

6 *Staging* Tristan und Isolde

STEWART SPENCER

Theatre historians attempting to trace the early production history of *Tristan und Isolde* are confronted by a frustrating lack of documentary material.[1] The technical limitations of nineteenth-century photography meant that photographers could not abandon their studios for the theatre until the end of the century,[2] while surviving set designs and contemporary lithographs may bear little resemblance to what audiences saw onstage.[3] Nonetheless, the set designs and models for the 1865 Munich première suggest that visually at least the staging was enthusiastically indebted to the prevalent aesthetic of lavishly detailed historical realism.[4] Acts I and III were designed by Angelo (ii) Quaglio (1829–90) and Act II by Heinrich Döll (1824–92).[5] Quaglio specialized in architectural designs, Döll in landscapes,[6] but both were essentially scene-painters rather than designers: throughout the nineteenth century, sets were painted, rather than built, the designers' skill being applied to creating the illusion of three-dimensional designs using two-dimensional cloths (see Ill. 1).

The designs of Quaglio and Döll were acclaimed throughout Germany, and there is no evidence that in 1865 Wagner was unhappy with their meticulously detailed work, although it is perhaps worth noting in passing that he may have envisaged a less specific approach. In 1852 he had drawn up a set of instructions for staging *Der fliegende Holländer* and insisted that 'the treatment of the ship cannot be naturalistic enough'.[7] Writing to the director of the Karlsruhe Court Theatre on 23 January 1859, by contrast, Wagner had observed that 'to return to the ship, I seem to be better at artistic symbolism than at its technical reality'.[8] While it is tempting to read into this remark a response to the metaphysics of Calderón de la Barca[9] and to the musical hegemony of Schopenhauer,[10] it would be wrong, I believe, to attach too much significance to it, as it prefaces an apology for Wagner's ignorance of nautical terminology and has no counterpart

Ill. 1. Set model for Act I by Angelo (ii) Quaglio (1829–90) for the Nationaltheater, Munich, 10 June 1865.

in his other comments on the staging of his works. Indeed, he continued, as it were, to pin his colours to the mast of historical realism throughout the rest of his career.[11]

Although we know that Wagner delegated the conducting duties to Hans von Bülow (1830–94) in order for him to be able to concentrate on the actual production,[12] it remains unclear exactly how Wagner worked with his singers. A clue may be afforded by a passage in his later tribute to the tenor Ludwig Schnorr von Carolsfeld (1836–65), who played the part of Tristan in the work's inaugural production:[13]

> Never has the most bungling singer or musician allowed me to give him such detailed instructions as this hero who had attained to the highest mastery of the art of singing; my apparently petty insistence on those instructions was always welcomed by him in the friendliest possible manner as their meaning was instantly clear to him, so that I would have felt that I was being dishonest if – perhaps in the belief that I might seem too sensitive – I had withheld the slightest criticism. But the reason for this was that the ideal meaning of my work had already revealed itself to my friend as if of its own accord and had truly become his own.

Wagner seems to have relied on Schnorr to create a character on the basis of an improvisatory response to the music and text, with the result that for long periods he did not need to interfere at all in the singer's performance:[14]

> Throughout the rehearsals for the first and second acts I had kept both ear and eye firmly fixed upon my performers, but with the start of the third act I involuntarily averted my gaze from the fatally wounded hero stretched out on his bed of anguish and sat motionless in my seat, eyes half closed, lost in the performance. At the first rehearsal in the theatre, the unusual length of my apparent total disinterest – for I never once turned to him or even so much as stirred in the course of this whole tremendous scene, even at the singer's most vehement accents – seemed to have left Schnorr so inwardly inhibited that when I finally rose to my feet after his curse on love and staggered over to him before bending down and emotionally embracing the singer who was still lying stretched out on his couch in order to tell my wonderful friend that no words could express my estimate of the ideal that he had achieved, his dark eye flashed like the star of love; a scarcely audible sob – and we never spoke another serious word about this third act.

This improvisatory approach to direction in the pursuit of detailed psychological realism is clear from later accounts of Wagner's work in rehearsal: with Mathilde Mallinger (1847–1920) in Munich in 1868,[15] with the casts of *Tannhäuser* and *Lohengrin* in Vienna in 1875,[16] and with several of the singers involved in the first Bayreuth *Ring* in 1876.[17] It was to find expression in his theoretical writings of the early 1870s as 'fixed mimetic improvisation'.[18] So keen was Wagner that audiences should appreciate the realistic detail of this acting style that he briefly toyed with the idea of staging *Tristan und Isolde* in the intimate confines of the 550-seat Residenztheater (also known as the Cuvilliés-Theater), but acoustic considerations obliged him to revert to the 2000-seat Nationaltheater.[19]

The improvisatory nature of Wagner's work as director, presupposing, as it did, a creative contribution from his performers, clearly taxed to their limits singers unused to such demands. Earlier in the nineteenth century, the English actor and manager William Macready had complained that 'it was the custom of the London actors, especially the leading ones, to do little more at rehearsals than read or repeat the words of their parts, marking on them their entrances and exits, as settled by the stage-manager, and their respective places on stage. To make any display of passion or energy would be to expose oneself to the ridicule or sneers of the green-room'.[20] Later in the century, too, the accounts of Henry Chorley[21] and Charles Santley[22] indicate the continuing lack on the English stage of a director's guiding hand, while the publication of manuals such as Gustave Garcia's *The Actor's Art*, with its illustrations of the gestures that should be adopted in expressing various emotions, reflects a stylized, theatrical approach to acting far removed from the intensely individualized characterization favoured by Wagner.[23] In general, the history of stage direction throughout much of the nineteenth century was that of the heroic efforts of individual directors such as Johann Wolfgang von Goethe in Weimar, William Macready and Charles Kean in London and Duke Georg II in Meiningen, efforts repeatedly undermined by routine and the cult of the star performer.

Paradoxically, the production books issued by the Paris Opéra from 1826 and the pamphlets describing the staging instructions for Verdi's operas that first appeared in 1855 served, rather, to ossify a performing tradition that Wagner wanted to remain open-ended. If he wrote, or superintended the publication of, performance guides to *Tannhäuser*,[24] *Der fliegende Holländer*[25] and the *Ring*,[26] his aim was not so much to prescribe an inviolable performing tradition based on inalienable rules as to encourage the performer to create a character of all-consuming intensity within designs that were committed to the aesthetic of historical realism.[27]

When Cosima Wagner (1837–1930) introduced *Tristan und Isolde* to the Bayreuth Festival repertory in 1886,[28] she commissioned designs from Max Brückner (1836–1919) and his brother Gotthold (1844–92)[29] that were inspired by those seen in Munich twenty-one years earlier, arguing that 'the creator of dramas from the spirit of music has left us with everything for the performance of his works in the most precise detail. ... It is not a question of discovering new things, merely of perfecting individual details' (see Ill. 2).[30] If Wagner himself had for the most part been pleased with the Munich production,[31] Cosima had reservations about the hyper-realism of the acting style that her late husband had coaxed from his performers, and demanded acting that banished every element of realism as inimical to the spirit of the work. Above all, she argued that the congruity of gesture between stage and orchestra that had been an integral part of Wagner's aesthetic since at least the time of *Opera and Drama*[32] was inappropriate to a work like *Tristan und Isolde*.[33]

Whatever the merits of Cosima Wagner's aims, the results – as Felix Weingartner pointed out[34] – foundered on a mixture of inexperience and misplaced arrogance. If Cosima's influence was neither as reactionary nor as malign as is generally claimed,[35] it gave rise to a growing sense of tension between the 'authentic' Bayreuth style and the more experimental stagings that began to emerge in the early years of the twentieth century, as photography and the cinema usurped the role of the theatre as a purveyor of realism, prompting more adventurous directors and designers to explore the fields of symbolism, impressionism, expressionism and abstraction that were successively opening up in the world of art. Their more conservative counterparts, meanwhile, continued to plume themselves with Bayreuth's feathers, staging their productions in designs indistinguishable from those first seen in 1886.[36]

One of the first designers to question Bayreuth's approach was the Swiss artist and theorist Adolphe Appia (1862–1928).[37] He had attended the world première of *Parsifal* in 1882 and returned for *Tristan und Isolde* in 1886, on both occasions expressing his disappointment at stagings that he felt fell short of his own particular vision of these works. In an appendix to his seminal study, *La musique et la mise en scène*,[38] he discussed his own approach to *Tristan und Isolde*, arguing that it was necessary to stage the 'inner action' and enable the audience to 'see the drama through the eyes of the hero and heroine'. In as much as the external world is a mere illusion for Tristan and Isolde, the settings should be reduced to their absolute minimum. In Act II, for example, 'the mild summer night gleaming through the tall

Ill. 2. Set design for Act II by Max Brückner (1836–1919) and Gotthold Brückner (1844–92) first seen at the Bayreuth Festival on 25 July 1886. This design was commissioned by Cosima Wagner (1837–1930) in an attempt to recreate what she believed had been the 'ideal' production in Munich in 1865. It was to remain canonical for more than half a century.

trees has lost its meaning for Isolde': two things alone still matter for her, 'the absence of Tristan' and – the reason for that absence – 'the torch'.[39] In the event, it was not until 1923 that Arturo Toscanini invited Appia to realize his designs at La Scala.[40] No photographs of this production have survived, but there is no doubt that Milanese audiences, used to a more pictorial style of production, were disenchanted by the austerity of Appia's work, quite apart from the fact that neither symbolism nor abstraction was common currency any longer (see Ill. 3). Above all, however, Appia's vision presupposed a metaphysical reality that no production, shackled and trammelled by the constraints of the stage, can ever aspire to achieve.

But Appia's ideas bore fruit in the work of other designers. In 1903 Alfred Roller (1864–1935) collaborated with Gustav Mahler on a production of *Tristan und Isolde* at the Vienna Court Opera that marks the first tentative attempt to produce designs that were more than merely decorative.[41] Roller was a founding member of the Vienna Secession, and his designs were typically anti-salonesque, their bejewelled and mosaic-like beauty redolent of the Jugendstil art of the period, the use of light and colour facilitated by recent developments in theatre technology.[42] Act II was particularly memorable, its opening scene dominated by the flame-red torch. During the love-duet the deep blue night sky – rather than the usual dense forest of leaves – was suffused with purple.[43] Following Melot's betrayal, a new day dawned with the pale sulphurous rays of the rising sun. In Act III, too, lighting was used to bathe the rough grey walls and massive gate of the castle in a bright flat light to create an atmosphere of desolation and solitude.[44] Mahler not only conducted but also directed the singers, ensuring that music and staging were fully integrated. The extent of Mahler's contribution was necessarily limited by the fact that, according to the reminiscences of Erwin Stein, Mahler directed the staging from the conductor's desk.[45] Nonetheless, there is some evidence that he sought to recreate the improvisatory style of Wagner's own productions while avoiding their literalness: not every gesture in the orchestra needed to be reproduced on the stage.[46] The first small step had been taken in the direction of an interpretative production.

A further step was to follow in 1909, when Vsevolod Meyerhold (1874–1940) directed *Tristan und Isolde* – his very first opera – in St Petersburg.[47] Like Roller, Meyerhold was familiar with Appia's ideas, quoting from the Swiss reformer's writings in his essay on *Tristan und Isolde*:[48]

Ill. 3. Set design for Act II by Adolphe Appia (1862–1928), La Scala, Milan, 20 December 1923. Appia's pioneering attempt to recreate the spirit of the work as opposed to the leafy literalism of the stage directions was the realization of an aim that he had pursued for thirty years but one that found few imitators until the New Bayreuth productions of the 1950s.

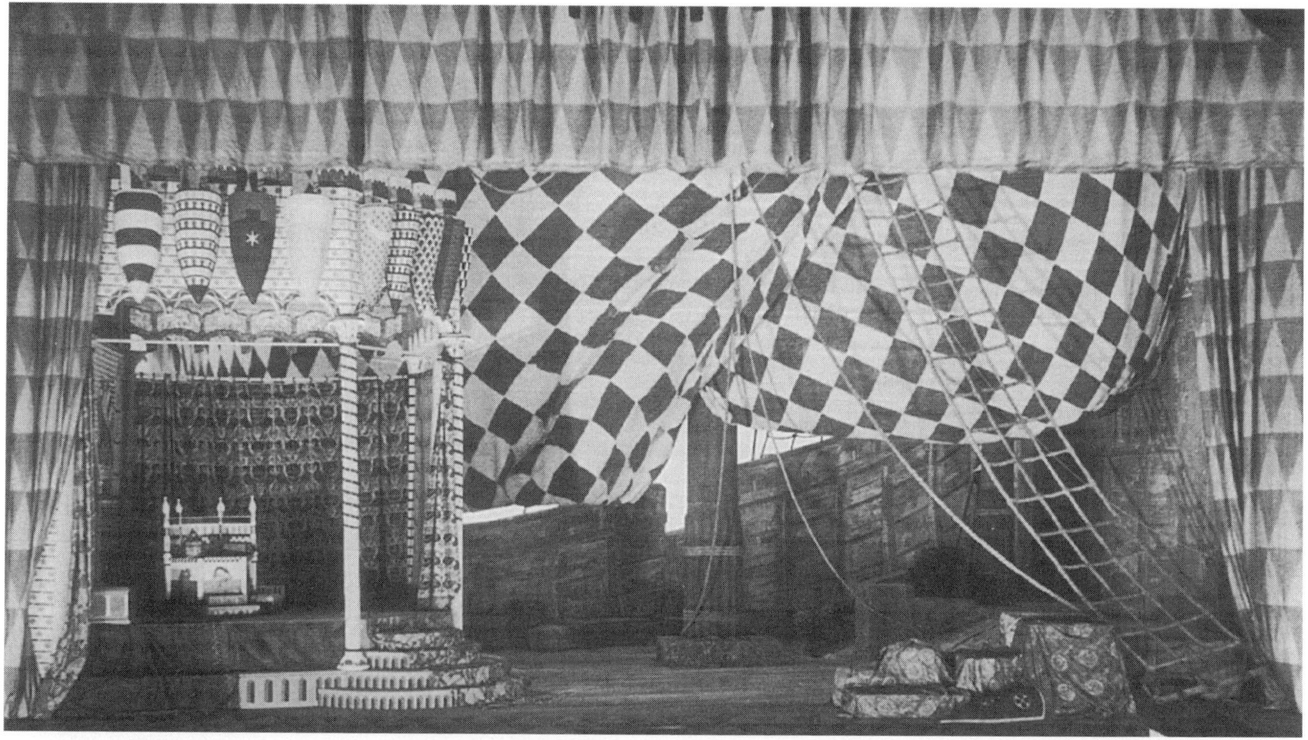

Ills. 4a and 4b. Set designs for Acts I and II by Alexander Shervashidse (1867–1949) for the production by Vsevolod Meyerhold (1874–1940) at the Mariinsky Theatre, St Petersburg, 30 October 1909 (OS). Their colours were designed, in Meyerhold's words, 'to recall the crumbling pages of ancient tomes' and 'persuade us that at some time in the past everything was like this'.

Ills. 4a and 4b (cont.)

The only way of realizing a dramatic conception is to immerse oneself first in the world of the emotions, the realm of music. . . . Music, which determines the tempo of every occurrence on the stage, dictates a rhythm which has nothing in common with everyday existence. The life of music is not the life of everyday reality. 'Neither life as it is, nor life as it ought to be, but life as we see it in our dreams.'[49]

As Meyerhold explains, there is nothing more 'absurd' than characters behaving in a lifelike manner on the stage, only to burst into song.[50] Movements and gestures should therefore be rhythmic in character and carefully choreographed, presupposing a certain balletic elegance on the part of the performers.[51] The work, he went on, was based on a myth, which is why he regarded Bayreuth's historicist style as a mistake: it was 'completely devoid of mystery'.[52] Meyerhold concludes that 'Wagner's dramas were composed from within' and that 'a huge stage may be packed with every conceivable detail, yet you still refuse to believe that there is a ship in front of you. . . . All you need is one sail filling the entire stage to build a ship in the spectator's imagination'.[53] Similarly, in Act II 'the garden with the rustling of leaves blending with the sound of the horns is miraculously evoked by the orchestra. The mere contemplation of real foliage on the stage would be as flagrantly tasteless as illustrating Edgar Allan Poe'.[54] Once again, however, the gap between vision and reality proved unbridgeable. The sets for all three acts reveal considerable topographical detail[55] (see Ills. 4a and 4b) resulting in a not entirely fruitful tension with the 'artificiality' and 'affectation' of the direction,[56] while the costumes, inspired by the miniatures in the fourteenth-century Heidelberg (or 'Manesse') Manuscript,[57] likewise reflect a historical specificity at odds with Meyerhold's mythical view of the work. Nonetheless, as Meyerhold himself insisted in defending his production against the criticisms of Alexander Benois, 'the object does not exclude the symbol'.[58] As Ivan Sollertinsky later asserted, Meyerhold's staging was claimed by 'the Russian symbolists as peculiarly their own',[59] investing it with an influence disproportionate to the relatively small number of performances that it received.

Lacking the political and social dimension of the *Ring* and the troubling ideology of *Die Meistersinger von Nürnberg* and *Parsifal*, Wagner's 'opus metaphysicum of all art'[60] has tended to encourage conservative stagings. The work entered the repertory of the Paris Opéra on 14 December 1904 in designs by Marcel Jambon (1848–1908) and Alexandre Bailly (1866–1947) that were not replaced until

1966.[61] The Metropolitan Opera witnessed only three different productions between 1886 and 1959, all of them literalist in style.[62] And the uncredited Covent Garden designs first seen at the end of the nineteenth century remained in the repertory until 1958.[63] It was left to other theatres, especially in Germany, to explore the theoretical and practical avenues opened up by Appia, Roller and Meyerhold, and while many smaller opera houses were content to recycle old sets and costumes or to hire copies of the Brückners' designs from Coburg,[64] there was a perceptible shift at this time, as designers abandoned the leafy literalism of the nineteenth century and sought a more interpretative approach to the work, paring away its period trappings in their search for what they regarded as its quintessential concerns.[65] And yet, as Oswald Georg Bauer rightly points out, no director or designer was willing to forgo at least a vestige of Romantic realism in an essentially lyrical work.[66]

Among the finest examples of this austere yet intensely poetical lyricism are the designs that Emil Preetorius (1883–1973) produced for no fewer than seven productions of *Tristan und Isolde* in Paris in 1936, Bayreuth in 1938, Florence in 1941, Rome in 1943, Amsterdam in 1948, Munich in 1958 and Vienna in 1959.[67] Wagner's son Siegfried (1869–1930), whose own production of *Tristan und Isolde* in Bayreuth in 1927 was compromised by decorative two-dimensional designs by Kurt Söhnlein (1894–1985),[68] saw Preetorius's *Lohengrin* in Berlin in 1929 and invited him to work in Bayreuth, where his designs, generally produced in collaboration with Heinz Tietjen (1881–1967),[69] were to leave their mark on the Bayreuth production style of the 1930s and 1940s. The claustrophobic compactness of his sets for Acts I and II of *Tristan und Isolde* is counterbalanced by the bleak desolation and openness of the set for Act III (see Ills. 5a and 5b); their formal interrelationship is understated but nonetheless clearly designed to function as a unifying factor, while their contribution to the drama is symbiotic and dynamic.[70] The rationale behind Preetorius's approach is worth quoting at length:[71]

> Think of the way in which the hushed and lovingly protecting night and the leafy seclusion of the second act of *Tristan und Isolde*, with its powerful sense of pictoriality, takes its place between the other two acts: the restlessly echoing, wind-swept ship, open on all sides to the sea, and the crumbling castle on the autumnal, abandoned shore. These are grandiose and broadly expansive visions that tell of a fertile imagination. What they are *not* is clearly delineated, sharply definable, concrete visual images. This must make an

Ills. 5a and 5b. Set designs for Acts I and III by Emil Preetorius (1883–1973) first seen at the Bayreuth Festival on 24 July 1938. Similar designs by Preetorius were also used in no fewer than seven different productions in various European centres over a twenty-three-year period and represent a first tentative step in the direction of greater abstraction on the Bayreuth stage. Particularly interesting is the use of the same basic design for all three acts.

important difference. Wagner was not a visual person in the proper sense of the word, a point he repeatedly and freely admitted. . . . He meant it as a form of praise when he said that the German spirit built from within. Music, he believed, was the supreme redemptive art, the living God within our hearts, which revealed the innermost vision of the essence of the world. All these remarks suggest a man for whom the ultimate authority was not the eye but the ear. And all his thoughts, ideas and instructions concerning the scenery in the narrower sense of the word prove this point in a way that has hitherto been only inadequately noticed. Only rarely does he speak with any certainty of colours and forms or of the character of individual sets, little is said in terms of their size in absolute or relative terms; and his instructions for the scenery in general – unlike the production! – are often lacking in cogent clarity; at the same time, some of the demands which he makes on the designer are attractive as ideas and appealing to the inner eye but, as outward realisations, they are not advisable if the image is to create an effect that is stylistically pure and correct. . . . The realism that Wagner wanted . . . must be rendered with moderation, for otherwise we run the risk of compromising the remote and mythical unearthliness of the whole.

If we accept the premise of this argument, then the interpretative role of the designer and director working in a post-nineteenth-century context follows as a matter of course. From now on directors and designers were required to mediate between the work of art and its audience, breathing new life into an artefact that had outgrown the immediate circumstances of its birth and transcended the performing tradition in which its creator had worked.

Among later designers who were clearly influenced by Preetorius are Günther Schneider-Siemssen (born 1926)[72] and Roberto Oswald (born 1933).[73] But so, too, were Wieland Wagner (1917–66)[74] and his brother Wolfgang (1919–2010)[75] in their productions for New Bayreuth, when post-war austerity conspired with the need to free Wagner from his National Socialist associations to generate a production style notable less for what it said than for what it did not say. Wieland directed and designed productions of *Tristan und Isolde* at Bayreuth in 1952 and 1962, in Stuttgart in 1958, at the Holland Festival in 1959, in Hamburg in 1960, in Berlin in 1961, in Brussels in 1962, in Geneva in 1963, in Milan in 1964, in Rome in 1965 and in Paris in 1966, although all were essentially try-outs or revivals of the two Bayreuth productions. If his 1952 staging was notable for its gaunt beauty and desolation, his 1962 interpretation was a mystery play about the destructive force of love. As Wieland himself observed:[76] ‘Myth is always topical; and this is true whether it deals with an obsolete morality and the ordered world of chivalry . . . or with our modern, allegedly emancipated society. Every passion is a threat to the order which has been achieved and represents a fatal danger to society.'

If such thinking risked reducing the work to a disquisition on purely temporal concerns, Wieland's designs, inspired by Henry Moore (1898–1986), reintroduced a totemic, timeless, archetypal quality. Act I was dominated by the suggestion of a towering ship's prow dimly discerned in the night sky – for Wieland, the lovers' crossing from Ireland to Cornwall was a journey across the Styx, the underworld river of oblivion. For Act II, Wieland derived his inspiration from the standing stone at Fowey in Cornwall[77] to create a huge stela or Celtic monolith that doubled as Brangaene's watchtower and also as a phallic symbol in whose shadow the lovers stood (see Ill. 6). Isolde likewise died standing, arms upraised as she achieved 'total passion in death'[78] and the sun sank behind the third of Wieland's mighty monoliths. A complex and subtle lighting plot in intense shades of green, blue and red was perfectly timed to what was happening onstage and in the pit.[79]

Wieland's production found many imitators, the cosmological element in particular influencing the work of directors such as August Everding (1928–99), who oversaw productions in Vienna (1967 and 1971), New York (1971), Bayreuth (1974) and Munich (1980).[80] But a reaction against it was inevitable, especially when the ideas of Jung began to go out of fashion and were replaced by more convincing explanations of human behaviour. At the same time, the heady optimism of the 1960s and 1970s, when man first walked on the moon, was giving way to a bleaker view of the world that was reflected first and foremost in the work of two of the followers of Walter Felsenstein (1901–75) in the former German Democratic Republic: Götz Friedrich (1930–2000)[81] and Harry Kupfer (born 1935).[82] Common to all of Götz Friedrich's productions was their metallic blackness and sense of menace. In all three, moreover, the discovery of the lovers in Act II resembled nothing so much as a brutal interrogation, with batteries of searchlights on watchtowers blinding the adulterous couple. Above all, Friedrich's aim was to explore the characters' psyche, laying bare their vulnerability and showing how they are torn apart by their own desires and fears.

But such psychological realism did not preclude symbolism, which added new layers of meaning to the work: in the Scheveningen production, for example, the spirals that dominated the sets by Heinrich

Ill. 6. Act II in the production by Wieland Wagner (1917–66) first mounted at the Bayreuth Festival on 24 July 1962 and revived in six subsequent seasons. This image, with Birgit Nilsson and Wolfgang Windgassen as the lovers, dates from 1963. The central image is modelled on the standing stone at Fowey in Cornwall that Wieland believed marked Tristan's wayside grave.

Ills. 7a and 7b. Acts II and III in the production by Jean-Pierre Ponnelle (1932–88) first staged at the Bayreuth Festival on 25 July 1981. The cast in 1981 included Johanna Meier and René Kollo as the lovers, Hermann Becht as Kurwenal and Helmut Pampuch as the Shepherd. As was the case with Preetorius's designs in 1938, the sets are based on the same basic image, the stern of the ship in Act I transmuting into the tree which, leafy and luminescent in Act II, is withered and fissured in Act III.

Wendel (1915–80) symbolized incompleteness, implying a journey towards completeness that was achieved at the end of the work. And in Günther Schneider-Siemssen's design for Act III of the 1980 Berlin production, a deep fissure in the rock represented Tristan's incurable, open wound. In his Dresden production in 1975, Harry Kupfer reintroduced elements of the nineteenth century: Isolde's tent in the opening act was furnished with Biedermeier bric-à-brac, the tragedy suffered by the lovers the source of a very real trauma designed to highlight the nineteenth century's fatally tragic error in seeking to deny the world. Unlike Hans Sachs and Parsifal, Tristan and Isolde are destroyed by their inability to engage with the world, a reading of the work which significantly – for every production must seek to engage in a dialogue with the *Zeitgeist* – reflected the social concerns of its audience in 1975. Traditional readings of the work were subtly subverted in an attempt to tease from it a meaning that it may nonetheless

Ills. 7a and 7b. (cont.)

contain, even if it had not been envisaged by Wagner himself. The composer, after all, had admitted to August Röckel in 1856 that the artist 'stands before his own work of art – if it really *is* a work of art – as though before some puzzle, which is just as capable of misleading *him* as it can mislead the other person'.[83]

Subversion of another kind was found in Bayreuth in 1981, when Jean-Pierre Ponnelle (1932–88) directed *Tristan und Isolde* in his own harrowingly beautiful designs (see Ills. 7a and 7b).[84] Ponnelle followed Preetorius in imposing a unifying form on each of the work's three acts, and he also sought to explore its mythic dimension. Most memorably of all, however, he suggested that Isolde's arrival at the end of the work is no more than a figment of Tristan's fevered imagination.[85] Other directors who have adopted a sceptical view of the work's underlying Romanticism include David Alden (born 1949) for the English National Opera in 1996 and Herbert Wernicke (1946–2002) at the Royal Opera House, Covent Garden, in 2000. In Alden's production, the sets by Ian MacNeil (born 1960) became increasingly spare with each passing act, for in the director's view Act III is not about madness but 'clarity',[86] as Tristan comes to believe that in order to experience love he must die. The heart-rending futility of this belief was summed up in the final image of Isolde walking slowly upstage, away from Tristan's body, on an otherwise empty and wanly lit stage. At Covent Garden, Herbert Wernicke explored the selfish desire of two lovers to use one another as a way of finding fulfilment, their exploitation of each other symbolized by their permanent separation. For a modern generation, it seems that the Romantic Oneness posited by Wagner is no longer a viable option.

Directing the work at Bayreuth in 1993, the German dramatist Heiner Müller (1929–95) dismissed its Romanticism as 'nonsense' and strove instead to achieve a sense of 'coldness'[87] that was manifestly intended to provoke the viewer but offered nothing in its place. Conceivably Müller, who had never previously directed an opera, would have revised the production if he had lived, but his increasing disregard for narrative linearity would always have been difficult to reconcile with a work whose trajectory is compellingly prescribed by the music. Müller's production was replaced in 2005 by a staging by Christoph Marthaler (born 1951) that was designed by Anna Viebrock (born 1951)[88] and takes as its starting point the emotional paralysis of characters ground down by the drabness of their surroundings (see Ill. 8). When the lovers meet in Act II, the climax of their assignation comes when Isolde unbuttons her nylon blouse and Tristan loosens his tie. And when Marke discovers his wife's adultery, his helpless response is to rebutton her blouse. Such an analytical domesticization of the drama is at odds with the music's soaring lyricism, but the tension is a fruitful one and in a curious way it echoes the concerns of a composer who felt that the emotional lives of his nineteenth-century contemporaries had been stultified by the society in which they lived.

Two other mainland European productions deserve at least a brief mention.[89] In 2005 Peter Sellars (born 1957) and the American video artist Bill Viola (born 1951) collaborated on a production at the Opéra Bastille in Paris.[90] As Bill Viola has explained, the project interested him because it gave him an opportunity to explore the 'Hindu and Buddhist traditions of Tantra that lie submerged in the Western cultural consciousness'. The image world that he created was intended to exist 'in parallel to the action on the stage' and to 'trace the movement of human consciousness through one of its most delicate, poignant states: the surrender to an absolute, all-consuming love'.[91] But the video imagery so dominated the action that the singers were effectively reduced to giving a concert performance at

Ill. 8. Act III in the production by Christoph Marthaler (born 1951) first seen at the Bayreuth Festival on 25 July 2005. Here, too, a unit set was used, each act sinking further in the bowels of the ship-like building of Anna Viebrock's sets. Tristan, played by Robert Dean Smith, is seen here on his deathbed, where he is visited by a series of his followers. Upstage right is the Shepherd (Arnold Bezuyen), centre left the kilted figure of Kurwenal (Andreas Schmidt).

the front of the stage, in the process undermining the integrity of the piece. Significantly, the video took on a life of its own as an international exhibition, *The Tristan Project*.

Two years later, on 7 December 2007, Patrice Chéreau (born 1944) staged *Tristan und Isolde* at La Scala, Milan.[92] Chéreau had already refused to direct the work in Milan in 1978 and in Bayreuth in 1981 and 1993, arguing that '*Tristan* can't be staged; it's a radio play',[93] but ultimately he was unable to resist the fascination of a piece that in Richard Strauss's words represents 'the end of all Romanticism'.[94] In monumental but historically non-specific sets by his regular designer, Richard Peduzzi (born 1943), Chéreau pursued an idea advanced by Slavoj Žižek and Mladen Dolar in their book *Opera's Second Death*,[95] exploring the death wish on the part of two 'depressed' people 'who have got to know each other while undergoing detox' and who, believing that they are going to die, abandon themselves to 'madness' and 'hysteria'. By the end of Act II, they have learned to 'invent a common language, that of this strange death drive'. Their 'depression' leads the lovers down 'the corridor to death', ending in their suicides. In the light of the work's more recent performance history, such a clinical dissection of the lovers' psychoses and of the 'broken' and 'blinded' lives of the other characters inevitably has a slightly reductive feel to it, a reductivism exacerbated by the extraordinary intensity of the acting. This domesticization of the drama was also found in the new production by Claus Guth (born 1964) that opened at the Zurich Opera on 10 December 2008. Here the main characters were clearly modelled on Wagner himself and on Mathilde Wesendonck and her husband Otto.

It remains briefly to mention the work's performance history in the United States of America, a brevity due in part to the fact that the country has largely remained aloof from a continental European style of production often referred to as 'Eurotrash'.[96] As we noted above, productions have tended to linger in North American opera house repertories for far longer than their European counterparts, while also remaining more inherently conservative in character. The Metropolitan Opera designs of 1920 by Josef Urban (1872–1933) outlived their creator by twenty-six years, while August Everding's Metropolitan Opera production of 1971, for example, was not replaced until 22 November 1999, when the German director Dieter Dorn (born 1935) and his regular designer Jürgen Rose (born 1937) joined forces on a quasi-abstract production of evasive minimalism that recalled

Wieland's set designs without recapturing the intensity of his singers' performances.[97] Visually more interesting were the retro Pop-Art designs of David Hockney (born 1937) that were first seen at the Los Angeles Music Center on 6 December 1987. Hockney's designs were seen again in Chicago in January 2009 and in Barcelona in January 2010. In both instances, new directors were credited: José Maria Condemi (born 1969) in the case of the Chicago production, Thor Steingraber (1966) in that of the Barcelona revival. But the Pop-Art sets again prevented the work from generating the visceral intensity that Wagner felt would 'drive people mad' if the work were to be adequately performed.[98]

Writing in 1889, George Bernard Shaw claimed with his usual provocative perversity that 'To enjoy Parsifal, either as a listener or as an executant, one must be either a fanatic or a philosopher. To enjoy Tristan it is only necessary to have had one serious love affair; and though the number of persons possessing this qualification is popularly exaggerated, yet there are enough to keep the work alive and vigorous'.[99] Wagner himself would have argued, conversely, that it is not so much the possession of this qualification that constitutes the work's emotional charge, but rather the desire to possess it.[100] But if art is not to descend into the merely culinary, then director and designer alike owe it to both the composer and to his audience to ensure that *Tristan und Isolde* is more than an escapist fantasy for the emotionally underprivileged.

7 *Tristan's traces*

STEVEN HUEBNER

Die Meistersinger and beyond

At the beginning of *Die Meistersinger von Nürnberg*, Walther wants to find out whether Eva is betrothed. Surprised, she responds: 'Mir ist, als wär' ich gar wie im Traum! / Er frägt, ob ich schon Braut?' ('It seems as if I were in a dream! He asks whether I am already betrothed?') The 'Tristan' chord (spelled as F/B/G♯/D♯ and coloured by oboe, clarinet and bassoon) punctuates the last sentence. The pitches and orchestration (excluding cor anglais) duplicate the first harmony in the Prelude to *Tristan und Isolde*, G♯ even leading to A to produce a French augmented sixth chord that resolves to E-major harmony. The allusion is fleeting, perhaps a knowing wink: Eva as bride-to-be, Isolde as bride-to-be. On a more profound level, 'dream' acts as a conduit to noumena in Wagner's Schopenhauer-influenced thinking: Eva's ephemeral 'Tristan' chord hints at the more fantastical things to come in the opera – the results of dreaming but also of *Wahn* ('delusion').

Flash forward to Walther's lesson with Sachs in Act III. The problem with Walther's Act I Trial Song, sings Sachs, is that 'mit solchem Dicht- und Liebesfeuer / verführt man wohl Töchter zum Abenteuer' ('With such poetry and passion one seduces daughters into misadventure'). Half-diminished harmony sounds on the strings during the last word. The inversion, pitches, spelling and orchestration are now different from Eva's earlier 'Mir ist, als wär' ich gar wie im Traum!', but the violins round out the phrase with a four-note chromatic rising figure. Once again *Tristan* seems near, especially because the earlier Trial Song to which Sachs refers ('So rief der Lenz in den Wald') mimics *Tristan*'s musical style. Walther's description of spring's voice in the Trial Song as 'Es schwillt und schallt, / es tönt der Wald / von holder Stimmen Gemenge; / nun laut und hell, / schon nah' zur Stell' ('The woods swell and resound with a sweet chorus, now loud and clear, and drawing near') seems like a brash and earthy antinomy to the 'Weise . . . so wundervoll und leise' ('the melody . . . so wonderful and soft') and its synaesthetic continuation in Isolde's *Liebestod*. At the end of *Tristan* the outer voices slowly pull apart to produce a sensation of opening into the infinite. Likewise, the orchestral soprano and bass that accompany Walther move in contrary motion, even culminating with a downbeat major-mode added-sixth harmony (at 'Wie Glockenhall / ertos't des Jubels Gedränge') like the crest of Isolde's passage. But Walther sings impulsively and with unbridled enthusiasm. As an emulator of the earlier opera, he does not get it quite right. One might say that he reinterprets – even energizes – the death-driven music of the precursor with the life-affirming fertility of a character inhabiting the comic mode.

The most obvious reference to *Tristan* in *Meistersinger* (few critics have hesitated to call it a quotation) is Sachs's renunciation of his claim to Eva's heart in Act III: 'Mein Kind, / von Tristan und Isolde / kenn' ich ein traurig Stück' ('My child, I know a sad story about Tristan and Isolde'). Here the orchestral winds play through the initial sequence of the *Tristan* Prelude. The passage is solemn, almost ritualistic – a moment that seemingly seeks to elicit reverence for the earlier work. Near the end of each act in *Tristan* this sequence sounds at its original pitch level and close to its initial orchestration. Sachs's transposed quotation seems an antonym to the end of Act II when Tristan looks up to Marke and sings, with pity, 'O König, das / kann ich dir nicht sagen; / und was du frägst, / das kannst du nie erfahren' ('O King, this I cannot tell you, and what you would ask, you can never experience'). For Sachs distances himself from Marke not merely by relinquishing any claim to Eva, but also by his greater intuition about the human condition, as also attested by Sachs's Act III 'Wahn' monologue.[1] An analysis of the ways in which *Tristan* colours *Meistersinger* could certainly be extended much further. Carl Dahlhaus's description of the diatonicism in the latter opera as something of a 'reconstruction' after the chromaticism of *Tristan* is especially compelling.[2]

In short, with the many resonances of *Tristan* in *Meistersinger* (and why not the latter part of the *Ring* or *Parsifal* as well? – *vide* the half-diminished sonority at Kundry's kiss), Wagner himself presaged the later popularity of *Tristan* as a signifier and stylistic touchstone.

Even my narrow selection of examples so far suggests rich intertextual fabric. Musical reminiscences of *Tristan* in *Meistersinger* range from a single chord and motif to more generalized style, and from quotation to allusion (recognizing the hazy border between these two categories in music, and, in this case, another fuzzy distinction between allusion and personal compositional style). These reminiscences engage the position of the critic, or *ethos* as Linda Hutcheon calls it in her theoretical outline that persuasively makes a case for a broad understanding of parody.[3] Thus the attitude of parody may be respectful of the model or playful (to infer the intent of Wagner as author). Or it may contest the model, gently mock it, or scorn and deride, as Beckmesser implicitly does (to infer the intent of characters as reader-fabricated authors). Intertextual traces become signs in the new work, feeding its ideology and its new agglomeration of meanings and problems constructed by composers, critics and performers. *Die Meistersinger*, for example, famously posits the following question: *Tristan* may well produce a satisfying quasi-spiritual experience, but how might this be incorporated into a functional society? Another series of questions sparked by the links between these operas might turn around compositional history after Wagner's death as related to music that both radically challenges conventional syntax and is historically grounded.

This essay is about the reception of *Tristan und Isolde* as reflected in the intertextual world the opera inhabits. As a source or parallel text, *Tristan* occupies a special position because it has repeatedly been given epochal significance, perhaps more than any other work in the history of music. This importance has been variously attributed to its representation of sexual desire, its pre-Freudian insights, and its putative quality as, in Nietzsche's words, an *opus metaphysicum*, but mainly to its role as a conspicuous marker in the evolution of style. In 1920, Ernst Kurth emphasized what had by then already become a commonplace in narratives about Western style, at least in Germany, when he called his most important theoretical work *Die romantische Harmonik und ihre Krise in Wagners 'Tristan'*.[4] The opera, or at least its Prelude, became absorbed into the pedagogical canon long ago, almost impossible for musicians in the West to avoid in the acquisition of syntactical fluency. (Once again, *Die Meistersinger* is prescient for subsuming *Tristan*, via the Trial Song, into a didactic project.) But current pedagogy often unwittingly and erroneously extends Joseph Kerman's characterization of the *Tristan*-style as 'symphonic'[5] into the study of a non-referential musical object, a specimen of 'absolute' music divorced from plot, to be taken apart like a Bach fugue on the theorist's work table of virtual (re)composing – with nary a thought of Schopenhauer.

In discussions about the musical echoes of *Tristan*, then, syntax and semantics have received varying degrees of emphasis, particularly with reference to modernist language as it emerged at the end of the nineteenth century. One example is the seminal role often attributed to Wagner's opera as a source of expressionism. Luigi Rognoni characterized Schoenberg's goal in *Verklärte Nacht* as 'a search for an opening in the chromaticism of *Tristan und Isolde*',[6] a line of inquiry not unreasonable to pursue on its own terms in a study of compositional history where the antecedent acquires an elusive musical presence in the later work. Others have given greater weight to the inner drama of the protagonists in Wagner's opera as harbingers of expressionist explorations of interiority, drawing a parallel between, say, Tristan's Act III hallucinations and Schoenberg's *Erwartung*.[7] But regardless of the weight we may assign to the syntactical or hermeneutic side in intertextual exegesis, more sustained attention to the former will be necessary fully to comprehend the most significant referential signposts from Wagner's opera.

The chord

For well over a century critics have funnelled the compositional importance of *Tristan und Isolde* into a single sonority. The 'Tristan' chord has come to assume a large burden in pedagogy and criticism because of a multivalence that succinctly illustrates the erosion of the tonal system. This multivalence, its character as 'wandering chord' to cite Schoenberg,[8] variously gave rise to hostility, debate, acceptance or reverence. Alban Berg was said by one of his students to have been so fascinated by the sonority that he played it whenever he saw a piano, a kind of sonic talisman for the modernist.[9] Not so another progressive musician sixty years before: Hector Berlioz admired Wagner in many respects, but his complaint about the *Tristan* Prelude in 1860 as a long 'gémissement chromatique' ('chromatic moan') reflects his conviction that fundamental principles of his art had been assaulted.[10] He confessed to having 'read and reread' the music with utter incomprehension, a reaction that undoubtedly included the opening bars. What almost certainly mystified Berlioz was not the sound of the half-diminished chord *per se*, by then often used, but its spelling and use.

More productive debates about function began even before Wagner's death.[11] Cyrill Kistler (1879) advocated hearing the G♯ as a chord tone in a 'minor triad with diminished seventh' on scale degree VII in A. Karl Mayrberger (1881) initiated the tradition of hearing the G♯ as nonchordal, which came to include interpretations of the first sonority as a seventh chord on B (either as some sort of subdominant in A or tonicization of E).[12] Mayrberger's approach enjoyed implicit approval from the Bayreuth establishment by virtue of its publication in the *Bayreuther Blätter*. Despite the case for changing function across the bar line that he tried to make (from a chord on VII to one on V), Kistler's interpretation makes little grammatical sense: with the G♯ heard as a leading tone there is no real change of harmony between the second bar and the third. It was an explanation that the baffled Berlioz, had he been alive, might have held up to buttress his point. Yet Kistler's approach unwittingly contained the seeds of the future, for when the parameter of tonal function is neutralized, chromatic voice leading, voice exchange and motivic development acquire a greater role in analytical constructions of coherence. Free atonality around the time of the First World War validated this approach, giving rise to such observations as Hugo Leichtentritt's that the beginning of Schoenberg's atonal piano pieces Opus 11 'hardly differs from the Wagnerian *Tristan* melos'.[13]

Leonard Meyer distinguishes between a 'critical' (read hermeneutic and aesthetic) understanding of the G♯ as a long appoggiatura to the A, that is a literal representation of painful yearning, and an interpretation that is 'preferable historically' because it hears the 'G♯ as a structural element in an independent harmony' leading to later 'emancipation of the dissonance' in atonal music.[14] In an extended analysis of Schoenberg's *Gurrelieder*, Alban Berg briefly drew attention to a passage in Waldemar's song 'Es ist Mitternachtszeit' where the half-diminished chord informs the harmonic succession and is also 'melodically paraphrased'.[15] Such a Schoenbergian/Brahmsian approach recalls the horizontal prominence of the 'Tristan' chord at the beginning of Wagner's Prelude (the strong articulation of G♯–B–D–F♯ in the chromatic ascent in bars 2–11) where the G♯ is 'structural' in a motivic sense, as well as its other horizontal manifestations in the opera. The motivic perspective fed traditions where the half-diminished chord appears as a set [0, 2, 5, 8] in set-theoretical analyses of chromatic, bitonal or atonal music, as in Tethys Carpenter's understanding of the first sonority at Clytemnestra's 'Ich habe keine guten Nächte' in Richard Strauss's *Elektra*.[16] A related analytical impulse is Milton Babbitt's pithy description of the first two chords in *Tristan* as inversionally related around a mid-point without reference to roots and function.[17] What he meant is that in closed position the 'Tristan' chord of the second bar is a succession of two minor thirds and a major third built upwards, and that the same interval succession unfolds downwards from D to produce the 'dominant seventh' on E in the third bar.

Charles Rosen's characterization of discussions about the harmonic function of the first 'Tristan' chord as 'uninteresting' in *The Romantic Generation* also lends weight to the motivic-contrapuntal analytical tradition.[18] Rosen, however, argues backwards in time by illustrating how half-diminished chords provided a new compositional resource after the exhaustion of possibilities offered by the full-diminished seventh. Yet the very amenability of half-diminished harmony to both subdominant and dominant function in late nineteenth-century style would also seem to be a new resource and perforce validate those 'uninteresting' debates about the opening bars. And notwithstanding Meyer's incisive remarks, a teleological view of history has not always entailed an understanding of the first half-diminished sonority in *Tristan* as 'structural'. Ernst Kurth advanced the functional, unprepared dissonance argument for the G♯ and proposed that the chromatic alteration of diatonic pitches in *Tristan* more generally exemplified the 'energetic' harmonic style that led to Schoenberg's expressionism. He sensibly identified functional harmonic 'pillars' separated by chromatic flux as integral to this style.[19] For Kurth, moments when tertian characteristics of the chord are foregrounded (such as the spelling of the half diminished chord as F/A♭/C♭/E♭ at 'O sink' hernieder, Nacht der Liebe' or the climax of the Prelude) constituted 'sensuous' harmony that found its fullest realization in impressionism.

The role of *Tristan* in Kurth's history may strike us today as overly reductive, though not without merit and broadly consonant with the significance ascribed to the opera. Such compositional/grammatical importance lends rhetorical force to quotations or allusions to Wagner's opera in subsequent art, and to critical exegesis about them, especially when critics invoke compositional intent. All of this, however, brings us (at last) to our important methodological point. When is a half-diminished chord merely a standard item in late Romantic chromatic harmony, and when is it, to cite Mark DeVoto, 'emblematic: in whatever context, it never fails to announce to the listener that the composer knows that *Tristan und Isolde* has been there before'?[20] Some sort of supporting index usually goes a long way in drawing a bridge between a half-diminished harmony and Wagner's opera, that is, the same pitches as the beginning of the *Tristan* Prelude, or the same voicing if different pitches, or a verbal cue in texted music.

But firm guidelines are impossible to establish. DeVoto hears the pounding second inversion half-diminished chord in closed position (E/G♯/B♭/C♯) that propels the scherzo of Bruckner's Ninth Symphony as an emblematic 'Tristan' chord. The chord begins the movement, but it resolves differently than Wagner's bar 3 to a D-major tonic harmony. Idiosyncratic spelling here (like the beginning of the *Tristan* Prelude, though in a different way) illustrates the rich potential of this sonority. In Bruckner's scherzo it sounds like an added-sixth harmony (that is, a chord with a root of C♯), not a half-diminished seventh (built up from B♭ = A♯), but is actually spelled as a variation of a dominant-functioning diminished-seventh harmony (i.e., C♯/E/G♯/B♭ instead of C♯/E/G/B♭). The eventual contraction of the G♯ and B♭ to A exemplifies the Kurthian energetic melodic ductus created by chromatic alteration. Nevertheless, considering the context of late nineteenth-century harmony and the absence of a verbal programme it is difficult to see this harmony as an emblem of *Tristan*, except as an illustration of the broad stylistic impact of the opera on hundreds of compositions and, concomitantly, Bruckner's admiration for Wagner.[21]

Brahms's relationship to Wagner was of course much different. He disliked *Tristan* – 'If I look at [the score] in the morning I'm cross for the whole day', he is once reported to have remarked[22] – but that would not by itself necessarily preclude quotation or allusion. He may well have noticed Wagner's various uses of half-diminished harmony and absorbed them in the Second Symphony, as Raymond Knapp has shown,[23] although his approach may not have depended on the existence of *Tristan*. Similarly, it is not entirely clear that the half-diminished harmony in the intermezzo Op. 117, No. 2 (bars 8–9) can be productively understood as a Wagnerian allusion, as has been suggested.[24] An even more striking example of the gravitational pull of Wagner's opera in Brahms criticism is James Webster's observation that the emphatic diminished seventh chord in the ninth bar of the *Alto Rhapsody* is a 'variant' of the 'Tristan' chord: the pitches are B/D/F/A♭ (D♯ instead of D would create exact pitch congruence).[25] Webster compares the misery-to-hope/C minor-to-major trajectory of Brahms's work to the same trajectory in Act I of *Tristan* in as much as it relates to Isolde's psychology (Wagner's own use of C major at the end of the act, however, seems richer for its portrayal of both a celebratory arrival in society and, in an interplay with A major, the lovers' separation from the world around them). There were other well-known models for this tonal map in the nineteenth century, as Webster recognizes, so specific motivic and harmonic details are vital to the intertextual link he seeks to create. These, however, hardly stand out from Brahms's language. Arrival on a diminished seventh with root B is normative in a C minor piece and the subsequent shift to another diminished-seventh harmony before a tonic does not bear the distinctly Wagnerian mark that Webster suggests.

And what should be made of Carpenter's invitation, cited earlier, to hear the harmony at Clytemnestra's 'Ich habe keine guten Nächte' as a half-diminished chord that recalls *Tristan*? The sound is of a minor-mode triad with added sixth (F/A♭/C/D in closed position) in a bitonal context. It does not immediately bring Wagner's opera to mind, but a verbal cue unmentioned by the author does have potential for intertextual critical exegesis: are Clytemnestra's harrowing guilt-racked *nights* an antipode to the guiltless night of Tristan and Isolde? If so, this passage might trigger reflection about different representations of sexuality in each opera.

Like Brahms, Dvořák often used half-diminished-seventh harmony, and the last movement of his Seventh Symphony presents the problem of proximity to *Tristan* from another angle. The development section begins with the exact voicing and pitches of the first chord in *Tristan* (bar 173, though with D♯ spelled as E♭) yet the connection is difficult even for acute ears to pick up because Dvořák scored the harmony low on the trombones and bass. However understated, it is unlikely that an accomplished post-Wagnerian musician could have written a half-diminished chord in this way and *not* think of *Tristan*. The absence of a verbal cue here makes it difficult to gauge a particular attitude towards Wagner's opera on the basis of the text itself. The very surreptitiousness of the moment suggests a spirit of musical play: against the current of our own critical culture so taken with hermeneutics and social grounding, such semantic non-specificity reminds us of the 'purely compositional' significance of the model.

In conceiving intertextual connections it seems most useful to think of works in the nineteenth and early twentieth centuries as circling around *Tristan und Isolde* along different orbits. Given the place of the opera in the collective musical consciousness of this period as witnessed (in part) by extended debates about how to analyse the beginning, it is difficult to disconfirm stylistic similarities as distant echoes, perhaps the route of outer satellites in the intertextual system. The mere use of the term 'Tristan' chord, however, sends a strong intertextual signal and would be used best for instances of this sonority in closer orbit than the Bruckner and Brahms examples I have cited. The Strauss and Dvořák fall within a more proximate range, determined by the weight assigned to such factors as verbal evidence internal to the work, syntax, inferred intent and compositional context and process. The Dvořák appears closer than the Strauss; in my view it is the only instance in my restricted selection of examples so far that may be persuasively called a 'Tristan' chord, yet ironically it is one with minimal experiential impact. The orbital model might apply to references within a single composition as well, extending in *Die Meistersinger* from Sachs's distant or perhaps mid-range half-diminished 'Mit solchem Dicht- und Liebesfeuer / verführt man wohl Töchter zum Abenteuer' to the close reminder of *Tristan* at 'Mein Kind, / von Tristan und Isolde / kenn' ich ein traurig Stück'.

Love and the erotic

I now turn to other traces, though in a way that can do justice neither to the frequency of reference – and to much more than a single chord – nor to the complexity of individual cases. Allusions to sexual desire and eroticism often spawned citations of *Tristan* (as in *Die Meistersinger*), especially because these themes have loomed large in the public and critical reception of the opera. Clara Schumann was particularly outspoken on this point, not surprisingly so, given her general antipathy towards Wagner. In 1875 she described the work in her diary as 'the most disgusting thing I have ever seen ... To be forced to see and hear such crazy lovemaking the whole evening, in which every feeling of decency is violated ... is the saddest thing I have ever experienced in my artistic life'.[26] In a formal paper on the opera for the Royal Musical Association in 1881, the critic H. F. Frost tried to demonstrate that *Tristan* was not 'hideously immoral' by suggesting that King Marke and Isolde had not consummated their relationship.[27]

Representation of desire in *Tristan* has resonated with different sexualities. George Bernard Shaw heard a style that exuded virility. He described the opera as 'one transport; deafness and impotence *combined* [emphasis mine] could alone resist it'[28] – humorously suggesting an impact so visceral on the male body that it could indeed bypass the ear. Ferruccio Busoni, on the other hand, interpreted the style as feminine: 'Wagner's music [in *Tristan*] is sexual, inactively erotic, thus: *lascivious*. This also explains why its inordinate duration is tolerated. *Potency acts swiftly*.'[29] In a caricature short story, the writer Oskar Panizza critiqued the *mores* of opera-goers and performers at a Parisian staging of *Tristan* at the turn of the century, contrasting their frivolous attitude with those of native German audiences. Yet the epigrammatic, almost breathless, style of the story, the speaker's obvious attraction to advertisements for corsets in the programme book, his description of the Isolde's physique and attitude – 'you have taken as a model some of Charcot's hysterical *convulsionnaires* … your costume with extra *décolletage* … a real *danse du ventre*'[30] – betray the voyeur.

It is but a short distance from this to Aubrey Beardsley's illustration *The Wagnerites* of the same year. The performance is *Tristan*, as announced by a programme book casually splayed in a corner. A male viewer, transfixed by events on stage, sits in the parterre submerged in a sea of conspicuous bare shoulders and thickly glossed lips belonging to women of questionable social standing.[31] Beardsley not only implies an ironic reversal of high society Wagnerian snobbishness, but also an unbroken stream of promiscuity from the stage into the pit and out into the house. In his drawing *How Sir Tristram Drank of the Love Drink*, an illustration for Malory's *Le Morte d'Arthur* but clearly with Wagner in mind, Beardsley depicts an Isolde with a Medusa-like crop of hair and prominent vaginal flower who towers over an effeminate Tristan.[32] Such illustrations of Wagner's heroine as a *femme fatale*, an extension of interpretations that see her in control of the action, seem echoed in later feminist descriptions of an Isolde who exhibits 'Salome's pathology' because 'she does befuddle and seduce poor Tristan by means of her chromatic excess'.[33] Following this line of criticism, one might want to trace the ubiquitous conflation of death, eroticism, feminine sexuality and the avant-garde in early twentieth-century art back to *Tristan*. Yet to juxtapose Isolde's *Liebestod* to Salome's grizzly final monologue in Strauss's opera, as is sometimes done, more readily draws attention to different artistic goals and results, particularly as they relate to the male subject.

Tristan also figured in homosexual desire, as in Hanns Fuchs's novel *Eros zwischen euch und uns* (1909) recently described by Mitchell Morris. Georg is playing *Tristan* when he first casts eyes upon the love of his life, Hans Wandelsloh. The author moves deftly back and forth between events in the opera and real life, those 'two pairs of eyes that dive deep into one another'.[34] The homosexual Polish composer Karol Szymanowski, a man of many talents, wrote a novel pointedly entitled *Efebos* in which a circle of male friends discuss an opera that Szymanowski's alter-ego in the plot is working on. One of the characters praises *Tristan* as 'the most elevated work ever created about love', but also suggests that 'the impenetrable wall of gender that divides' Wagner's protagonists shows how the 'animal mechanism of love is not suited to unearthly feelings'.[35] He thus appears to position the *Liebestod* as a mere stepping-stone to same-sex love embodying an even purer union of the physical with the aesthetic. Whether one pursues homosexual implications or not, this line of criticism obviously moves in a different direction from the excesses of Isolde as *femme fatale* towards a critical construction of desire disassociated from gender, a view of the opera where, in Lawrence Kramer's words, 'as desiring subjects, Tristan and Isolde are indistinguishable'.[36]

In Edvard Grieg's piano piece *Erotik* (Op. 43, No. 5) an ostensibly ungendered representation of libido includes an allusion to Isolde's 'Mild und leise' in an impassioned middle section leading to a reprise of the main melody. Grieg's language is relatively conservative here and, as with most of the composer's *Lyriske stykker* ('Lyric Pieces'), the technical demands are tailored for bourgeois home music-making. Surrounded on each side by *Småfugl* ('Little Bird') and *Til våren* ('To Spring'), *Erotik* may seem out of place in the collection. Yet that *Tristan* made its way into this benign domestic environment as an erotic emblem appears consonant with Wagner's more general commodification, to pursue Adorno's well-known line of thought. Likewise – and surely innocent of any critical or philosophical musing about the opera – Benjamin Britten slipped a Wagnerian sign of rapturous death into the end of *Chanson d'automne* as a fourteen-year-old student of Frank Bridge. Here, Paul Verlaine's 'sobbing violins' give way to the image of a soul floating forever in the wind 'pareil à la feuille morte' ('like a dead leaf') accompanied by the final progression of *Tristan* (spelled as F♭ harmony with added sixth moving to a C♭ chord). But the prodigy's intent is thoroughly quotidian: he presented the piece as a wedding anniversary gift to his parents.

The allusions of Grieg and Britten seem analogous to a current of criticism that sees the opera as a glorification of romantic love and sensual desire, *tout court*. 'Anyone who could write *Tristan* must surely have believed in love with the uttermost conviction', wrote Alban Berg to his future wife Helene Nahowski in 1907.[37] In Thomas Mann's essay 'The Sorrows and Grandeur of Richard Wagner' (1933), still one of the most insightful short appreciations of the composer, the author censured critics who 'tell us that *Tristan und Isolde* is a love drama, which as such implies the supreme affirmation of the will to life, and consequently has nothing to do with Schopenhauer'.[38] Mann does not name his target, but from the official Bayreuth circle in the pre-Nazi period, Houston Stewart Chamberlain's forceful repudiation of the influence of Schopenhauer's thought on *Tristan* – 'certainly here there is neither pessimism nor optimism at issue, but only love that speaks'[39] – would seem a likely candidate.

Indeed, a history of the opera's reception could profitably be written around varied appreciations of Schopenhauer's impact. To cite just one more example, albeit a conspicuous one: in describing the work as pessimistic and subversive, the writer Denis De Rougemont implicitly folded Schopenhauer into a more comprehensive view of the medieval myth's reverberation in Western culture, where Wagner's opera 'restored the mislaid significance of the legend in all its virulence'.[40] For De Rougemont, denial of the work's darkness and projection of the anathema of desire was nothing less than 'a deceit which society puts forth in self-defense'.[41] In this light, Clara Schumann exhibited merely trivial prudishness, soon out of place in rapidly changing *mores* of the *fin de siècle*. Grieg and Britten would seem to be more germane to De Rougemont's critique. The social 'necessity' or, at any rate, utility, of the drawing-room piano piece and wedding anniversary gift conjoin the apparently positive role of an erotic dimension re-enforced by innocuous Wagnerian allusion. Containment of *Tristan* also occurs in Hugo Wolf's setting of Mörike's poetry in *Gebet* ('Prayer'). The speaker entreats God to send both 'Freuden' and 'Leiden' in moderation – the line juxtaposing this Tristanesque antimony receives several half-diminished harmonies – because the greatest rewards in human existence lie somewhere in the middle ('Doch in der Mitten / liegt holdes Bescheiden'). This final line launches the piano on a passage that mimics the *Liebestod*, now compressed into a kind of *juste milieu* of bourgeois optimism.

Sexuality is more explicit in Jules Massenet's opera *Esclarmonde*. The eponymous princess heroine collapses on a bed of petals with a lover she has magically attracted. A resplendent half-diminished chord sounds – the pitches and spelling are the same as at Brangaene's first warning when Tristan and Isolde sink into flowers – and an offstage chorus of spirits intones 'Hymen! hymen!'[42] This quotation triggers an orchestral passage that simulates coitus. But far from engaging the more troubling aspects of the Wagnerian antecedent, a succession of *coups de théâtre* leads to the happy ending of a socially acceptable marriage blessed by the opera's patriarch. The conclusion is grimmer in Puccini's *Manon Lescaut*, but desire no less foregrounded and society no more threatened. The wayward heroine dies and Des Grieux (we assume from the opera and know from Abbé Prévost's novel) gets on with his life. Half-diminished harmonies in Act II have not gone unnoticed in the critical literature,[43] although it bears emphasizing that the harmony gains semantic clarity because it is rhetorically and structurally marked and also attached to desire, or, more to the point, *feminine* desire. Whereas Beardsley's courtesans soak in the eroticism of the opera while presumably plying their trade, Puccini's heroine contrasts her life as a mistress with her *Tristan*-coded attraction to Des Grieux. As Manon Lescaut reminiscences about her lover, she decorates the final cadence of both sections in her Act II duet with her brother with half-diminished harmony (at Lescaut's 'Poichè tu vuoi saper' and following her final 'Vien, resister più non so!'). Surely money is more important than love, her brother suggests. This makes for a materialistic refraction of the day/night dichotomy in Wagner, soon rearticulated musically when Manon interrupts her minuet lesson – a social dance *par excellence* – with a half-diminished chord, now with the same pitch content as the first harmony in *Tristan*. 'Voglio il tuo perdono', she soon begs Des Grieux, also with the same pitches. He responds 'O tentatrice!', his own carnal instincts fired up by Manon's obvious sexual attraction to him.

Richard Strauss's *Capriccio* harnesses desire to a didactic project. The characters reflect on the relationship of words to music in opera, a venerable problem. Flamand is a composer, Olivier a poet, and both vie for the affection of the Countess Madeleine, a personification of the spirit of opera. Ironically, it is the poet Olivier whom Strauss associates with *Tristan*. In Scene 5 he repeatedly returns to the motif encompassing a falling seventh of 'Lausch, Geliebter!' from Wagner's Act II duet. Wagner's argument about the primacy of music in *Tristan* evidently did not convince Strauss. During the composition of *Capriccio*, he noted that in many parts of Wagner's opera the text seemed of equal importance to the music, actually citing 'Lausch, Geliebter!' as an example.[44] Seventy-five years after Wagner wove *Tristan* into *Meistersinger* as a kind of dangerous presence, its more conventional operatic elements had become apparent, not the least of which was its relevance to the central aesthetic debate represented in *Capriccio*. Almost as if to tame the transcendental significance often attributed to the *Tristan* music, it is Strauss's *poet* who cites its erotically charged love music during the simultaneous act of seduction and persuasion of the superiority of *his* art.

Tristan also evokes desire in Debussy's *Prélude à l'après-midi d'un faune* around the musings of Mallarmé's priapic lyric protagonist. Social implications remain muted and Debussy (who knew Wagner's opera well enough to play it at the piano)[45] folds *Tristan* allusions into a more modern musical discourse than, say, Massenet or Grieg. Different degrees of removal from the model coexist in the *Prélude*. In bar 46, half-diminished harmony voiced with a B♭-minor triad (as at the beginning of Act III of *Tristan*)[46] contributes to a phrase that recalls the general style of the antecedent. The progression to the next harmony, a D♭-major chord with added sixth, would not have been out of place in Wagner. Debussy's melodic line is chromatic, and in bar 48 even continues with obsessive repeated surging characteristic of the *Tristan* sound. But the harmonies suddenly turn whole-tone, frustration evoked not through evaded cadence as in Wagner but by evaporation into an entirely different, and more modern, tonal space. The famous opening oboe and clarinet sonority beneath a chromatic flute solo in Debussy's *Prélude* is also a minor chord with added sixth (this time with a C♯ as root). Not ostensibly Wagnerian in itself, it is the later B♭-minor/added-sixth harmony that recalls its pedigree, but not as much as the final bars where the C♯-minor/added-sixth sonority reappears (above an E pedal) in the iconic spacing of the 'Tristan' chord (that is, with A♯ as a bass beneath E/G♯/C♯). This chord gives way to the prevailing E tonic. The progression transposes Wagner's own outer harmonic posts, recalling the 'Tristan' chord (F as bass) at the beginning of the Prelude and the B-major harmony at the final curtain (or, alternatively, the progression in his last five bars). Debussy even hangs on to an added sixth above E-major harmony almost until the end, as in the descending motif associated with Isolde's Transfiguration. He told the Wagnerian critic Willy (Henry Gauthier-Villars) that the conclusion of his *Prélude* 'is the last line [of Mallarmé's poem] prolonged: "Couple adieu, je vais voir l'ombre que tu devins"' ('Farewell couple, I will see the shadow that you became').[47] The last progression suggests not only the prolongation of desire beyond the aural boundaries of the piece but also that we should take Debussy at his word concerning Mallarmé. For by using the 'Tristan' chord he connects the 'couple' who would collapse into the single entity 'tu' to Wagner's united protagonists, creating a shadow ('l'ombre') of their presence/absence. And the shadow falls in another way too, for the 'Tristan' chord here does double duty as the self-referential aesthetic statement by a composer who stood poised to push beyond Wagnerian syntax, now a mere memory.

This dusky image of *Tristan* modulates into a night that has 'des douceurs de femme' ('a woman's sweetness') in *De Rêve*, the first song of *Proses lyriques* for which Debussy wrote both text and music. 'Mon âme! c'est du rêve ancien qui t'étreint' ('My soul! it is an ancient dream that grips you'), he writes as the concluding line. Folded within a dream of nostalgia and desire is the 'Tristan' chord with Wagner's initial pitches and voicing, giving rise to fanfare figures at 'casque d'or / Maintenant ternis, à jamais ternis' ('golden helmets now tarnished, forever tarnished'). These become muted as Debussy darkly modifies the conclusion to another Wagner opera: 'Les chevaliers sont morts / Sur le chemin du Grâal' ('The knights have died in search of the Grail').

'April is the cruelest month, breeding / Lilacs out of the dead land, mixing / Memory and desire', writes T. S. Eliot in a similar vein at the beginning of *The Waste Land*. He continues shortly with three juxtaposed elements that quote or allude to *Tristan*: a German-language excerpt from the Act I sailor's song; the (temporary) speaker's tryst with a hyacinth girl that leaves him mute 'Living nor dead, and I knew nothing, / Looking into the heart of light, the silence'; and the shepherd's Act III 'Öd' und leer das Meer!' Eliot thus succinctly summarizes Wagner's whole opera and, like Debussy in *De Rêve*, also distances himself from the model. For he ends his encapsulation of *Tristan* not with a Transfiguration but with the inky expanse of the sea. Although he *looks* into silence, he seems implicitly to invite his reader to *hear* the music at 'Öd' und leer das Meer!', a reprise of the shepherd's dark English horn strain of memory and desire. The black waters conjoin the pall of death at Tristan's (Eliot's speaker's?) birth: 'April is the cruelest month.'

Decadence and subversion

Mallarmé's and Debussy's symbolist aesthetic, or T. S. Eliot's, engage art forms removed from romantic and/or purely libidinous images of *Tristan*. Militant aestheticism; scorn for the marketplace and utilitarianism; exaggerated ecstasy; morbidity; obsessive behaviour; perceptions of art as dangerous yet intoxicating, visceral, debilitating, painful: such were the values often grouped under the umbrella of *fin-de-siècle* decadence. The aesthete confronted bourgeois complacency with numerous challenges, not the least of which was a reversal of normative values justified by a life lived aesthetically. Critics have frequently described how Wagnerism harmonized with these sensibilities.[48] In his fine account of the literary impact of *Tristan*, Elliott Zuckerman even coined the term 'Tristanism', as a distinct subset of Wagnerism, in large part because of such reactions.[49] Zuckerman's epithet perhaps overstates the case for the particularity of the opera in the reception of Wagner's oeuvre: there were few 'Tristanists' who were not also 'Wagnerists' and *Tristan* was often taken as the *summum bonum* of the composer's style and aesthetic. Yet it does also contain some truth, in as much as criticism of the opera has often revolved around its particular paradox of pain and pleasure as well as its daunting hold on the listener. The Italian critic Alberto Savinio once wrote of an organic web from which it was 'physiologically impossible to *escape*' (emphasis mine) until the end of the opera.[50]

In *Beyond Good and Evil* Nietzsche describes the 'Wagnerienne who "submits to" *Tristan und Isolde*, her will suspended' in the same breath as the 'Roman in the arena, the Christian in the ecstasies of the cross' as an instantiation of the 'spiritualization of cruelty'.[51] The effect of tragedy in general, and the bliss/agony of Wagner's lovers in particular (he implies), lies not in the stimulation of tragic pity, but rather in a displacement of the self's masochistic cruelty as it attempts to suppress irrepressible animal instincts. Rather than surrender to these, the Wagnerienne submits to the opera. Wagner was at his most depraved when he wrote it, the philosopher later maintained in *Ecce Homo*, observing that the 'world is poor for anyone who has never been sick enough for this "voluptuousness of hell"'.[52] Nietzsche loved the work deeply even after his 'break' with Wagner, writing of the necessity of *Tristan* in human experience while also warning of its dangers and irrationality – the cankers of decadent culture. Proust's narrator in *La Prisonnière (À la recherche du temps perdu)* perceptively draws attention to Nietzsche's quaking before the seductiveness of the opera by suggesting that Adolphe Adam's lighthearted *Le Postillon de Lonjumeau* (1836) might have served him as a protective straightjacket.[53] The passage seems like an ironic reversal of Nietzsche's excoriation of the ascetic's self-denial in *Beyond Good and Evil*: rather than play with the fire of the particular 'spiritualisation of cruelty' embodied in *Tristan*, better to avoid the matter altogether in Adam. Proust's narrator himself, however, does not seek to resist Wagner's opera. He abandons himself willingly to aesthetic masochism, to the motifs that circulate freely, that are omnipresent, 'so pressing and so close, so internal, so organic, so visceral, that one has the impression less of motivic reprise than neuralgia'.[54] (His characterization might also serve well as a succinct summary of the links between the opera and German expressionism.)

Thomas Mann caricatured the decadent appeal of *Tristan* in his eponymous short story. A marginally talented writer named Detlev Spinell takes a cure at a sanatorium and welcomes the arrival of Gabriele, a young married woman with a pale Pre-Raphaelite countenance. Her health appears to improve until they sit down at the piano and read through Wagner's opera. Spinell, possessed and enraptured, encourages her along 'the metaphysical certainty pressing forward chromatically'.[55] He explains, cajoles. Gabriele smiles uncomprehendingly. After the beginning of the *Liebestod*, the 'shadows had deepened in the corners of her eyes'. She lifts her hands from the keyboard and prosaically covers her face so that she may peer into darkness, see what her companion sees. Unwittingly, she has presaged her own demise. Spinell feels aesthetically fulfilled as she spits up blood over the next few days, a confirmation of the association between beauty and death that he enjoyed when he first cast eyes upon her. When Gabriele's husband is summoned because of her worsening condition, Spinell derides his blindness – the blindness of the day – to the morbid fascination of his wife, a synecdoche for the general artistic insensitivity of the bourgeois. But the conclusion of the story subverts the aesthetic bliss of death. Humming the 'Yearning' motif Spinell leaves the sanatorium to revel in the early evening light and the lengthening shadows, to contemplate the superiority of his sensibilities. Suddenly, Gabriele's baby boy and his nurse disrupt the quiet atmosphere. His self-indulgent bubble punctured, Spinell can barely 'hide the fact that he is – inwardly – on the run'.[56]

In a more poignant register, Mann fashions Aschenbach's death at the end of *Death in Venice* – the city of Wagner's death and the composition of some of *Tristan* – into an aesthetic experience not unlike Isolde's vision. The sight of Tadzio in the sea – isolated, surrounded by azure and vague mists – parallels Isolde's fulfilment in 'Wogen wonniger Düfte' ('clouds of wonderful fragrance'). Although sex and death (real or metaphorical) had long been conjoined in artistic expression, the decadent frame of mind was drawn to that equation as a moment of aesthetic rapture, a rapture so intense and pervasive as to break down the barriers among the senses in Isolde's synaesthetic gateway to primal unity. In their setting of Mann's story, Benjamin Britten and his librettist Myfanwy Piper responded to its various Wagnerisms. The beginning of Act II reflects Aschenbach's solitude by recalling the initial music of Wagner's Act III in its tempo, sustained bass and motif. Here, Britten's allusion is perhaps best heard via Debussy's to the same music between Scenes 2 and 3 in Act II of *Pelléas et Mélisande*, the desolation of Venice and Allemonde meeting the desolation of Kareol. More important, Philip Rupprecht has recently drawn attention to how the pitches of the 'Tristan' chord inform the phrases of Aschenbach's opening aria 'My mind beats on'.[57] 'Why am I now at a loss?' he asks: Wagner's opera seems to collude with Eros to create his writer's block and also to serve as a point of departure for a voyage of self-discovery that ends in a *mort exquise*.

Similarly, the 'mort parfumé du souffle de la bien-aimée' ('death made fragrant by the breath of the beloved') in Henri Duparc's song *Extase* (Jean Lahor) – not to mention the title of the *mélodie* – betray the background presence of Wagner's 'Wogen wonniger Düfte'. The composer responded with a Tristanesque language of rising chromatic sequences and conspicuously placed half-diminished sonorities. In Debussy's setting of 'La Mort des amants' (Charles Baudelaire) the pitches of the 'Tristan' chord articulate the end of the first four-bar phrase and the piece finishes with a rising four-note chromatic figure whispered in the tenor range of the piano. 'Nous aurons des lits pleins d'odeurs légères ... Nous échangerons un éclair unique, / Comme un long sanglot, tout chargé d'adieux' ('We shall have beds filled with light scents ... We shall exchange a single flash of light, like a sustained sob bearing the weight of farewell'): although Baudelaire did not necessarily have the synaesthetic *Liebestod* in mind as he fashioned his own *correspondances*, Debussy made the link for his listeners.

Pelléas et Mélisande was a favourite among decadents and its manifold and complex connections to *Tristan* have been often discussed.[58] The pale, lithe, Pre-Raphaelite-type protagonists, rather like Mann's Gabriele, wander through a plot with analogies to Wagner's opera. In Mann's realistic setting, the baby undermines the aesthete's detachment; in Debussy's and Maeterlinck's dream world, the birth of the child at the end promises a perpetuation of despair. The key image is one of blind circularity rather than the linear progression of awareness inherent in Mann's 'metaphysical certainty pressing forward chromatically'. The tone of *Pelléas* matches Eliot's truncation of *Tristan* at 'Öd' und leer das Meer'. *Tristan* reminiscences accumulate most thickly in the orchestral interlude between Scenes 2 and 3 in Act II mentioned earlier: following the allusion to the bleak Kareol music that precedes 'Öd' und leer das Meer', Debussy's music settles on a passage where the 'Tristan' chord in its iconic voicing sounds as the initial harmony of four bars in succession. The first of these transpositions recurs as the very last chord of the opera before the final C♯ pedal. At the end, the desolate life of Allemonde continues. Like Isolde, Mélisande has expired, (almost) inexplicably. Her baby, like Tristan, is born in the wake of death. Nevertheless, that the last 'Tristan' chord appears in approximately the same place as the final 'Tristan' chord in Wagner's opera underscores Debussy's opposing vision: whatever the unknown operations of fate, death does not represent higher bliss, subjective fulfilment and transcendence. 'L'âme humaine est très silencieuse / L'âme humaine aime à s'en aller seule' ('The human soul is very silent. The human soul prefers to depart alone') sings Arkel moments before, quite different from the seraphic sounds that permeate the environment as Isolde joins her lover. If anything is *exquise* about Mélisande's death, it is the silence of the attendants who appear at her bedside.

Tristan would soon be incorporated into even darker avant-garde visions. In a quotation whose fame rests on the detective work involved in ferreting out its significance, Alban Berg chiselled the 'Tristan' chord into the dark final movement of his *Lyric Suite* in reference to his extra-marital love for Hanna Fuchs-Robettin.[59] Associated in the same movement with Baudelaire's poem *De profundis clamavi*, the quotation takes on a hue of despair associated with Baudelaire's 'barren landscape' on the edge of 'chaos'. Paul Hindemith's setting of Oskar Kokoschka's 1909 one-act play *Mörder, Hoffnung der Frauen* (1921) represents another kind of chaos: sexuality as battle. In their erotic attraction, the Man and Woman inflict shocking violence on each other: she, branded with a hot iron, he, stabbed and confined to a cage around which his antagonist prowls. But she gradually weakens and the Man gains strength, ultimately ripping up the bars, killing the Woman and striding off into a wall of flames. Kokoschka's disjointed imagery, semantic discontinuity and syntactical freedoms all suggest irrational primal energies that subvert the rationality of language. Hindemith's reference to the 'Lausch, Geliebter!' music from the Act II *Tristan* duet (at 'Unsre Frau! / Unser Herr' and much emphasized after this) occurs as the followers of Man and Woman first address each other, a prelude to their violent mutually destructive orgy later in the work. In this perverse fantasy of the Man, the Woman ultimately collapses. *Mörder, Hoffnung der Frauen* might be understood as a representation of the truly subversive nature of Schopenhauerian Will, as if Wagner had not gone far enough – and by a wide margin.[60] As we have seen, *Tristan* had become ensconced in philistine culture, often as an idealized celebration of Eros. Hindemith and Kokoschka challenge the reactionary appropriation of Wagner, trumping the *mort exquise* of earlier composers.

Eros also feeds perversity in Berg's *Lulu*. In Act II, Scene 1 the composer Alwa declares love for Lulu to the accompaniment of the 'Tristan' chord in the transposition and voicing of bar 2 in Wagner's opera.[61] Some have suggested that Tristan is caught up in a completely solipsistic hysteria in Act III and that throughout the work Isolde is merely his 'fantasy'.[62] Berg's citation encourages such a reading of *Tristan* through Lulu's lovers. Half-diminished harmony in its characteristic 'Tristan' chord spacing also occurs as the last sonority before Lulu's scream of death at the hands of Jack the Ripper. She has become dispensable as a fantasy object: the phallic knife does its work, but not before confronting listeners with the vocal texture of the chaos with which each of her lovers has flirted, and to which most have succumbed. Brangaene screams at the culmination of Wagner's Act II duet, a chaotic impulse and glimpse into the horror of the Will that Isolde neutralizes, avoids or sublimates in the dulcet vision of her reprise of this music in the *Liebestod*.[63] Following Hindemith's *Mörder* and other avant-garde *femmes fatales*, Lulu restores the scream. Berg's 'Tristan' chord followed by a *Todesschrei* explosively fuse *femme fatale* and masochistic male fantasy readings of *Tristan* in an unambiguously misogynistic climate.

Desublimation

Such troubling extensions rub shoulders with utterly farcical appropriations of *Tristan* in the repertory. The young Hindemith, *enfant terrible* of Weimar musical culture, conceived *Mörder, Hoffnung der Frauen* as the first instalment of a triptych that also included the burlesque opera *Das Nusch-Nuschi*. Sexuality remains the central theme, but now with a link to *Tristan* that effectively challenges its cultural status. Blame for the adulterous flings of the women in the Burmese emperor's harem falls upon his most trusted general, Kyce Wang. At the climactic scene of denunciation, the emperor paraphrases both the words and music of King Marke's 'Mir dies? / Dies, Tristan, mir?' Freudian critical perspectives on *Tristan* hold King Marke as father, Isolde as mother, Tristan as son[64] (they seem especially convincing when Tristan returns to the love music of 'O sink' hernieder' later in Act II at 'Dem Land, das Tristan meint / der Sonne Licht nicht scheint. / Es ist das dunkel / nächt'ges Land, / dauraus die Mutter / mich enstandt'). Hindemith's desublimation becomes complete when the emperor orders the castration of his friend.

From Burma to Vienna: another turn around the mother-son axis ushers a gentler comic mode and the Marschallin's bedroom in Act I of Strauss's *Der Rosenkavalier*. With all of Octavian's impetuous bleating about the end of the night ('Warum ist Tag? Ich will nicht den Tag! / Für was ist der Tag!'), a wink at *Tristan* evidently proved too difficult for Strauss to resist. As Octavian joins hands with the Marschallin he distractedly ruminates about melded identity: 'das bin ich, das will zu dir, / aber das Ich vergeht in dem Du' ('It is I who seek you out / But the "I" is lost in the "You""). Strauss sets the last phrase with a half-diminished harmony voiced the same way as bar 2 of Wagner's Prelude.[65] In Ravel's comedy *L'Heure espagnole* the suitors for the happily adulterous prima donna are more numerous than in Strauss. In a rearticulation of medieval bonds of fealty, one of them, the corpulent banker Don Inigo, finances her husband's business. He improbably marshalls the 'Tristan' chord (sounding at the pitch of Wagner's bar 2) at the climax of his first amorous advance – only to be met by an indignant 'Excusez-moi seigneur' while the cuckoo clock sounds irreverently to poke fun at both him and his allusion. In Alexander Zemlinsky's lighthearted lied *Irmelin Rose* suitors are still more plentiful as witnessed by the sounding of the opening melodic motif from *Tristan* eight times in succession as they give voice to their shallow flattery ('Und mit zärtlichen Gebärden / klang ihr Schmeicheln ohne Rast'). Quotations such as these have something of the character of a prop pulled from the cupboard of musical and comedic stagecraft, and no more so when actually associated with a real prop. In Act II of Strauss's *Ariadne auf Naxos* a reference to Circe's magic drink spawns a 'Tristan' chord, as does the moment when callow Albert Herring in Britten's eponymous opera quaffs lemonade spiked with rum. Whereas in *Tristan* the potion unleashes the world of the night, in *Albert Herring* it disengages a small-town protagonist from his mother's apron strings.

As an example of desublimation perhaps no *Tristan* quotation has been cited more frequently than Debussy's reference in the piano piece 'Golliwogg's Cakewalk' from the suite *Children's Corner*. The yearning rising sixth sounds '*avec une grande emotion*' in the middle section, and the 'Tristan' chord at pitch infuses the rag time figuration elsewhere (including the opening gambit). The implied social distance traversed in this interpenetration of 'high' and 'low' art lends a particularly grotesque flavour to the borrowing. Yet the dividing line here between reverence and assertion of creative independence through satire is by no means clear. The same seems true of Emmanuel Chabrier's much earlier four-hand piano *quadrille* on themes from the opera entitled *Souvenirs de Munich* – the same Chabrier who voiced an under-the-skin type of possession by *Tristan* when, at the Munich performances, he was heard to sob: 'Oh! this is silly ... Can't help myself ... For ten years of my life I have waited for the cello A!'[66] Enthusiasm for art-religion became an important social posture in *fin-de-siècle* France among elegant company – but wit had been one of much longer standing. Reverence becomes completely submerged by iconoclasm in Erik Satie's quotation of the 'Tristan' chord (spelled F/A♭/D♯/B) as the penultimate sonority in the short piano piece *Choral inappétissant*.[67] Part of the joke is that the final resolution is to C major, sudden white-note 'purity' after the bizarre and wandering harmonies that fill the piece (including an E-major dominant-seventh chord, which is where the penultimate 'Tristan' chord 'should' resolve). More important, Satie equates his allusion with dull academicism, flattening the perspective between a distasteful four-part exercise and Wagnerian harmony in order to debunk both.

Satie's oeuvre, of course, funnelled obliquely into surrealism. Several decades later the film *L'Age d'or*, to a scenario by Luis Buñuel and Salvador Dali, also trafficked in grotesque Wagnerian appropriation, now with trenchant political connotations. An early scene shows pompous municipal officials setting about to lay the foundation stone for a magnificent edifice on a barren island. Behind the stately gathering, a young peasant couple copulates frenetically: the young woman's ecstatic moans provide a counterpoint to an excerpt from *Tristan* on the soundtrack. After scandalized townsfolk pry the two apart, she appears in a bathroom. A toilet flushes and images of a cesspool fill the screen while the *Tristan* music continues, something of an exponential intensification of Clara Schumann's bourgeois rectitude, described earlier. Later in the film, Buñuel and Dali insert another large passage from *Tristan* as diegetic music in a garden concert scene. A counterpoint to the earlier *Tristan* episode, the lovers enjoy their erotic tryst behind the backs of listeners whose glum demeanours mask any hint of absorption in sex or aesthetic rapture. A phone call from the Minister of the Interior calls away the male lover. He learns that many women and children have perished as a direct result of his unspecified brutalities. Sorely irritated at being disturbed by something so 'trifling', he returns to his paramour. But in the interim, pornography conjoins mockery of romantic transcendence: for she has found a ready replacement for her lover by slowly sucking on the toe of a garden statue.

In their applications of *Tristan* borrowings, others have linked social desublimation to a democratizing instinct by implicitly advocating the right of all levels of society to Wagnerian discourse. Responding to the funereal 'Bedeckt mich mit Blumen' in the folk poetry of the *Spanisches Liederbuch* – 'Ist ja alles doch dasselbe, / Liebesodem oder

Düfte von Blumen' ('Everything is just the same, love's breath or flowers' fragrance') – Hugo Wolf selected the key of A♭, often an emblem at the *fin de siècle* for Wagner's Act II duet, and cited the 'Tristan' chord at pitch. Gustave Charpentier announced that one of the premises in his opera *Louise* was to reuse Wagnerian themes in an urban and proletarian milieu in such a way that they would be made broadly relevant.[68] The love scene in Montmartre contains traces of *Tristan*, as does the love music for two humble fisher folk in Act II of Alfred Bruneau's *L'Ouragan*. In Manuel de Falla's *La vida breve*, the 'Tristan' chord (together with rising chromatic lines) follows a chorus for workers in an iron foundry and encapsulates the attraction of the poor gypsy Salud to the wealthier Paco. The chord sounds again (at the pitch of Wagner's bar 2) when Salud collapses before the assembled guests at Paco's wedding to another. Ruggiero Leoncavallo colours the Left Bank world of his *La bohème* with *Tristan* quotations (Act III prelude), but a more polemical transplantation of borrowings to a popular, modern milieu is surely the prologue of *Pagliacci*. Tonio's speech outlines the tenets of *verismo*, and when he refers to the agonies of love in the 'squarcio di vita' ('slice of life'), the music assumes a distinctly Tristanesque aura. Hanns Eisler did the 'squarcio di vita' one better by working quotations from *Tristan* into the quotidian subjects of his song cycle *Zeitungsausschnitte* ('Newspaper Clippings'), including a setting from the 'personal' ads of a widower seeking a new wife.

The left-leaning politics of Charpentier, Bruneau and Eisler were well known, as are Hans Werner Henze's. As he tells it, his large composition for piano, tape and orchestra entitled *Tristan* began existence as an extended piece for piano with harmonies that reminded him of Wagner's opera because they seemed 'to be moving towards an incommensurable goal, whose attainment keeps being deferred, so that a new constellation of enigmas can be posed in its place'.[69] But Henze feels that Wagner's music has something totalitarian about it. With a broad range of cultural references he (re)plays the enigmas of desire, loss and memory that culminate in a 'scream of death no longer simply that of Isolde or Tristan, but of the whole suffering world ... What can be heard on tape is an electronic elaboration of the scream'.[70] Once more Brangaene's shriek seems to leapfrog the *Liebestod*. As with the Enlightenment vision of Beethoven's Ninth Symphony, Wagner's romantic transcendence has not always been an easy sell in the twentieth century. The casual indifference of the garden lover in *L'Age d'or* to his own brutality complements his self-indulgent aesthetic and erotic absorption in Wagner's music. Henze, for his part, focuses on the texture of world events. Near the end of his piece a citation of the Kareol music occurs to the accompaniment of a human heartbeat (over speakers) and a recitation of the medieval Tristan legend with a Cockney accent. Chimes sound. 'Öd' und leer das Meer' again. The year is 1973. Henze recalls the 'football stadium in Santiago where political "suspects" are rounded up ... while the fascists' goose-step resounds through buildings deserted by the people, and the fly face of General Pinochet appears on the television screen'.[71]

Notes

Introduction

1. Winifred Wagner (ed.), *König Ludwig II. und Richard Wagner: Briefwechsel*, vol. I (Karlsruhe, 1936), 106.
2. Vladimir Nabokov, *Strong Opinions* (New York, NY, 1973), 304.
3. Roger Scruton, *Death-Devoted Heart: Sex and the Sacred in Wagner's 'Tristan und Isolde'* (New York, NY, 2003); Eric Chafe, *The Tragic and the Ecstatic: The Musical Revolution of Wagner's 'Tristan und Isolde'* (New York, NY, 2005).

Synopsis

1. See John Deathridge, Martin Geck and Egon Voss (eds.), *Wagner Werk-Verzeichnis* (Mainz, 1986), p. 431. There are editions in Richard Wagner, *Sämtliche Schriften und Dichtungen*, 5th edn., vol. XI (Leipzig, 1911), 326–43, and in a Programmheft for the Bayerische Staatsoper production of the opera (Munich, 1980), 31–40, which differ only in occasional variations of orthography. The translation follows their use of italics, but omits the footnotes by Hans von Wolzogen and some inessential variants. Missing quotation marks have been added. Since both editions use parentheses instead of square brackets for variants, I have not attempted to differentiate between these and possible parentheses in Wagner's original.

1 Public and private life: on the genesis of *Tristan und Isolde* and the *Wesendonck Lieder*

1. Richard Wagner, *Sämtliche Briefe*, vol. VI, ed. Hans-Joachim Bauer and Johannes Forner (Leipzig, 1986), 299. The editors of the volume suggest 16 December 1854 as an exact date of the letter. The translation is my own, as are subsequent translations unless otherwise indicated.
2. Letter of 23 August 1856 to August Röckel. Richard Wagner, *Sämtliche Briefe*, vol. VIII, ed. Hans-Joachim Bauer and Johannes Forner (Leipzig, 1991), 156.
3. Egon Voss, 'Die "schwarze und die weiße Flagge": Zur Entstehung von Wagners *Tristan*', *Archiv für Musikwissenschaft*, 54 (1997), 218. Two of the most thorough and interesting accounts of the genesis of the opera can

be found in Ernest Newman, *The Wagner Operas* (New York, NY, 1949), with many reprints [UK title: *Wagner Nights*] and Roger Scruton, *Death-Devoted Heart: Sex and the Sacred in Wagner's 'Tristan and Isolde'* (Oxford and New York, NY, 2003).

4. Letter of 16 December 1856 to Franz Liszt. Wagner, *Sämtliche Briefe*, vol. VIII, 228.
5. Letter of 30 September 1857 to the firm of Breitkopf & Härtel. Richard Wagner, *Sämtliche Briefe*, vol. IX, ed. Klaus Burmeister and Johannes Forner (Leipzig, 2000), 46–7.
6. Letter of 15 March 1858 to Alexander Ritter, in Hans von Bülow, *Briefe und Schriften*, ed. Marie von Bülow, 8 vols. (Leipzig, 1895–1908), vol. IV, 162.
7. Letter of 4 January 1858 to Dr Hermann Härtel. Wagner, *Sämtliche Briefe*, vol. IX, 107.
8. See letters dated 17 March and 6 April 1859 to the firm of Breitkopf & Härtel. Richard Wagner, *Sämtliche Briefe*, vol. X, ed. Werner Breig and Andreas Mielke (Wiesbaden, 2000), 375 and vol. XI, ed. Werner Breig and Martin Dürrer (Wiesbaden, 1999), 23.
9. Full details in Deathridge, Geck and Voss (eds.), *Wagner-Werk-Verzeichnis*, 433–42.
10. Letter of 5 June 1859 to the firm of Breitkopf & Härtel. Wagner, *Sämtliche Briefe*, vol. XI, 120.
11. The phrase used by the Wagner scholar Otto Strobel to describe the earliest musical sketches of *Tristan*. See Otto Strobel, '"Geschenke des Himmels." Über die ältesten überlieferten *Tristan*-Themen und eine andere – unbekannte Melodie Wagners', *Offizieller Bayreuther Festspielführer* (Bayreuth, 1938), 157–65.
12. To cite one instance: Breitkopf & Härtel acknowledged receipt of pp. 255–74 of the manuscript score of Act III on 21 June 1859. See Wilhelm Altmann (ed.), *Richard Wagners Briefwechsel mit Breitkopf & Härtel* (Leipzig, 1911; repr. Niederwalluf bei Wiesbaden, 1971), 164. On the same day Wagner wrote to Mathilde Wesendonck that 'the day before yesterday I started the composition [of Act III] again with enthusiasm: yesterday it came to a halt, and today I can't even get going at all' (Wagner, *Sämtliche Briefe*, vol. XI, 136). As he frequently did, Wagner blamed his difficulties on the weather (!) though the sketches themselves show that serious harmonic and especially structural difficulties with the music were the real cause. For a detailed account of Wagner's procedure in Act I, see Robert Bailey, *The Genesis of 'Tristan and Isolde' and a Study of Wagner's Sketches and Drafts for the First Act* (Ann Arbor, MI: University Microfilms, Inc., 1970).
13. For opposed views on the issue of recapitulation, see William Kinderman, 'Dramatic Recapitulation in Wagner's *Götterdämmerung*', *19th-Century Music*, 4 (1980–81), 101–12 and Chapter 12 of my *Wagner Beyond Good and Evil* (Berkeley, CA, 2008).
14. Richard Wagner, *My Life*, ed. Mary Whittall and trans. Andrew Gray, (Cambridge, 1983), 588.

15. In a letter of 12 July 1862 to the publisher Franz Schott, Wagner wrote that he had overcome his 'reluctance' to publish the songs, which he counted 'among his best works' (Richard Wagner, *Sämtliche Briefe*, vol. XIV, ed. Werner Breig and Andreas Mielke [Wiesbaden, 2002], 207). The simple reason for this change of heart was that Schott had advanced him a great deal of money for *Die Meistersinger von Nürnberg*, which was proving more difficult, and therefore taking longer, to compose than Wagner had anticipated. The offer to publish the songs was one way of mollifying Schott and preventing him from asking for his money back. Accounts of the *Wesendonck Lieder* are few and far between. The only more-than-cursory one in English is Malcolm Miller, *Wagner's 'Wesendonck Lieder': an analytic study, with consideration of the orchestral arrangements of Felix Mottl and Hans Werner Henze* (PhD diss., King's College London 1990), (copy deposited in the Chancery Lane Maughan Library, King's College London).
16. See Richard Wagner, *Sämtliche Werke*, vol. XVII (*Klavierlieder*), ed. Egon Voss (Mainz, 1976), vii.
17. See Egon Voss, 'Die Wesendoncks und Richard Wagner', in Axel Langer and Chris Walton (eds.), *Minne, Muse und Mäzen: Otto und Mathilde Wesendonck und ihr Zürcher Künstlerzirkel* (Zurich, 2002), 119.
18. For detailed information on the genesis of the songs between November 1857 and October 1858, some of which exist in as many as three versions, see Deathridge, Geck and Voss (eds.), *Wagner-Werk-Verzeichnis*, 448–58.
19. Franz Liszt, 'Robert Franz', *Neue Zeitschrift für Musik*, 43/22 (23 November 1855), 230.
20. Wagner himself sang some of Franz's lieder while Franz accompanied him on the piano. A conclusion difficult to resist from the mixture of faint praise and scorn lavished on Franz's visit in Wagner's autobiography is that although Wagner had been grateful to him in the early 1850s for helping to bring *Lohengrin* to public attention, he now (in summer 1857) clearly regarded Franz as a rival. See Wagner, *My Life*, 552. For a more generous evaluation of Franz, see A. W. Ambros, 'Robert Franz', in *Bunte Blätter. Skizzen und Studien für Freunde der Musik und der bildenden Kunst* (Leipzig, 1872), 295–325.
21. Liszt, 'Robert Franz', 229–35 *passim*.
22. Liszt, 'Robert Franz', 234.
23. See Deathridge, Geck and Voss, *Wagner-Werk-Verzeichnis*, 452. This was by no means Wagner's only attempt in public to downplay the significance of Mathilde Wesendonck. The piano sonata he wrote for her in 1853, which according to Wagner's own description at the time was his 'first composition since the completion of *Lohengrin* six years ago', is a far more ambitious composition than is suggested by the title Wagner gave to it when he agreed to let it appear in print in January 1878 in order to settle some of his debts with his publisher: *A Sonata for the Album of Frau M. W.* Not even with the greatest semantic licence

could anyone convincingly describe this lengthy one-movement sonata as an album piece. In private, Wagner tried to diminish its obvious ambition even more by calling it variously a 'sketch', a 'fantasy', and most damningly of all, an 'elegant triviality' ('elegante Nichtigkeit'). See Deathridge, Geck and Voss, *Wagner-Werk-Verzeichnis*, 348. Mathilde Wesendonck herself thought the discrepancy between the nature of the piece and its published title blatant enough to mention it in a short memoir, albeit without pointing to Wagner as the culprit. See Mathilde Wesendonck, 'Erinnerungen', *Allgemeine Deutsche Musik-Zeitung*, 23/7 (14 February 1896), 92. Answering a letter of 21 November 1884 from the Wagner collector Mary Burrell, who was equally suspicious of the title, she had already stated that it was not a question of an 'album sonata', adding that Wagner 'profoundly detested this mania for albums'. See Judith Cabaud, *Mathilde Wesendonck ou la rêve d'Isolde* (Arles, 1990), 371–2.

24. Martin Gregor-Dellin and Dietrich Mack (eds.), *Cosima Wagner's Diaries*, trans. and with an introduction by Geoffrey Skelton, 2 vols, (London, 1978/80), 15 January 1872.
25. Letter of 31 December 1858 to Franz Liszt. Wagner, *Sämtliche Briefe*, vol. X, 206–7.
26. Letter of 4 January 1859 from Liszt to Wagner. Hanjo Kesting (ed.), *Franz Liszt – Richard Wagner Briefwechsel* (Frankfurt/Main, 1988), 599. Liszt's reply and Wagner's original letter were omitted from nineteenth-century editions of their correspondence.
27. Kesting, *Franz Liszt – Richard Wagner Briefwechsel*, 589.
28. Beginning of the letter of 31 December 1858 to Liszt. Wagner, *Sämtliche Briefe*, vol. X, 206.
29. Undated letter, probably April 1859, to Mathilde Wesendonck. Wagner, *Sämtliche Briefe*, vol. XI, 58.
30. Slavoj Žižek, 'Afterword', in *Revolution at the Gates: A Selection of Writings from February to October 1917 [by] V. I. Lenin* (London and New York, NY, 2002), 207.
31. Mathilde Wesendonck, 'Erinnerungen', 92.
32. Dena Goodman, 'Enlightenment Salons: The Convergence of Female and Philosophic Ambitions', *Eighteenth-Century Studie*s, 22/3 (Spring 1989), 332.
33. Philip Dutton Hurn and Waverley Lewis Root, *The Truth About Wagner* (London, 1930), 164.
34. The portrait is usually reproduced without comment in the more lavishly presented Wagner biographies. See, e.g., Curt von Westernhagen, *Wagner: A Biography*, 2 vols. (Cambridge, 1978), 1, 8–9, illustration 10b.
35. William Ashton Ellis (trans.), *Richard Wagner to Mathilde Wesendonck* (London, 1905), xl.
36. See Cosima Wagner's letter to Golther dated 5 January 1904 in Dietrich Mack (ed.), *Cosima Wagner: Das zweite Leben* (Munich and Zurich, 1980), 650. Also Ellis's introduction to *Richard Wagner to Mathilde Wesendonck*, xxxix.

37. One event turned out to be politically extremely hazardous. The German victory celebration Mathilde organized with Otto Wesendonck's support in the Zurich Tonhalle in March 1871 at the end of the Franco-Prussian War resulted in a near-riot and an attempt to burn down their villa, after which they left Zurich for good. See Chris Walton, 'Wagner, Otto and the Three Mathildes', *The Musical Times*, 143 (Autumn 2002), 43.
38. Gregor-Dellin and Mack, *Cosima Wagner's Diaries*, 9 February 1871.
39. Letter of 6 October 1903 from Cosima Wagner to Wolfgang Golther, cited in Mack, *Cosima Wagner*, 859.
40. The letter was eventually sold to the collector Mary Burrell by Minna's daughter Nathalie and first published in English translation in John N. Burk (ed.), *Letters of Richard Wagner: The Burrell Collection* (London, 1951), 369–72. German text in Wagner, *Sämtliche Briefe*, vol. IX, 228–31.
41. The fate of Mathilde Wesendonck's side of the correspondence is still a mystery. Copies of some decidedly uninteresting letters written relatively late in her relationship with Wagner between 1861 and 1865, when the intensity of their exchange of views was in any case markedly diminishing, were discovered fortuitously by Cosima Wagner's daughter Eva and sent to Golther and the Wesendonck heirs to do with them what they liked. In an unpublished communication to Mathilde's grandson Fritz von Bissing, Cosima assumed (perhaps correctly) that Mathilde herself destroyed all her letters to Wagner after he had returned them – an act that has left posterity almost completely in the dark about the true extent of her contribution. 'Die Briefe Ihrer theuren Grossmutter wurden ihr Alle zurückgestattet u[nd] sie hat sie zerstört' ('Your dear grandmother's letters were all returned to her and she destroyed them'). Dictated letter of 28 December 1903 to Fritz von Bissing (not in Cosima's hand but signed by her) sold as part of Lot 167, Sotheby's, London, 19 May 2006. An admittedly inscrutable entry in Wagner's so-called Venice Diary addressed to Mathilde suggests that her letters to him were expected to be many: 'I've had a beautiful case made here, expressly to keep your keep-sakes and letters safe and secure. It can hold a great deal, and whatever is put there will not be given to naughty children. Take good care what you send me in future. You won't get any of it back . . .' Entry dated August 24 [1858], Julius Kapp (ed.), *Richard Wagner an Mathilde und Otto Wesendon[c]k. Tagebuchblätter und Briefe* (Leipzig, 1915), 110.
42. '[Ich] brachte das Opfer vor welchem Ihre Mutter sich scheute.' Dictated letter of 2 June 1904 to Karl von Wesendonck (not in Cosima's hand but signed by her) sold as part of Lot 167, Sotheby's, London, 19 May 2006.
43. Stanley Sadie (ed.), *The New Grove Dictionary of Opera* (London, 1992), vol. IV, 819.
44. Philippe Ariès and Georges Duby (eds.), *A History of Private Life*, vol. IV, *From the Fires of Revolution to the Great War*, ed. Michelle Perrot (Cambridge, MA, and London, 1990), 2.

2 Between memory and desire: Wagner's libretto and late Romantic subjectivity

1. Portions of the following summarize discussions in two earlier articles, Arthur Groos, 'Wagner's *Tristan und Isolde*: In Defence of the Libretto', *Music & Letters*, 69 (1988), 465–81, and 'Appropriation in Wagner's *Tristan* Libretto', in Arthur Groos and Roger Parker (eds.), *Reading Opera* (Princeton, NJ, 1988), 12–33.
2. Ernest Newman, *The Wagner Operas* (New York, NY, 1949; repr. 1983), vol. I, 202. For examples of this commonplace throughout Wagner scholarship, see Richard David, 'Wagner the Dramatist', in Peter Burbidge and Richard Sutton (eds.), *The Wagner Companion* (New York, NY, 1979), 129, and Joseph Kerman, 'Opera as Symphonic Poem', in *Opera as Drama*, rev. edn. (Berkeley and Los Angeles, CA, 1988).
3. See Carolyn Abbate, 'Opera as Symphony, a Wagnerian Myth', in Carolyn Abbate and Roger Parker (eds.), *Analyzing Opera: Verdi and Wagner* (Berkeley, CA, 1989), 92–124.
4. See the *Mitteilung an meine Freunde*, in Richard Wagner, *Sämtliche Schriften und Dichtungen*, 6th edn. (Leipzig, [1911–16]), vol. III, 266 and 316.
5. The title page is reproduced in Horst F. G. Klein, *Erst- und Frühdrücke der Textbücher von Richard Wagner* (Tutzing, 1979), 30.
6. The exception is Dieter Borchmeyer, *Das Theater Richard Wagners: Idee – Dichtung – Wirkung* (Stuttgart, 1982); trans. Stewart Spencer as *Richard Wagner: Theory and Theatre* (Oxford, 1991).
7. See Piero Weiss, '"Sacred Bronzes": Paralipomena to an Essay by Dallapiccola', *19th-Century Music*, 9 (1985), 42–9.
8. Robert Boxberger (ed.), *Immermann's Werke* (Berlin, 1883), vol. XIII, 233.
9. See Thomas Mann, 'Leiden und Größe Richard Wagners', trans. as 'The Sorrows and Grandeur of Richard Wagner', in Thomas Mann, *Pro and Contra Wagner*, trans. Allan Blunden (Chicago, IL, 1985), 124–6; Dieter Borchmeyer, 'Welt im sterbenden Licht – *Tristan* und der Mythos der Nacht', in *Das Theater Richard Wagners*, 261–87 (English trans., 326–67); Jürgen Maehder, 'Ein Klanggewand für die Nacht – Zur Partitur von *Tristan und Isolde*', Bayreuth Programmhefte II/1982, 27–9.
10. See Groos, 'Appropriation', 25–9, and Peter Wapnewski, 'Rivale Faust: Beobachtungen zu Wagners Goethe-Verständnis', *Jahrbuch des Freien Deutschen Hochstifts* (1984), 128–56.
11. See Albrecht Riethmüller, 'Nikolaus Lenau's "The Bust of Beethoven"', in J. M. McGlathery (ed.), *Music and German Literature: Their Relationships since the Middle Ages* (Columbia, SC, 1992), 306f. The poem's function is suggestively interpreted by John Deathridge, 'Postmortem on Isolde' in *Wagner Beyond Good and Evil* (Berkeley, CA, 2008), 133–55.
12. As divided in the brilliant translation of A. T. Hatto, Gottfried von Straßburg, *Tristan, with the Surviving Fragments of the Tristran of Thomas* ([Harmondsworth], 1965).

13. See Volker Mertens, trans. Stewart Spencer, 'Wagner's Middle Ages', in Ulrich Müller and Peter Wapnewski (eds.), *Wagner Handbook* (Cambridge, MA, 1992), 236–68. Nearly half of Wagner's Dresden library consisted of medieval texts and history, and his documented reading includes Friedrich Heinrich von der Hagen, *Gottfrieds von Straßburg Werke aus den beßten Handschriften mit Einleitung und Wörterbuch herausgegeben* (Breslau, 1823); Hans Ferdinand Massmann, *Tristan und Isolt von Gottfried von Straßburg* (Leipzig, 1843); Hermann Kurtz, *Tristan und Isolde: Gedicht von Gottfried von Straßburg. Übertragen und beschlossen von Hermann Kurtz* (Stuttgart, 1844); and Georg Gottfried Gervinus, *Geschichte der poetischen National-Literatur der Deutschen*, 2nd edn., vol. I (Leipzig, 1840), 434–54.
14. Cf. Robert Schumann's scenario for the opera, written in 1845–6 by Robert Reinick, published in *Die Musik*, 17 (1925), 753–60.
15. Wagner, *Mein Leben*, 2nd edn. (Munich, 1915), vol. III, 84; cited from the translation of Andrew Gray, *My Life*, ed. Mary Whittall (Cambridge, 1983), 511. Cf. the similar reference to *Parzival* in the letter to Mathilde Wesendonck of 30 May 1859.
16. See Stewart Spencer and Barry Millington (trans. and eds.), *Selected Letters of Richard Wagner* (New York, NY, 1988), 458.
17. Wagner, *Sämtliche Schriften*, vol. IV, 47f.
18. Wagner, *Sämtliche Schriften*, vol. IV, 8.
19. Lines 11645ff. in the edition of Friedrich Ranke, Gottfried von Straßburg, *Tristan und Isold* (Zurich and Berlin, 1965).
20. In recent scholarship the nature of this striving has received emphases ranging from primal urges to mystical union. See especially Linda Hutcheon and Michael Hutcheon, 'Eros and Thanatos: Richard Wagner's *Tristan und Isolde*', in *Opera: The Art of Dying* (Cambridge, MA, 2004), 45–72; Morten Bartnæs, *Richard Wagners 'Tristan und Isolde': Literarische Alleinswerdung als literaturwissenschaftliches Problem* (Hannover, 2001).
21. The libretto will be cited according to Richard Wagner, *Sämtliche Schriften und Dichtungen*, 6th edn. (Leipzig, n.d.), vol. VII. All translations are the author's.
22. See the entry in Jacob and Wilhelm Grimm, *Deutsches Wörterbuch*, vol. VI (Leipzig, 1886), 951. *Liebeslust* expresses the hero's dual nature, anticipating momentary sensual delights which his striving for the ultimate totality of human experience will not permit him to enjoy. The three passages consist of Faust's famous definition of the 'two souls' conflicting within his breast: 'Die eine hält, in derber *Liebeslust*, / sich an die Welt mit klammernden Organen' (1114f.); Faust's command to Mephisto after meeting Gretchen to procure him 'ein Halstuch von ihrer Brust, / Ein Strumpfband meiner *Liebeslust*!' (2661f.); and the petition of the Doctor Marianus in the final scene of *Faust II* that the Mater Gloriosa accept 'was des Mannes Brust / Ernst und zart beweget / Und mit heiliger *Liebeslust* / Dir entgegenträget' (12001ff.).

23. See 'The Circuitous Journey', in M. H. Abrams, *Natural Supernaturalism: Tradition and Revolution in Romantic Literature* (New York, NY, 1973), 141–324.
24. On the dawn-song, see A. T. Hatto, *Eos: An Inquiry into the Theme of Lovers' Meetings and Partings at Dawn in Poetry* (London, 1965); on the genre in *Tristan*, Peter Wapnewski, *Richard Wagner: Die Szene und ihr Meister*, 2nd edn. (Munich, 1983), 42.
25. 'Zeitlos und raumlos ist der Nacht Herrschaft' ('Time-less and space-less is the rule of night'), in Novalis, *Schriften*, ed. Paul Kluckhohn and Richard Samuel, vol. I (Stuttgart, 1960), 132.
26. See the discussion of this nexus in Peter Wapnewski, *Der traurige Gott: Richard Wagner in seinen Helden*, 2nd edn. (Munich, 1980), 71–9, and Ulrich Weisstein, 'The Little Word *und*: *Tristan und Isolde* as Verbal Construct', in Leroy R. Shaw *et al.* (eds.), *Wagner in Retrospect: A Centennial Reappraisal* (Amsterdam, 1987), 70–90.
27. Max Frischeisen-Köhler (ed.), *Über den Tod und sein Verhältnis zur Unzerstörbarkeit unsers Wesens an sich*, in Schopenhauer, *Sämtliche Werke*, vol. III (Berlin, n.d.), 526.
28. On the androgynous implications of this scene, see Jean-Jacques Nattiez, *Wagner Androgyne* (Princeton, NJ, 1993), 140–46.
29. Kerman, 'Opera as Symphonic Poem', 158–78, esp. 163–8.
30. See Michel Poizat, *L'Opéra ou Le Cri de l'ange: Essai sur la jouissance de l'amateur d'opéra* (Paris, 1986), 53–64 and 221–42, trans. Arthur Denner as *The Angel's Cry: Beyond the Pleasure Principle in Opera* (Ithaca, NY, 1992), 31–9 and 159–78; Slavoj Žižek and Mladen Dolar, *Opera's Second Death* (New York, NY, 2002), 103 *passim*.
31. Žižek and Dolar, *Opera's Second Death*, 123.
32. Cf. Nattiez's working out of the androgynous complementarity of the principals in Act III, supplementing Kerman's emphasis on Tristan with a brief reading of Isolde, Nattiez, *Wagner Androgyne*, 150–55.
33. Both 'Verklärung' and 'Liebestod' are historically justifiable. Deathridge draws attention to the fact that the latter is sanctioned by the first separate full score of the concert version of the Prelude and 'Liebestod' in 1882; see *Wagner Beyond Good and Evil*, 266.
34. On the importance of wind, breath, etc., see Friedrich Kittler, '*Weltatem*: On Wagner's Media Technology', in Shaw (ed.), *Wagner in Retrospect*, 203–12; repr. in David Levin (ed.), *Opera through Other Eyes* (Stanford, CA, 1993), 215–35, 261–4.
35. See Sieghart Döhring, 'Die Wahnsinnsszene', in Heinz Becker (ed.), *Die 'Couleur locale' in der Oper des 19. Jahrhunderts* (Regensburg, 1976), 279–314.
36. See Deathridge, 'Postmortem on Isolde', 139f.
37. See Borchmeyer, *Das Theater Richard Wagners*, trans. Spencer, 362f. On its later ramifications, see Camilla Bork, '"Tod und Verklärung": Isoldes Liebestod als Modell künstlerischer Schlußgestaltung', in Hermann Danuser and Herfried Münkler (eds.), *Zukunftsbilder: Richard Wagners Revolution und ihre Folgen* (Schliengen, 2002), 161–78.

38. See Patrick McCreless, 'Isolde's Transfiguration in Words and Music', in Deborah Stein (ed.), *Engaging Music: Essays in Music Analysis* (New York, NY, and Oxford, 2005), 122–35.
39. See Poizat, *L'Opéra*.

3 The Prelude and the play

1. On the history of the combination and the 'Liebestod' title, see Robert Bailey (ed.), *Richard Wagner: Prelude and Transfiguration from 'Tristan und Isolde'*, Norton Critical Score (New York, NY, 1985), 36–43.
2. Donald Tovey, *Essays in Musical Analysis*, vol. II (1935), 71.
3. Bailey (ed.), *Prelude and Transfiguration*. Also included are scores of the Prelude, the Transfiguration (without vocal part), and Wagner's concert ending to the former.
4. In programme notes prepared for concert performances; see *ibid.*, 47f.
5. Translated by Robert Jacobs in *Three Wagner Essays* (London, 1979), 53f.
6. See Joseph Kerman, *Opera as Drama*, rev. edn. (Berkeley, CA, 1989), Chapter 8, and *passim*.
7. Ernest Newman, *The Wagner Operas* (New York, NY, 1949), 239.
8. Jacobs, *Three Wagner Essays*, 63.
9. Especially if he also catches the *mitleidig* ('compassionate') look that Tristan bestows on the king, as per Wagner's stage direction. This direction presents a difficulty for my reading of this passage.
10. The change in the deceptive cadence is determined by the bass moving down, rather than up, as before: E–E♭ rather than E–F.

    Speaking of Ex. 3.6, Bailey observes that past the upbeat to bar 1 of the Prelude, this is the only time in the opera (including the Prelude) where the initial motif begins with the note A♮ rather than A♭ (p. 126). He argues that Wagner wrote A♮ at the beginning of the Prelude to maximize the contrast with G♯ in bar 1, this contrast adumbrating the large-scale tonal shift A to A♭ (G♯) which occurs at many important points in the opera. In Ex. 3.6, the restored A/G♯ contrast supports the new destination of the Prelude complex at this point: A♭ rather than C and A, as before.

    Further support is provided by the 'extra' chords. The bass line F–E–D♯ in bars 2–5 of Ex. 3.6 anticipates the bass E–E♭ of the changed deceptive cadence that opens into the new destination.
11. Albert Lavignac, *The Music Dramas of Richard Wagner and His Festival in Bayreuth*, trans. Esther Singleton (New York, NY, 1898), 307.

4 In the realm of the senses: sight, sound and the music of desire in *Tristan und Isolde*

1. Richard Wagner, *Gesammelte Schriften und Dichtungen* (Leipzig, 1887–1911), vol. IX, 306. Cf. *Richard Wagner's Prose Works*, trans. W. A. Ellis (1896; repr. Lincoln, NE, 1995), vol. V, 303. The translation is my own, as

are subsequent translations (including those of the libretto, which is quoted according to the score), unless otherwise indicated.

2. In the original: 'ersichtlich gewordene Taten der Musik.' Wagner, *Gesammelte Schriften*, 306; Ellis (trans.), *Prose Works*, 303.
3. Wagner, *Gesammelte Schriften*, 307; Ellis (trans.), *Prose Works*, 303.
4. Wagner, *Gesammelte Schriften*, 307; Ellis (trans.), *Prose Works*, 303f.
5. See the letter of 19 December 1856 to Marie Wittgenstein and the sketch of the same date, cited in Ernest Newman, *The Wagner Operas*, vol. I (New York, NY, 1949; repr. 1983), 193–5. See also Robert Bailey (ed.), *Wagner, Prelude and Transfiguration from 'Tristan und Isolde'* (New York, NY, 1985), 5. Also, two of the 'Wesendonck Lieder' were fashioned as 'studies' for *Tristan* (see Chapter 1). To that extent, we can say that their music had a quasi-independent existence from either Mathilde's poems or Richard's libretto.
6. The term was adapted for film theory by Michel Chion from its earlier application to the techniques and aesthetics of *musique concrète* by Pierre Schaeffer. See Michel Chion, *La voix au cinema* (Paris, 1972), and Claudia Gorbman (trans. and ed.), *Audio-Vision: Sound on Screen* (New York, NY, 1994). Carolyn Abbate touches on the 'acousmatic' effect of the sailor's song at the opening of *Tristan* and its anticipation in the young shepherd's piping in Act I, Scene 3 of *Tannhäuser* in 'Debussy's Phantom Sounds', *Cambridge Opera Journal*, 10 (1998), 74f., considering both as precedents for the various uncanny, elusive, ambiguous uses of acousmatic voice and sound in *Pelléas et Mélisande* and other works of Debussy. The shepherd in *Tannhäuser* of course also anticipates the shepherd, piping on the same instrument, in Act III of *Tristan*, though the resemblance is more to his later 'lustige Weise' than to the first, long-drawn-out 'traurige Weise' at the beginning of the act.
7. Connecting Schopenhauer's theory of the dream-state with his idea of music as a direct analogue of the Will, Wagner argues in the introductory portion of the essay 'Beethoven' for a wholly separate aesthetic foundation of music (not distinguishing instrumental music from song and opera). Echoing the metaphorical discourse of Tristan and Isolde's *Tagesgespräch* ('discourse on day') from Act II, Wagner argues for the inherent psychological truth of acoustic signs – the Rousseauvian *cri naturel* as it evolved into song and music – and their immediate access to the subconscious emotional faculties, as opposed to the 'deceptive appearance' ('täuschender Schein') of the visible world: the *Schallwelt* vs. the *Lichtwelt*. See Wagner, *Gesammelte Schriften*, vol. IX, 69f.; Ellis (trans.), *Prose Works*, vol. V, 68–70.
8. The libretto variously denotes the shepherd's sad tune as '*sehnsüchtig und traurig*' (stage directions at beginning of the act), '*klagend*' and '*ernst*' (stage directions and Tristan's disappointed response to this signal in the first scene), while it is most consistently identified as the 'alte Weise'.
9. Wagner, *Gesammelte Schriften*, vol. IX, 75–7. The idea of a 'dimming' or 'debilitation of sight' ('Depotenzierung des Gesichts') co-inciding with moments of intense 'inwardness' (and associated with states of heightened

aural/musical acuity) could also be exemplified by the reaction of Tristan and Isolde to the love potion at the climax of Act I, a moment of psychological and hence musical 'inwardness' and insight, apprehension, and clairvoyance. From this moment up to the end of the act they seem to loose sight of the outside world, while lost in their own troubled, conflicted, passion-ridden inner one, as manifested in the recrudescence and development of motifs from the Prelude to Act I.

10. On the text and music of Isolde's opening 'rage aria' ('Entartet Geschlecht!'), see also the opening section of Thomas Grey, 'Wagner the Degenerate: Fin de siècle Cultural "Pathology" and the Anxiety of Modernism,' *19th-Century Studies*, 16 (2002), 73–92 (here, 73–7).
11. More precisely: the four-note rising 'Desire' motif – whose connotations have in fact vacillated across Act I between the 'magic arts' of Isolde's mother and Isolde's pre-existing, though suppressed, desire for Tristan – emerges in the Act II prelude as the syntactic complement to a new idea (starting at bar 29 of the prelude) that begins as an inversion of the original 'Desire' motif. As Anthony Newcomb has suggested, these together form a kind of separable ritornello complex that structures the opening scene of Act II as a whole, reflecting also Isolde's determination to extinguish the torch and to rendezvous with Tristan. See Newcomb, 'Ritornello Ritornato: A Variety of Wagnerian Refrain Form', in Carolyn Abbate and Roger Parker (eds.), *Analyzing Opera: Verdi and Wagner* (Berkeley, CA, 1989), 202–21.
12. The shepherd's exotic and melancholy piping, as well as Tristan's reception of it in a state oscillating between waking and dreaming, recall Wagner's real-life experiences of uncannily penetrating 'acousmatic' effects (in the essay 'Beethoven'): in one case, the song of a Venetian gondolier heard, invisibly, during the night; in the other case, the antiphonal calls of those same Swiss shepherds whose characteristic melodies (in conjunction with their distinctive and influential landscape) became such a topos for early Romantic culture. See Wagner, *Gesammelte Schriften*, vol. IX, 74 and Ellis (trans.), *Prose Works*, vol. V, 73–4.
13. Tristan really does 'hear' the light here, in that his words are accompanied by frenzied iterations of the motif from Act II, Scene 1 associated with the torch and Isolde's desire to extinguish it. Like Isolde in her final moments (see below), Tristan is suddenly able to hear and interpret the 'noumenal' music of the orchestra and its leitmotivic signs, whose interpretation is normally reserved for the audience. This confounding of seeing and hearing at the moment of Tristan's death might help reconcile Wagner's idea of a Dionysian-musical 'dimming of vision' in moments of ecstatic receptivity with Nietzsche's at first seemingly contradictory claim that 'a supreme degree of visual intensity', unattainable in spoken drama, may be achieved in the musical drama (*The Birth of Tragedy*, sec. 21). For the heightened visual capacity generated by music, as Nietzsche goes on to explain, is more a matter of imagination than sight, an 'inward' directed gaze, or something like Tristan's 'night-vision' of Act II. Music allows us 'to see more, and in a more intensely inward manner than usual,

and to see the events on stage spread out like some delicate tissue[;] our spiritualized eye, gazing into the interior of things, sees the world of the stage both as infinitely enlarged and as illumined from within'. *The Birth of Tragedy*, ed. Roger Raymond Geuss and Ronald Speirs, trans. Ronald Speirs (Cambridge, 1999), 102.

14. The opening motivic complex of the Prelude – the 'Suffering' and 'Desire' motifs linked by the 'Tristan' chord – is arguably given a similarly distinct association with Isolde's magic potions in the course of Act I. But as suggested earlier, and as the traditional designations also suggest, the associative-dramatic meanings of this initial motif-complex are more ambiguous than their textural 'exposition' in the drama would indicate.
15. The association of the motif with the mutual, amorous 'gaze' of Tristan and Isolde is actually anticipated already near the beginning of Act I, Scene 2, though in a negative way, when the motif accompanies Isolde's scornful description of how Tristan deliberately evades her 'gaze' ('der meinen Blick den seinen birgt, in Scham und Scheue abwärts schaut'). As Joseph Kerman discusses (see Chapter 3 above), this is the first of several important re-playings of the whole initial motivic series of the Act I Prelude (bars 1–17, or 1–21). In this case, the 'Death' motif (not heard in the Prelude) intervenes, significantly, between the 'Glance' and the preceding series.
16. The dramatic-psychological motif of the glance or 'gaze' in *Tristan* would seem to be less an instance of Freudian scopophilia, or of the visual 'pleasure' of the (male) cinematic gaze theorized by Laura Mulvey (*Visual Pleasure and Narrative Cinema*, 1975), than a visual manifestation of repressed desire.
17. 'Tristan's honor – highest faith! Tristan's sorrow – bold defiance! ... Draught of dear oblivion, I drink you without regret.'
18. Cf. Chapter 3, Joseph Kerman, 'The Prelude and the play'.
19. Tristan and Isolde have been ruminating on the act of drinking the potion (in Act I) and its consequences (thus, 'then we were, or became, votaries of the night'). Wagner's somewhat confusing syntax in the final lines quoted here might be more literally rendered: '... are derided by him, to whom night has dedicated its sight [glance, gaze]'.
20. Wagner, *Gesammelte Schriften und Dichtungen*, vol. IX, 74 (and cf. above, notes 7 and 9).
21. Revisiting and refining his famous dichotomy (advanced in *The Birth of Tragedy*) of the 'Apollonian' and the 'Dionysian' in *The Twilight of the Idols*, Nietzsche associates the Dionysian with something like this heightened, pan-sensory receptive state, as opposed to the primarily visual (hence more studied, more objective) Apollonian mode of reception: 'In the Dionysian state ... the whole affective system is excited and enhanced, so that it discharges all its means of expression at once.' The Dionysian state, as he goes on to describe it, suggests something rather like Isolde's ecstasy at the end of *Tristan*, though in a way that also acknowledges the artifice of such a 'staging' of Dionysian frenzy: a state that unites 'the power of representation, imitation, transfiguration,

transformation, and every kind of mimicking and acting'. See Friedrich Nietzsche, *Twilight of the Idols* (sec. 10), in Walter Kaufmann (trans.), *The Portable Nietzsche* (Harmondsworth, 1959), 519–20. Gary Tomlinson cites and discusses this passage in considering Nietzsche's turn away from Platonic/Schopenhauerian metaphysics and towards an aesthetics grounded more specifically in the body and the immediate, physical dimension of *aesthesis* (aesthetic reception). Gary Tomlinson, *Metaphysical Song: An Essay on Opera* (Princeton, NJ, 1998), 118–19.

22. While there is good philological justification for insisting on the correct identification of Isolde's final scene as the 'Transfiguration' (*Verklärung*) rather than the traditional 'Love-Death' (*Liebestod*), the earlier climactic development of the material here in Act II does provide a significant association between this music and the concept (and term) *Liebestod*. On the terminology of *Liebestod* and *Verklärung*, see Robert Bailey (ed.), *Wagner: Prelude and Transfiguration from 'Tristan und Isolde'* (New York, NY, 1985), 41–3.
23. Dieter Borchmeyer comments on the synaesthetic character of the 'Transfiguration', alluding to Wagner's influence on the French symbolists and ultimately Skryabin's multi-media extravaganza, *Prometheus*, *Richard Wagner: Theory and Theatre* (Oxford, 1991), 358. 'For "to see" here', he adds, 'means to perceive with every sublimated sense' (360); Isolde perceives the ascension of Tristan's soul with an 'all-sensuous eye' (361).
24. Isolde's ability to hear the leitmotivic discourse of the orchestra in her final moments would parallel Tristan's similar ability at the brink of his death, when he 'hears' the motif recalling Isolde's torch ('Wie, hör' ich das Licht?'), as suggested above (likewise a moment of synaesthetic epiphany).
25. Nietzsche also suggests, in the passage from *Twilight of the Idols* quoted above (n. 21), that 'modern' music in general tends toward a recuperation (if necessarily partial or incomplete) of what he imagines as the original 'Dionysian' state of utmost sensory receptivity. 'Music, as we understand it today, is also a total excitement and a total discharge of the affects, but even so only ... a mere residue of the Dionysian histrionicism.' Relating this Dionysian state to modern notions of 'certain hysterical types who also, upon suggestions, enter into *any* role', Nietzsche's account of the metamorphic character of the Dionysian frenzy again suggests a close affinity with Isolde's heightened/altered consciousness in the 'Transfiguration', as well as the underlying aesthetic artifice of its mode of presentation. Kaufmann (trans.), *The Portable Nietzsche*, 519; cf. Tomlinson, *Metaphysical Song*, 118.
26. Note the differences in the original printed text of the libretto in these final lines. While Wagner seems to have wanted to make them a bit more succinct, the original version places more emphasis on the combination or synthesis of sensory modes: 'In des Wonnemeeres / wogendem Schwall, / in der Duftwellen / tönendem Schall, / in des Weltatems / wehendem All –' (etc.). Wagner, *Gesammelte Schriften und Dichtungen*, vol. VII, 80–81.

27. This is the burden of the famous letter to Schopenhauer drafted by Wagner in 1858 but left incomplete and never sent, indicative of the composer's diffidence about direct contact with Schopenhauer in the philosopher's later years, likely from a fear of rejection or misunderstanding by one of the few contemporaries he admired unreservedly. See Borchmeyer, *Richard Wagner: Theory and Theatre*, 365, and Bryan Magee, *Wagner and Philosophy* (London, 2000), 222.

5 A mantle of sound for the night: timbre in Wagner's *Tristan und Isolde*

1. See Adriana Guarnieri Corazzol, *Tristano, mio Tristano. Gli scrittori italiani e il caso Wagner* (Bologna, 1988); A. Guarnieri Corazzol, *Sensualità senza carne. La musica nella vita e nell'opera di d'Annunzio* (Bologna, 1990); Adriana Guarnieri, *Musica e letteratura in Italia tra Ottocento e Novecento* (Milan, 2000).
2. See Karsten Witte, '"Das ist echt! Eine Burleske!" Zur *Tristan*-Novelle von Thomas Mann', *German Quarterly*, 41 (1968), 660–72; Frank M. Young, *Montage and Motif in Thomas Mann's 'Tristan'* (Bonn, 1975); Bruno Rossbach, *Spiegelungen eines Bewußtseins. Der Erzähler in Thomas Manns 'Tristan'* (Marburg, 1989); Heinz Gockel *et al.* (eds.), *Wagner – Nietzsche – Thomas Mann: Festschrift für Eckhard Heftrich* (Frankfurt, 1993); Thomas Klugkist, *Glühende Konstruktion. Thomas Manns 'Tristan' und das 'Dreigestirn' Schopenhauer, Nietzsche und Wagner* (Würzburg, 1995).
3. Cf. Mario Praz, *La carne, la morte e il diavolo nella letteratura romantica*, 3rd edn. (Florence, 1948); Erwin Koppen, *Dekadenter Wagnerismus, Studien zur europäischen Literatur des Fin de siècle* (Berlin and New York, NY, 1973), 199f.; Michael Zimmermann, '*Träumerei eines französischen Dichters'. Stéphane Mallarmé und Richard Wagner* (Munich and Salzburg, 1981); Carolyn Abbate, 'Die ewige Rückkehr von *Tristan*', in Annegret Fauser and Manuela Schwartz (eds.), *Von Wagner zum Wagnérisme. Musik, Literatur, Kunst, Politik* (Leipzig, 1999), 293–313.
4. 'In the surging swell of an ocean of bliss, in the ringing sound of waves of scent, in the World-breath's wafting universe: to drown – sink down – unconscious – highest bliss/desire!' Richard Wagner, *Sämtliche Schriften und Dichtungen* (Leipzig, 1887–8), vol. VII, 80f.; the edition of Wagner's writings does not always correspond to the version set to music.
5. Charles Baudelaire, *Œuvres complètes*, ed. Y.-G. Le Dantec (Paris, 1954), 65. The translation is from James McGowan (trans.), *The Flowers of Evil* (Oxford, 1993), 139.
6. Baudelaire, *Œuvres*, 1213; McGowan (trans.), *The Flowers of Evil*, 19.
7. Gabriele d'Annunzio, *Il Trionfo della Morte*, ed. Giansiro Ferrata (Verona, 1973), 363.
8. Julia Kristeva, *Revolution in Poetic Language*, trans. Margaret Waller (New York, NY, 1984); Zimmermann, '*Träumerei*'.

9. Ernst Bloch, *Geist der Utopie* (Frankfurt, 1973), 108f. The translation is by Anthony A. Nassar, *The Spirit of Utopia* (Stanford, CA, 2000), 83.
10. 'This Tristan is turning into something *terrible*! This final act!!! – – – I fear the opera will be banned – unless the whole thing is parodied in a bad performance – : only mediocre performances can save me! Perfectly *good* ones will be bound to drive people mad, – I cannot imagine it otherwise.' Wagner to Mathilde Wesendonck, mid-April 1859. Stewart Spencer and Barry Millington (eds.), *Selected Letters of Richard Wagner* (New York, NY, 1988), 452.
11. Theo Hirsbrunner, 'Schwierigkeiten beim Erzählen der Handlung von Richard Wagners *Tristan und Isolde*', *Schweizerische Musikzeitung*, 58 (1973), 137–43; Wolfram Steinbeck, 'Die Idee des Symphonischen bei Richard Wagner. Zur Leitmotivtechnik in *Tristan und Isolde*', in Christoph-Hellmuth Mahling and Sigrid Wiesmann (eds.), *Bericht über den internationalen musikwissenschaftlichen Kongreß Bayreuth 1981* (Kassel, 1984), 424–36; Ralf Eisinger, *Richard Wagner: Idee und Dramaturgie des allegorischen Traumbildes* (PhD diss., Munich, 1987).
12. On Wagner's *Tristan* poem and its multiple relationships with Gottfried von Straßburg, see Arthur Groos, 'Wagner's *Tristan*: In Defence of the Libretto', *Music & Letters*, 69 (1988), 465–81; A. Groos, 'Appropriation in Wagner's *Tristan* Libretto', in Arthur Groos and Roger Parker (eds.), *Reading Opera* (Princeton, NJ, 1988), 12–33; Volker Mertens, 'Richard Wagner und das Mittelalter', in Ulrich Müller and Ursula Müller (eds.), *Richard Wagner und sein Mittelalter* (Anif, 1989), 9–84.
13. Theodor W. Adorno, 'Versuch über Wagner', in *Gesammelte Schriften*, vol. XIII (Frankfurt, 1971), 64; cited according to Theodor Adorno, *In Search of Wagner*, trans. Rodney Livingstone (New York, NY, and London, 1991), 67.
14. A minimal selection of scholarly literature on Wagner's 'Tristan'-chord would have to name the following: Ernst Kurth, *Romantische Harmonik und ihre Krise in Wagners 'Tristan'* (1923; repr. Hildesheim, 1985); Heinrich Poos, 'Die *Tristan*-Hieroglyphe. Ein allegoretischer Versuch', in Heinz-Klaus Metzger and Rainer Riehn (eds.), *Richard Wagner: 'Tristan und Isolde'* (Munich, 1987), 46–103; Sebastian Urmoneit, *Tristan und Isolde – Eros und Thanatos. Zur 'dichterischen Deutlichkeit' der Harmonik von Richard Wagner's 'Handlung'* Tristan und Isolde (Sinzig, 2005); Hermann Danuser, 'Tristanakkord', in *Musik in Geschichte und Gegenwart*, 2nd edn. *Sachteil*, vol. IX (Kassel, Stuttgart, Weimar, 1998), cols. 832–44.
15. Cf. Carl Dahlhaus, 'Wagners Begriff der dichterisch-musikalischen Periode', in Walter Salmen (ed.), *Beiträge zur Musikanschauung im 19. Jahrhundert* (Regensburg, 1965), 179–94; Stefan Kunze, 'Über Melodiebegriff und musikalischen Bau in Wagners Musikdrama, dargestellt an Beispielen aus *Holländer* und *Ring*', in Carl Dahlhaus (ed.), *Das Drama Richard Wagners als musikalisches Kunstwerk* (Regensburg, 1970), 111–48; Rudolf Stephan, 'Gibt es ein Geheimnis der Form bei Richard Wagner?', *ibid.*, 9–16.

16. Martin Vogel, *Der Tristan-Akkord und die Krise der modernen Harmonielehre* (Düsseldorf, 1962).
17. This fact is reflected in the title of Ernst Kurth's famous *Romantische Harmonik und ihre Krise in Wagners 'Tristan'* (1923).
18. The idea that a methodology of musical analysis necessarily reflects the experience of its contemporary music is not yet sufficiently accepted among musicologists, although any study of the epistemological foundations of the 'discovery of ancient music' during the twentieth century would reveal its validity.
19. Stefan Kunze, *Mozarts Opern* (Stuttgart, 1984).
20. Richard Toop, 'Messiaen / Goeyvaerts, Fano / Stockhausen, Boulez', in *Perspectives of New Music*, 13 (1974), 141–69; Jürgen Maehder, 'Olivier Messiaen au seuil de la musique sérielle – ordre numérique et création', in Carlo Ossola (ed.), *Création, Renaissance, ordre du monde*, Actes du Colloque au Collège de France 2008, in preparation.
21. Alban Berg used a similar technique at the end of the first of his *Lieder nach Ansichtskartentexten von Peter Altenberg* (1912); the choice of the identical pitch G as recurrent note was probably not intentional, although a direct reference to the 'Tristan' score may be possible. Cf. Jürgen Maehder, 'Verfremdete Instrumentation – Ein Versuch über beschädigten Schönklang', *Schweizer Beiträge zur Musikwissenschaft*, 4 (1980), 147–9.
22. Other examples of 'semantic logic' in Wagner's text setting are discussed in Jürgen Maehder, 'Studi sul rapporto testo-musica nell'*Anello del Nibelungo* di Richard Wagner', *Nuova Rivista Musicale Italiana*, 21 (1987), 43–66 and 255–82; Jürgen Maehder, 'Form- und Intervallstrukturen in der Partitur des *Parsifal*', Programmheft der Bayreuther Festspiele 1991, 1–24.
23. On 'negativity' in German Romantic opera, see Jürgen Maehder, 'Die Poetisierung der Klangfarben in Dichtung und Musik der deutschen Romantik', *Aurora: Jahrbuch der Eichendorff-Gesellschaft*, 38 (1978), 9–31.
24. Jürgen Maehder, *Klangfarbe als Bauelement des musikalischen Satzes – Zur Kritik des Instrumentationsbegriffes* (diss., Bern, 1977), Chapter 4 ('Formen der Instrumentenverwendung in szenischer Musik').
25. For a discussion of the orchestrational technique of 'added instruments', see Jürgen Maehder, 'Klangfarbendramaturgie und Instrumentation in Meyerbeers Grands Opéras – Zur Rolle des Pariser Musiklebens als Drehscheibe europäischer Orchestertechnik', in Hans John and Günther Stephan (eds.), *Giacomo Meyerbeer – Große Oper – Deutsche Oper* (Dresden, 1992), 125–50; Jürgen Maehder, 'Giacomo Meyerbeer und Richard Wagner – Zur Europäisierung der Opernkomposition um die Mitte des 19. Jahrhunderts', in Thomas Betzwieser *et al.* (eds.), *Bühnenklänge. Festschrift für Sieghart Döhring zum 65. Geburtstag* (Munich, 2005), 205–25.
26. Jürgen Maehder, 'Die Poetisierung der Klangfarben'; Michael C. Tusa, 'Richard Wagner and Weber's *Euryanthe*', *19th-Century Music*, 9 (1986),

206–21; Jürgen Maehder, 'Klangzauber und Satztechnik. Zur Klangfarbendisposition in den Opern Carl Maria v. Webers', in Friedhelm Krummacher and Heinrich W. Schwab (eds.), *Weber – Jenseits des 'Freischütz'* (Kassel, 1989), 14–40.

27. Novalis, *Gesammelte Werke*, ed. Hildburg and Werner Kohlschmidt (Gütersloh, 1967), 446.
28. Jürgen Maehder, '*Banda sul palco* – Variable Besetzungen in der Bühnenmusik der italienischen Oper des 19. Jahrhunderts als Relikte alter Besetzungstraditionen?', in Dietrich Berke and D. Hanemann (eds.), *Alte Musik als ästhetische Gegenwart. Kongreßbericht Stuttgart 1985* (Kassel, 1987), vol. II, 293–310.
29. On spatial disposition in Grand Opéra staging, cf. Jürgen Maehder, 'Historienmalerei und Grand Opéra – Zur Raumvorstellung in den Bildern Géricaults und Delacroix' und auf der Bühne der Académie Royale de Musique', in Sieghart Döhring and Arnold Jacobshagen (eds.), *Meyerbeer und das europäische Musiktheater* (Laaber, 1999), 258–87.
30. Carolyn Abbate, 'Erik's Dream and Tannhäuser's Journey' in Groos and Parker (eds.), *Reading Opera*, 129–67; Carolyn Abbate, *Unsung Voices, Opera and Musical Narrative in the Nineteenth Century* (Princeton, NJ, 1991), 156–249 and *passim*; Jürgen Maehder, '*Lohengrin* di Richard Wagner – Dall'opera romantica a soggetto fiabesco alla fantasmagoria dei timbri', Teatro Regio di Torino, programma di sala (Turin, 2001), 9–37.
31. Reinhold Brinkmann, 'Mythos – Geschichte – Natur. Zeitkonstellationen im *Ring*', in Stefan Kunze (ed.), *Von der Oper zum Musikdrama* (Bern, 1978), 61–77; Richard Benz, *Zeitstrukturen in Richard Wagners 'Ring des Nibelungen'* (Frankfurt and Bern, 1994); Tobias Janz, *Klangdramaturgie. Studien zur theatralen Orchesterkompositon in Richard Wagners 'Ring des Nibelungen'* (Würzburg, 2006).
32. Jürgen Maehder, 'Verfremdete Instrumentation'.
33. Jürgen Maehder, 'Hector Berlioz als Chronist der Orchesterpraxis in Deutschland', in Sieghart Döhring *et al.* (eds.), *Berlioz, Wagner und die Deutschen* (Cologne, 2003), 193–210.
34. Richard Wagner, *Gesammelte Schriften*, vol. IV, 166; trans. W. Ashton Ellis as *Richard Wagner's Prose Works* (1893; repr. Lincoln, NE, 1995), 308.
35. Stéphane Mallarmé, *Œuvres complètes* (Paris, 1945), 857.
36. Mallarmé, *Œuvres*, 543f. The translation is from Mallarmé, *Selected Prose Poems, Essays, & Letters*, trans. Bradford Cook (Baltimore, MD, 1956), 76f.
37. Hector Berlioz, rev. Richard Strauss, *Instrumentationslehre* (Leipzig, 1904), 50.
38. Dorothea Baumann, 'Wagners Festspielhaus – ein akustisch-architektonisches Wagnis mit Überraschungen', in Volker Kalisch *et al.* (eds.), *Festschrift Hans Conradin zum 70. Geburtstag* (Bern and Stuttgart, 1983), 123–50; Dorothea Baumann, *Musik und Raum. Eine Untersuchung*

zur Bedeutung des Raumes für die musikalische Aufführungspraxis (Habilitationsschrift, University of Zurich, 2003).

39. Cf. Alfred Schütz, 'Making Music Together: A Study in Social Relationship', *Social Research*, 18 (1951), 76–97; also in: Alfred Schütz, *Collected Papers*, vol. II (Den Haag, 1964), 159–78.
40. Adorno, 'Versuch über Wagner', 82; trans. Livingstone, *In Search of Wagner*, 84.
41. Giselher Schubert, *Schönbergs frühe Instrumentation* (Baden-Baden, 1975), especially the chapter 'Mischklang als tragender Grund', 46–50.
42. A comparison between the 'pastoral' characterizations of the cor anglais by Berlioz and Gevaert and Richard Strauss's 'modern' view under the influence of Wagner's scores is especially elucidating; cf. Hector Berlioz, *Grand Traité d'Instrumentation et d'Orchestration modernes* (Paris, 1844); François A. Gevaert, *Nouveau Traité d'Instrumentation* (Paris and Brussels, 1887), 152–4; Hector Berlioz, rev. Richard Strauss, *Instrumentationslehre* (Leipzig, 1904), 199–203.
43. Berlioz, rev. Strauss, *Instrumentationslehre*, 279.
44. Cf. Hans-Peter Reinecke, *Über den doppelten Sinn des Lautheitsbegriffs beim musikalischen Hören* (diss., Hamburg, 1953).
45. The first example of this use of the trombones appears in the 'scène lyrique' *La Mort de Cléopâtre* (1829) by Hector Berlioz; cf. Jürgen Maehder, 'Orchesterbehandlung und Klangregie in *Les Troyens* von Hector Berlioz', in Ulrich Müller *et al.* (eds.), *Europäische Mythen von Liebe, Leidenschaft, Untergang und Tod im (Musik)-Theater. Vorträge und Gespräche des Salzburger Symposiums 2000* (Anif, 2002), 511–37.
46. Peter Wapnewski, *Der traurige Gott. Richard Wagner in seinen Helden* (Munich, 1978), 54ff.
47. Manfred Hermann Schmid, *Musik als Abbild. Studien zum Werk von Weber, Schumann und Wagner* (Tutzing, 1981), 195ff.
48. For a similar interpretation of Wagner's use of timbre in the second act of *Tristan*, see Richard Klein, 'Farbe versus Faktur. Kritische Anmerkungen zu einer These Adornos über die Kompositionstechnik Richard Wagners', *Archiv für Musikwissenschaft*, 48 (1991), 87–109; Richard Klein, *Solidarität mit Metaphysik? Ein Versuch über die musikphilosophische Problematik der Wagner-Kritik Theodor W. Adornos* (Würzburg, 1991), 254–7; Tobias Janz, *Klangdramaturgie. Studien zur theatralen Orchesterkompositon in Richard Wagners 'Ring des Nibelungen'* (Würzburg, 2006).
49. Cf. Stefan Kunze, 'Naturszenen in Wagners Musikdrama', in Carl Dahlhaus *et al.* (eds.), *Bericht über den internationalen musikwissenschaftlichen Kongreß Bonn 1970* (Kassel, n.d.), 199–207; and 'Richard Wagners imaginäre Szene. Gedanken zu Musik und Regie im Musikdrama', in Rudolf Bockholdt and Erika Kunze (eds.), *Stefan Kunze, De musica. Ausgewählte Aufsätze und Vorträge* (Tutzing, 1998), 441–51.
50. Gabriele d'Annunzio, *Canto novo. Intermezzo* (Milan, 1924), 143f.
51. Jürgen Maehder, 'Erscheinungsformen des Wagnérisme in der italienischen Oper des Fin de siècle', in Fauser and Schwartz (eds.), *Von Wagner*

zum Wagnérisme, 575–621; Jürgen Maehder, 'Klangfarbenkomposition und dramatische Instrumentationskunst in den Opern von Richard Strauss', in Julia Liebscher (ed.), *Richard Strauss und das Musiktheater. Bericht über die Internationale Fachkonferenz Bochum, 14.–17. November 2001* (Berlin, 2005), 139–81; Jürgen Maehder, 'Orchesterklang als Medium der Werkintention in Pfitzners *Palestrina*', in Rainer Franke *et al.* (eds.), *Hans Pfitzner und das musikalische Theater. Bericht über das Symposium Schloß Thurnau 1999* (Tutzing, 2008), 87–122.

52. Adorno, 'Versuch über Wagner', 145; trans. Livingstone, *In Search of Wagner*, 156.

6 Staging *Tristan und Isolde*

1. At least two writers have been reduced to repeating barely relevant anecdotes describing Wagner's acrobatic exuberance during the Munich rehearsals; see Sebastian Röckl, *Ludwig II. und Richard Wagner*, vol. I (Munich, 1913), 133; and Detta Petzet and Michael Petzet, *Die Richard Wagner-Bühne König Ludwigs II.* (Munich, 1970), 42. Entertaining though it may be to know that Wagner stood on his head and climbed trees when particularly pleased with his performers, such knowledge brings us no closer to what went on in the rehearsal room. Nonetheless, the Petzets' volume remains by far the best introduction to the 1865 production. For a general, if selective, production history, see Brigitte Heldt, *Richard Wagner, 'Tristan und Isolde': Das Werk und seine Inszenierung* (Laaber, 1994); see also the chapter in Oswald Georg Bauer, *Richard Wagner: Die Bühnenwerke von der Uraufführung bis heute* (Frankfurt/Main, 1982), 124–53, trans. by Stewart Spencer as *Richard Wagner: The Stage Designs and Productions from the Premières to the Present* (New York, NY, 1983), 130–61.
2. Claudia Balk, *Theaterfotografie: Eine Darstellung ihrer Geschichte anhand der Sammlung des Deutschen Theatermuseums* (Munich, 1989), 43f. Balk argues that the first photographs were not taken in an actual theatre until 1896.
3. This point is well made by Oswald Georg Bauer, *Josef Hoffmann: Der Bühnenbildner der ersten Bayreuther Festspiele* (Munich and Berlin, 2008).
4. The surviving designs and models are reproduced in Petzet and Petzet, *Die Richard Wagner-Bühne*, pls. III–IV and ills. 36–45, 53–4, 59–60. Also reproduced are contemporary paintings by Michael Echter prepared at the request of King Ludwig and closely modelled on the stage designs (ills. 46–7, 55–6, 61–3).
5. On Quaglio and Döll, see Petzet and Petzet, *Die Richard Wagner-Bühne*, 334f.
6. See Kurt Hommel, *Die Separatvorstellungen vor König Ludwig II. von Bayern* (Munich, 1963), 284–7, 290f.
7. Richard Wagner, 'Bemerkungen zur Aufführung der Oper: *Der fliegende Holländer*', *Gesammelte Schriften und Dichtungen* (Leipzig, 1911), vol. V,

160; trans. William Ashton Ellis, *Richard Wagner's Prose Works* (1893–9; repr. Lincoln, NE, 1993–5), vol. V, 209.

8. Richard Wagner, *Sämtliche Briefe*, vol. X, ed. Andreas Mielke (Wiesbaden, 2000), 254 (letter to Ludwig Devrient, 23 January 1859): 'Um auf das Schiff zurückzukommen, so scheine ich mich besser auf dessen Kunstsymbolik, als auf dessen technische Realität zu verstehen.'
9. In 1858, Calderón catapulted to the top of Wagner's list of preferred authors; see Richard Wagner, *Sämtliche Briefe*, vol. IX, ed. Klaus Burmeister and Johannes Forner (Leipzig, 2000), 146f.; see also Alexander Coleman, 'Calderón/Schopenhauer/Wagner: The Story of a Misunderstanding', *The Musical Quarterly*, 69 (1983), 227–43.
10. See, for example, Édouard Sans, *Richard Wagner et la pensée schopenhauerienne* (Paris, 1969); Bryan Magee, *The Philosophy of Schopenhauer*, 2nd edn. (Oxford, 1997); and Heldt, *Richard Wagner*, 9–25.
11. The most recent full-length study is Patrick Carnegy's *Wagner and the Art of the Theatre* (New Haven, CT, and London, 2006), esp. 3–132; but see also Thomas Grey's perceptive review in *The Opera Quarterly*, 23 (2007), 360–67.
12. See Otto Strobel (ed.), *König Ludwig II. und Richard Wagner: Briefwechsel*, vol. I (Karlsruhe, 1936), 74 (letter to Ludwig II, 12 March 1865) and 75 (letter to Richard Wagner, 20 March 1865).
13. Richard Wagner, 'Meine Erinnerungen an Ludwig Schnorr von Carolsfeld', *Gesammelte Schriften*, vol. VIII, 184; cf. Ellis (trans.), *Prose Works*, vol. V, 234.
14. Wagner, *Gesammelte Schriften*, vol. VIII, 185; Ellis (trans.), *Prose Works*, vol. V, 234f.
15. Anonymous report on rehearsals for *Die Meistersinger von Nürnberg* first published in the *Neue Freie Presse* (21 June 1868) and reproduced by Ludwig Nohl, *Neues Skizzenbuch: Zur Kenntnis der deutschen, namentlich der Münchener Musik- und Opernzustände der Gegenwart* (Munich, 1869), 357–62.
16. Angelo Neumann, *Erinnerungen an Richard Wagner* (Leipzig, 1907), 9–14; trans. Edith Livermore, *Personal Recollections of Wagner* (London, 1909), 9–14.
17. Richard Fricke, *Bayreuth vor dreißig Jahren: Erinnerungen an Wahnfried und aus dem Festspielhause* (Dresden, 1906), 93f. (entry of 8 June), 101–4 (17 and 18 June), 107 (22 June); trans. by Stewart Spencer as 'Bayreuth in 1876', *Wagner*, 11 (1990), 93–109, 134–50 and *Wagner*, 12 (1991), 25–44. The translation by George Fricke published by Pendragon Press in 1998, *Wagner in Rehearsal 1875–1876: The Diaries of Richard Fricke*, verges on the disastrous, with annotation plagiarized from the translation in *Wagner*.
18. Richard Wagner, 'Über die Bestimmung der Oper', *Gesammelte Schriften*, vol. IX, 143; Ellis (trans.), *Prose Works*, vol. V, 144; see also Dieter Borchmeyer, *Richard Wagner: Theory and Theatre*, trans. Stewart Spencer (Oxford, 1991), 29–39, esp. 35.

19. Strobel, *König Ludwig II. und Richard Wagner*, vol. I, 90 (letter to Ludwig II, 1 May 1865). The cast at the 1865 performances included Ludwig Schnorr von Carolsfeld (1836–65) as Tristan, Malvina Schnorr von Carolsfeld (1832–1904) as Isolde, Anna Deinet (1843–1919) as Brangaene, Anton Mitterwurzer (1818–76) as Kurwenal and Ludwig Zottmayr (1828–99) as Marke. The costumes were designed by Franz Seitz (1817–83).
20. Frederick Pollock (ed.), *William Charles Macready, Reminiscences, and Selections from His Diaries and Letters*, vol. I (London, 1875), 145.
21. Henry F. Chorley, *Thirty Years' Musical Recollections*, vol. I (London, 1862), 58f.
22. Charles Santley, *Student and Singer* (New York, NY, 1892), 187–90.
23. Gustave Garcia, *The Actor's Art*, 2nd edn. (London, 1888). The outstretched arm, hand clasped to the heart and look of entreaty, for example, are intended to express 'the idea of religion enunciated with veneration' (50). See also George Taylor, *Players and Performances in the Victorian Theatre* (Manchester, 1989). For a brief history of the role of the director, see Helen Krich Chinoy, 'The Emergence of the Director', in Toby Cole and Helen Krich Chinoy (eds.), *Directors on Directing: A Source Book of the Modern Theatre*, 2nd edn. (Indianapolis, IN, 1976), 3–77.
24. Wagner, 'Über die Aufführung des *Tannhäuser*', *Gesammelte Schriften*, vol. V, 123–59; Ellis (trans.), *Prose Works*, vol. III, 167–205.
25. Wagner, 'Bemerkungen zur Aufführung der Oper *Der fliegende Holländer*', 160–68; Ellis (trans.), *Prose Works*, vol. III, 207–17.
26. Heinrich Porges, 'Die Bühnenproben zu den Festspielen des Jahres 1876', *Bayreuther Blätter*, 3 (1880), 141–8, 149–58, 193–9, 252–8, 301–7; 4 (1881), 89–98, 198–206, 233–8, 259–72; 7 (1884), 70–77; 9 (1886), 337–45; 13 (1890), 373–80; 19 (1896), 155–68, 329–57; trans. by Robert L. Jacobs as *Wagner Rehearsing the 'Ring'* (Cambridge, 1983).
27. In *Opera and Drama*, Wagner had adopted a theoretical standpoint and decried 'realistic actuality' onstage; see Wagner, *Oper und Drama* in *Gesammelte Schriften*, vol. IV, 19f.; Ellis (trans.), *Prose Works*, vol. II, 138f. But his exposure to the theatre in London in 1855, when he saw hyper-realistic productions of *The Merry Wives of Windsor* at the Royal Marylebone Theatre on 9 April and *Romeo and Juliet* at the Haymarket Theatre on 27 April, seems to have persuaded him to revise his opinion.
28. There had been four performances of the work in Munich in 1865, followed by a restudied production in 1869 that was revived in 1872, 1874, 1875, 1880, 1881, 1883 and 1884. In the meantime, there had also been productions in Weimar (14 June 1874), Berlin (20 March 1876), Königsberg (10 December 1881), Leipzig (2 January 1882), London (20 June 1882), Hamburg (23 November 1882), Vienna (4 October 1883), Bremen (26 December 1883), Dresden (21 May 1884), Frankfurt (15 October 1884), Karlsruhe (3 December 1884), Sondershausen (9 July 1885) and Prague (29 April 1886). By the end of the century the work was in the repertory of over thirty other theatres. Unfortunately details of the pre-1886 productions are frustratingly vague, although it is reported that

for the Vienna production in 1883 the sets were borrowed from existing stagings of *L'Africaine* and *Il trovatore*: see Petzet and Petzet, *Die Richard Wagner-Bühne*, 67. See also Alfred Loewenberg, *Annals of Opera 1597–1940*, 3rd edn. (London, 1978), cols. 974f.

29. The Brückner brothers ran a studio in Coburg and created designs that were seen all over Europe. Nonetheless, their work was by no means standardized and mass-produced but was subjected to often substantial stylistic revisions over the years; see Fritz Mahnke, 'Die Theatermalerfamilie Brückner in Coburg', in Harald Bachmann and Jürgen Erdmann (eds.), *150 Jahre Coburger Landestheater 1827–1977* (Coburg, 1977), 173–97.
30. Dietrich Mack (ed.), *Cosima Wagner, Das zweite Leben: Briefe und Aufzeichnungen 1883–1930* (Munich, 1980), 630 (letter to Hermann Keyserling, 11 April 1903).
31. He seems to have been disappointed only by the wooden acting of Ludwig Zottmayr as Marke and by the exaggerated histrionics of Anton Mitterwurzer as Kurwenal; see Petzet and Petzet, *Die Richard Wagner-Bühne*, 52.
32. Richard Wagner, *Oper und Drama*, 217–20; Ellis (trans.), *Prose Works*, vol. II, 364–7.
33. Mack (ed.), *Cosima Wagner*, 68f. (letter to Hermann Levi, 8 September 1886): 'Ich komme nun auf das einzelne Gebärdenspiel in *Tristan*: Ihr Bedürfnis einer Mimik vor "*die kein Himmel erlöst*" teile ich bis zu einem gewissen Grade nur; denn, bemerken Sie, daß die Figur sich gleichsam wiederholt. Soll nun Marke da wieder vor "Elend" Gesten machen? Hier liegen, meines Erachtens, die ungeheuren Schwierigkeiten der Darstellung von *Tristan*, wo das verzweigteste Seelenleben durch die Musik kundgegeben, kaum eine entsprechende Gebärde ohne Absurdität zuläßt und wo kaum ein Physiognomiespiel der Gewalt der Töne entspräche. [...] Wir müßten alles Banal-Konventionelle, Realistische, verbannen und dafür eine erhabene Konvention – den Stil – eintreten lassen.' See also Dietrich Mack, *Der Bayreuther Inszenierungsstil 1876–1976* (Munich, 1976). See also Shaw's comments on Cosima's static and attitudinal production style in his review of the 1894 Bayreuth Festival reproduced in Dan H. Laurence (ed.), *Shaw's Music*, vol. III (London, 1989), 287: 'Madame Wagner is a clever stage manager; but one of the faults of her qualities is to conceive a dramatic representation as a series of *tableaux vivants*, and to invent attitudes for people instead of continuous and natural action, the result being that artists get stuck for ten minutes at a time into poses that become ridiculous after ten seconds.'
34. Felix Weingartner, *Bayreuth (1876–1896)*, 2nd edn. (Leipzig, 1904), 14–18; trans. by Stewart Spencer as 'Bayreuth (1876–1896)', in *Wagner*, 14 (1993), 38–48 and 70–93. Weingartner is not an entirely impartial witness, but his testimony is sufficiently compelling to bear repeating. See also Susanna Großmann-Vendrey, *Bayreuth in der deutschen Presse*, III/1: *Von Wagners Tod bis zum Ende der Ära Cosima Wagner (1883–1906)*

(Regensburg, 1983), 49–64. The work entered the Bayreuth repertory on 25 July 1886 with a cast that included Heinrich Gudehus and Heinrich Vogl as Tristan, Therese Malten and Rosa Sucher as Isolde, Gisela Staudigl and Pelagie Sthamer-Andriessen as Brangaene, Fritz Plank and Karl Scheidemantel as Kurwenal and Eugen Gura, Gustav Siehr and Heinrich Wiegand as Marke. The work remained in the repertory until 1906, during which time twenty-four performances were given. All the performances, with the exception of two in 1906, were conducted by Felix Mottl.

35. For a more positive assessment of her achievements, see Sabine Sonntag, '"...das Burgtor etwas vorrücken...": Die Intendantin Cosima Wagner', *wagnerspectrum*, 1 (2005), 67–76.
36. The Royal Opera House, Covent Garden, was one of the most reactionary in this respect; see Stewart Spencer, '*Tristan und Isolde* in Great Britain', *wagnerspectrum*, 1 (2005), 145–63.
37. Richard C. Beacham, *Adolphe Appia: Artist and Visionary of the Modern Theatre* (Chur, 1994).
38. Appia wrote his essay in French between 1892 and 1897. It was published in 1899 as *Die Musik und die Inscenierung* in a not altogether reliable translation by Elsa Bruckmann. The French original was finally published in 1986 in Adolphe Appia, *Œuvres complètes*, ed. Marie L. Bablet-Hahn, vol. II (Paris, 1986), 43–207. The English translation used here is a collation of the French and German originals: Barnard Hewitt (ed.) and Robert W. Corrigan and Mary Douglas Dirks (trans.), *Adolphe Appia's Music and the Art of the Theatre* (Coral Gables, FL, 1962).
39. Hewitt (ed.), *Adolphe Appia's Music*, 198f.
40. Beacham, *Adolphe Appia*, 139–57. The production opened on 20 December 1923 with Nanny Larsén-Todsen and Stefan Belina-Skupiewski as the lovers and Ezio Pinza as Marke.
41. See Oswald Georg Bauer, '... "daß der Ausdruck Eindruck werde." Gustav Mahler und Alfred Roller: Die Reform der Wiener Wagner-Szene', *Bayerische Akademie der Schönen Künste: Jahrbuch 11* (Munich, 1997), 55–95; see also Manfred Wagner, *Alfred Roller in seiner Zeit* (Salzburg and Vienna, 1996). The production opened on 21 February 1903, and leading roles were sung by Anna von Mildenburg, Hermine Kittel, Erik Schmedes, Hans Melms and Richard Mayr. Mahler conducted twenty-one of the twenty-seven performances that were given in Vienna between 1903 and his departure for America in 1907. This production remained in the Viennese repertory until 1944; see Heldt, *Richard Wagner*, 141.
42. In many respects Roller was opposed to technological innovations that distracted from the quintessential drama of the work; see Alfred Roller, 'Bühnenreform?', *Der Merker*, 1 (1909), 193–7, esp. 196f.; and 'Bühne und Bühnenhandwerk', *Thespis: Das Theaterbuch 1930* (Berlin, 1930), 137–45, esp. 144.
43. Interestingly, Wagner himself described violet as the colour of *Tristan und Isolde*; see Martin Gregor-Dellin and Dietrich Mack (eds.), *Cosima*

Wagner, Die Tagebücher, vol. II (Munich, 1977), 106; trans. Geoffrey Skelton, *Cosima Wagner's Diaries*, vol. II (London, 1980), 83 (entry of 3 June 1878).

44. Roller's other innovation was the realignment of the ship in the opening act, so that for the first time it was possible to see the light playing on the surface of the waves.
45. Erwin Stein, 'Mahler and the Vienna Opera', in Harold Rosenthal (ed.), *The Opera Bedside Book* (London, 1965), 296–317, esp. 313. It is possible that Stein's observations were confined to the stage-and-orchestra rehearsals and that, as a result, they are not entirely representative of Mahler's working method. An earlier observer, the baritone Jacques Manheit (1858–1918), who worked with Mahler in Olmütz in 1883, reports that the conductor kept jumping up on to the stage from the pit and that he physically moved the singers around; Manheit's reminiscences from the *Montags-Revue* of 18 May 1908 are reproduced in Herta Blaukopf and Kurt Blaukopf, *Gustav Mahler: Leben und Werk in Zeugnissen der Zeit* (Stuttgart, 1993), 42–4. The soprano Marie Gutheil-Schoder (1874–1935) likewise refers to Mahler's improvisatory style of directing in her contribution to Paul Stefan (ed.), *Gustav Mahler: Ein Bild seiner Persönlichkeit in Widmungen* (Munich, 1910), 34–7.
46. See Alfred Roller, 'Mahler und die Inszenierung', *Musikblätter des Anbruch*, 2 (1920), 272–5; see also Alfred Heuß, 'Musik und Szene bei Wagner: Ein Beispiel aus *Tristan und Isolde* und zugleich ein kleiner Beitrag zur Charakteristik Gustav Mahlers als Regisseur', *Die Musik*, 12 (1912–13), 207–13.
47. See Rosamund Bartlett, *Wagner and Russia* (Cambridge, 1995), 94–103; Edward Braun, *Meyerhold: A Revolution in Theatre*, 2nd edn. (London, 1995), 86–95; and Bärbel Hamacher (ed.), *Wagner in St. Petersburg* (Bayreuth, 1993). The sets and costumes were designed by Prince Alexander Shervashidse.
48. 'Tristan and Isolde', in Edward Braun (trans. and ed.), *Meyerhold on Theatre* (London, 1998), 80–98.
49. *Ibid.*, 84–5. As Edward Braun points out in his note to this passage, the final quotation is a paraphrase of Treplev's words in the opening act of *The Seagull*.
50. *Ibid.*, 81.
51. Meyerhold quotes approvingly from *Der Tanz* (Stuttgart, 1906) by the director of the Munich Künstler-Theater, Georg Fuchs: 'The Germans' failure to recognize even today the beauty of the human body is revealed no more clearly than here, where its absurd distortions are unbearable to watch: Siegfrieds with tight corseted "Bierhaus" bellies; Siegmunds with sausage-shaped legs crammed into tights; Valkyries who appear to spend their leisure time in Munich beer halls over plates heaped with steaming offal and steins of foaming beer; Isoldes whose sole ambition is to play the part of fairground fat ladies and exercise their irresistible charms on the imagination of butchers' shop assistants' (Braun [trans. and ed.], *Meyerhold on Theatre*, 93f.).

52. *Ibid.*, 95.
53. *Ibid.*, 96f. Also worth quoting here is Meyerhold's comment that 'An author's stage directions depend on the level of stage technique at the time when the play is written. Stage techniques change, and an author's directions should be considered in the light of modern developments'; *ibid.*, 97.
54. *Ibid.*
55. They were described by contemporaries as 'the apogee of naturalism': see *Teatr i iskusstvo*, 45 (8 November 1909), quoted by Heldt, *Richard Wagner*, 166.
56. 'Khronika', *Russkaya muzykal'naya gazeta*, 45 (1909), 1036–40, quoted by Bartlett, *Wagner and Russia*, 101.
57. The manuscript has been in the Heidelberg University Library since 1888. The miniatures have been reproduced many times, most conveniently in Walter Koschorreck (ed.), *Minnesinger* (Frankfurt/Main, 1974). The manuscript also inspired the costume designs for Bayreuth's 1891 *Tannhäuser*.
58. V. E. Meierkhold, *Staty, pisma, rechi, besedy*, vol. I (Moscow, 1969), 198f., quoted by Braun, *Meyerhold: A Revolution*, 92. As Braun points out, the director's vision was further compromised by the difficulties in converting the Mariinsky stage into the 'relief stage' that Meyerhold believed was integral to his concept.
59. Quoted by Braun, *Meyerhold: A Revolution*, 90.
60. Friedrich Nietzsche, 'Richard Wagner in Bayreuth', in Giorgio Colli and Mazzino Montinari (eds.), *Sämtliche Werke*, vol. I (Munich, 1988), 479; trans. R. J. Hollingdale, 'Richard Wagner in Bayreuth', *Untimely Meditations* (Cambridge, 1983), 232.
61. The French première had taken place in Aix-les-Bains on 10 September 1897. Ten performances were given at the Nouveau-Théâtre in Paris in 1899 under the direction of Charles Lamoureux. For full details, see Martine Kahane and Nicole Wild, *Wagner et la France* (Paris, 1983), 169.
62. See Gerald Fitzgerald (ed.), *Annals of the Metropolitan Opera* (Boston, MA, and New York, NY, 1989); see also David Hamilton (ed.), *The Metropolitan Opera Encyclopedia* (New York, NY, and London, 1987), 368f. The work was first performed at the Met on 1 December 1886 with Lilli Lehmann, Marianne Brandt, Albert Niemann, Adolf Robinson and Emil Fischer. The conductor was Anton Seidl, the designer Henry E. Hoyt and the director a Mr van Hell.
63. See Spencer, '*Tristan und Isolde* in Great Britain'. *Tristan und Isolde* was first staged in London at the Theatre Royal, Drury Lane, on 20 June 1882 as part of the Grand German Opera Season conducted by Hans Richter. The main roles were taken by Rosa Sucher, Marianne Brandt, Hermann Winkelmann, Emil Krauss and Eugen Gura. The opera entered the Covent Garden repertory on 2 July 1884.
64. These designs were also published by Ernst Eulenburg in the form of coloured lithographs, enabling theatres to reproduce their own copies.

65. Significantly, perhaps, *Tristan und Isolde* failed to engage the attention of the leading avant-garde directors and designers of the 1920s, whose work is commemorated by Walter Panofsky, *Protest in der Oper: Das provokative Musiktheater der zwanziger Jahre* (Munich, 1966): the concerns of the opera were evidently felt to be too private and non-political.
66. Bauer, *Richard Wagner: Die Bühnenwerke*, 148; trans. Spencer, *Richard Wagner: The Stage Designs*, 159.
67. See Emil Preetorius, *Das szenische Werk*, 3rd edn. (Berlin and Vienna, 1944), esp. 42–4 and pl. facing p. 32; Preetorius's *Wagner: Bild und Vision*, 3rd edn. (Frankfurt/Main, 1949) first appeared in 1942, translated by the present writer as 'Richard Wagner: Stage Picture and Vision', *Wagner*, 12 (1991), 75–86. Thomas Mann's response to Preetorius appeared in the *Süddeutsche Zeitung* on 6/7 March 1950 and was reproduced in Erika Mann (ed.), *Wagner und unsere Zeit: Aufsätze, Betrachtungen, Briefe* (Frankfurt/Main, 1963), 167–9; for an English translation, see Thomas Mann, *Pro and contra Wagner*, trans. Allan Blunden (London, 1985), 208–11. See also Geoffrey Skelton, *Wagner at Bayreuth*, 2nd edn. (London, 1976), 153–6.
68. See Mack, *Der Bayreuther Inszenierungsstil*, 23 and pls. 203–10; and Heldt, *Richard Wagner*, 173–8. Siegfried's production replaced the 1886 staging, last seen in 1906. If visually unremarkable, it was memorable for the conducting of Arturo Toscanini in 1930 and of Wilhelm Furtwängler in 1931.
69. Tietjen's work has yet to be properly assessed, his complicated relations with National Socialism seemingly still an obstacle in the way of a detailed study; see Frederic Spotts, 'Phantom of the Opera', *Opera*, 57 (2006), 135–43.
70. Preetorius, 'Das Bühnenbild', in *Geheimnis des Sichtbaren: Gesammelte Aufsätze zur Kunst* (Munich, 1963), 72–80, esp. 74f.: 'Das Bühnenbild *ist* nicht – es *geschieht*!'
71. Preetorius, *Wagner: Bild und Vision*, 10–13; Engl. trans. 76 (emended).
72. See Günther Schneider-Siemssen, *'Die Bühne – mein Leben': Günther Schneider-Siemssen in Gesprächen mit Kurt Pahlen*, 2nd edn. (Vienna and New York, NY, 2001); Schneider-Siemssen's designs for *Tristan und Isolde* have been seen in Vienna (1967), New York (1970), Salzburg (1972), Berlin (1980) and Cape Town (1981).
73. Oswald has designed productions of *Tristan und Isolde* in Buenos Aires (1971), Montreal (1975 and 1986) and Chicago (1979).
74. The literature on Wieland Wagner is extensive; see, for example, Walter Erich Schäfer, *Wieland Wagner: Persönlichkeit und Leistung* (Tübingen, 1970); Geoffrey Skelton, *Wieland Wagner: The Positive Sceptic* (London, 1971); Heldt, *Richard Wagner*, 187–99; and Oswald Georg Bauer (ed.), *Wieland Wagner: Sein Denken* (Bayreuth, 1991).
75. See Oswald Georg Bauer, *Wolfgang Wagner: Arbeitsprinzipien eines Regisseurs* (Bayreuth, 1979); also Wolfgang Wagner, *Lebens-Akte: Autobiographie* (Munich, 1994), trans. by John Brownjohn as *Acts*

(London, 1994). Wolfgang directed the work in Bayreuth in 1957 and again in Milan in 1978.

76. Originally published in the booklet accompanying the Deutsche Grammophon recording of the 1966 Bayreuth Festival production and reproduced in Bauer (ed.), *Wieland Wagner*, 49–53, esp. 49.
77. Wieland believed – wrongly – that the stone marks the wayside grave of Tristan, who he believed was Marke's son. See Stewart Spencer, 'Tristan in Medieval Britain', *Wagner*, 11 (1990), 84–93. Flawed though Wieland's thinking may have been, the image remains extraordinarily potent.
78. Bauer (ed.), *Wieland Wagner*, 52.
79. In 1967, Wieland's production was filmed by Japanese television at the Osaka Festival under Pierre Boulez. Although available only in black and white and poor sound (Legato Classics LCV 005), the video nonetheless makes palpable the febrile intensity of the acting.
80. See Heldt, *Richard Wagner*, 207–23; see also Klaus Jürgen Seidel (ed.), *Die ganze Welt ist Bühne: August Everding* (Munich and Zurich, 1988); and Stefan Jaeger, 'August Everding: Das gescheiteste Vergnügen der Welt', in Norbert Ely and Stefan Jaeger (eds.), *Regie heute: Musiktheater in unserer Zeit* (Berlin, 1984), 89–110.
81. See Heldt, *Richard Wagner*, 227–46; see also Peter Riesterer *et al.*, *Zeit für Oper: Götz Friedrichs Musiktheater* (Frankfurt/Main, 1991). Friedrich directed productions of *Tristan und Isolde* at the Holland Festival in Scheveningen in 1974, in Berlin in 1980 and in Stuttgart in 1981. A restudied version of the 1974 production was seen in London in 1985. The Berlin production was filmed on tour in Japan in 1993 and is available on DVD (TDK DV-OTPUI).
82. See Dieter Kranz, *Der Regisseur Harry Kupfer: 'Ich muß Oper machen'* (Berlin, 1988). Kupfer first directed *Tristan und Isolde* in Dresden in 1975. Later productions were seen in Mannheim in 1982 and in Berlin in 2000. The third of the directors generally seen as Felsenstein's successors in the field of 'realistic music theatre', Joachim Herz (1924–2010) did not direct *Tristan und Isolde* in the course of his long and influential career.
83. Richard Wagner, *Sämtliche Briefe*, vol. VIII, ed. Hans-Joachim Bauer and Johannes Forner (Leipzig, 1991), 152 (letter to August Röckel, 23 August 1856).
84. See Max W. Busch, *Jean-Pierre Ponnelle 1932–1988* (Berlin, 2002); and Heldt, *Richard Wagner*, 267–88.
85. In Bayreuth in 1981 he was unwilling to have his Isolde appear onstage in the final scene but wanted her to sing her 'Transfiguration' from the orchestra pit. For 'logistical' reasons, this solution was not adopted. See the interview between Johanna Meier and Per-Erik Skramstad at www.wagneropera.net. Ponnelle's production was recorded in 1983 and is available on DVD from Deutsche Grammophon (00440 073 4321).
86. 'David Alden in conversation with Nicholas John', English National Opera programme (London, 10 February 1996).
87. Quoted by Mike Ashman in his introduction to the DVD recording released in 2008 by Deutsche Grammophon (00440 073 4439), p. 6. For

a full-length study of Heiner Müller, see Jonathan Kalb, *The Theater of Heiner Müller* (Cambridge, 1998). Unfortunately, Kalb clearly never saw the Bayreuth production.

88. The only full-length study of Marthaler's work, Klaus Dermutz, *Christoph Marthaler: Die einsamen Menschen sind die besonderen Menschen* (Salzburg and Vienna, 2000), was published too soon to take account of his Bayreuth production, but Anna Viebrock's *Materialbuch in drei Aufzügen: Das Bühnenbild zu 'Tristan und Isolde', Bayreuth 2005* (Eggersdorf, 2005) provides a detailed account of the designs for this production. Marthaler's production was filmed at the 2009 Bayreuth Festival and is available as a DVD from Opus Arte (OA 1033 D).
89. Other recent productions available on DVD include Peter Konwitschny's 1998 production at the Bavarian State Opera (Arthaus 100 056), Alfred Kirchner's 2005 staging from the Gran Teatre del Liceu (Opus Arte OA 0935 D), Olivier Py's 2005 staging at the Grand Théâtre de Genève (Bel Air BAC014), Nikolaus Lehnhoff's 2007 revival of his 2003 Glyndebourne production (Opus Arte OA 0988 D) and Johannes Felsenstein's 2008 production from the Anhaltisches Theater in Dessau (Arthaus 101 325).
90. A 'semi-staged' version had already been seen at the Walt Disney Concert Hall in Los Angeles, where it was presented one act at a time between 3 and 5 December and again between 10 and 12 December 2004.
91. Bill Viola, 'Moving Image World', Opéra National de Paris programme (Paris, 8 November 2005), 38. The Schopenhauerian Buddhism of the work has rarely been addressed.
92. Available on DVD (Virgin Classics 51931599) with a long introductory essay by Chéreau, 'Wann wird es Nacht im Haus?', from which the following quotations are taken.
93. Quoted by Mike Ashman, 'Nobody Really Yearns for Death', introduction to the Heiner Müller DVD (see note 87), 6; see also Wolfgang Wagner, *Lebens-Akte*, 284 and 399, trans. Brownjohn, *Acts*, 181 and 257.
94. Quoted by Willi Schuh, '*Tristan und Isolde* im Leben und Wirken Richard Strauß', in Walter Eichner (ed.), *Das Bayreuther Festspielbuch 1952* (Bayreuth, 1952), 70–90, esp. 88.
95. Slavoj Žižek and Mladen Dolar, *Opera's Second Death* (New York, NY, and London, 2002), 121–34.
96. Early productions are discussed by Hans Rudolf Vaget, '"Ohne Rat in fremdes Land?" *Tristan und Isolde* in Amerika: Seidl, Mahler, Toscanini', *wagnerspectrum*, 1 (2005), 164–85; and Carnegy, *Wagner and the Art of the Theatre* (n. 11), 197f.
97. This production was filmed in December 1999 and is available on DVD from Deutsche Grammophon (073 044–9). Minimalism was also the keynote of the clinically anti-Romantic new production by Christof Loy (born 1962) that opened at Covent Garden on 29 September 2009.
98. Richard Wagner, *Sämtliche Briefe*, vol. XI, ed. Werner Breig and Martin Dürrer (Wiesbaden, 1999), 58 (letter to Mathilde Wesendonck, April 1859).

99. Bernard Shaw, 'Tristan and Isolde', *The Star* (6 August 1889), quoted in Dan H. Laurence (ed.), *Shaw's Music*, vol. I (London, 1989), 723.
100. Richard Wagner, *Sämtliche Briefe*, vol. IV, ed. Gertrud Strobel and Werner Wolf (Leipzig, 1979), 248f.: 'I cannot help feeling that if we had *life*, we'd have no need of *art*. Art begins at precisely the point where life leaves off: when all around us ceases to exist, we call out in art, "I wish". I simply do not believe that a *truly happy* individual could ever hit upon the idea of creating "art".'

7 *Tristan*'s traces

1. Eduard Hanslick, who so resisted *Tristan* at its first Viennese performance in 1883, did inadvertently strike the right chord by castigating the entire opera with Sachs's words 'Wahn, überall Wahn!'; Henry Pleasants (trans.), *Hanslick's Music Criticisms* (New York, NY, 1988), 227.
2. Carl Dahlhaus, *Nineteenth-Century Music*, trans. J. Bradford Robinson (Berkeley and Los Angeles, CA, 1989), 205.
3. Linda Hutcheon, *A Theory of Parody: The Teachings of Twentieth-Century Art Forms*, rev. edn. (Urbana and Chicago, IL, 2000). Hutcheon restricts her view of intent to inferred intent of the creator, whereas I prefer to include a broader (reader/performer-controlled) perspective that gives agency to the characters on stage.
4. On *Tristan* in Kurth's theoretical system, see Lee A. Rothfarb, *Ernst Kurth as Theorist and Analyst* (Philadelphia, PA, 1988), 131–46.
5. Joseph Kerman, *Opera as Drama*, rev. edn. (Berkeley and Los Angeles, CA, 1988), 176.
6. Luigi Rognoni, *The Second Vienna School: Expressionism and Dodecaphony*, trans. Robert W. Mann (London, 1977), 3.
7. See Donald Mitchell, *Cradles of the New: Writings on Music 1951–1991*, ed. Mervyn Cooke (London and Boston, MA, 1995), 208f.; John C. Crawford and Dorothy L. Crawford, *Expressionism in Twentieth-Century Music* (Bloomington and Indianapolis, IN, 1993), 26f.
8. Arnold Schoenberg, *Harmonielehre* (1922), trans. Robert D. W. Adams, *Theory of Harmony* (New York, NY, 1948), 212f.
9. Stefan Askenase, cited in Joan Allen Smith, *Schoenberg and His Circle: A Viennese Portrait* (New York, NY, 1987), 154.
10. Hector Berlioz, 'Concerts de Richard Wagner: La Musique de l'Avenir', in *A Travers Chants* (Paris, 1862), 297.
11. For a succinct review see Jean-Jacques Nattiez, *Music and Discourse: Toward a Semiology of Music*, trans. Carolyn Abbate (Princeton, NJ, 1990), 223–38.
12. See Robert W. Wason, *Viennese Harmonic Theory from Albrechtsberger to Schenker and Schoenberg* (Ann Arbor, MI, 1985), 90–96.
13. Hugo Leichtentritt, *Musical Form* (Cambridge, MA, 1951), 427.
14. Leonard Meyer, *Style and Music: Theory, History, and Ideology* (Philadelphia, PA, 1989), 283.

15. Alban Berg, 'Gurrelieder Guide', trans. Mark DeVoto, *Journal of the Arnold Schoenberg Institute*, 16 (1993), 111–13.
16. Tethys Carpenter, 'The Musical Language of *Elektra*', in Derrick Puffett (ed.), *Richard Strauss: 'Elektra'* (Cambridge, 1989), 89f.
17. Milton Babbitt, [Reply to Edward T. Cone], repr. in Robert Bailey (ed.), *Richard Wagner: Prelude and Transfiguration from 'Tristan and Isolde'* (New York, NY, 1985), 290.
18. Charles Rosen, *The Romantic Generation* (Cambridge, MA, 1995), 475.
19. Rothfarb, *Ernst Kurth as Theorist*, 181–4.
20. Mark DeVoto, 'The Strategic Half-Diminished Chord and the Emblematic *Tristan* Chord: A Survey from Beethoven to Berg', *International Journal of Musicology*, 4 (1995), 144f.
21. For more references see Egon Voss, 'Wagner-Zitate in Bruckners Dritter Sinfonie? Ein Beitrag zum Begriff des Zitats in der Musik', *Die Musikforschung*, 49 (1996), 403–6.
22. Jan Swafford, *Johannes Brahms: A Biography* (New York, NY, 1997), 473.
23. Raymond Knapp, *Brahms and the Challenge of the Symphony* (Stuyvesant, NY, 1997), 266–9. Knapp suggests that Brahms had first-hand exposure to Wagnerian techniques because he helped copy out parts for the Viennese production of the Parisian revision of *Tannhäuser*.
24. Swafford, *Johannes Brahms*, 473.
25. James Webster, 'Der stilistische Ort der *Alt-Rhapsodie* und ihre Bedeutung für Brahms' künstlerische Entwicklung', in Friedhelm Krummacher and Michael Struck (eds.), *Johannes Brahms: Quellen – Text – Rezeption – Interpretation, Internationaler Brahms-Kongress Hamburg 1997* (Munich, 1999), 328.
26. Cited in Nancy B. Reich, *Clara Schumann: The Artist and the Woman*, rev. edn. (Ithaca, NY, and London, 2001), 203.
27. Cited in Anne Dzamba Sessa, *Richard Wagner and the English* (London, 1979), 45.
28. Bernard Shaw, 'Bayreuth and Back', in Dan H. Lawrence (ed.), *Shaw's Music*, vol. I (New York, NY, 1981), 745.
29. Ferruccio Busoni, letter to Philipp Jarnach, 7 June 1920, in Anthony Beaumont (trans.), *Selected Letters* (New York, NY, 1987), xx.
30. Oskar Panizza, '*Tristan und Isolde* in Paris', *Zürcher Diskussionen*, 25–6 (1900), 8.
31. See Emma Sutton, *Aubrey Beardsley and British Wagnerism in the 1890s* (Oxford, 2002), 99f.
32. For a slightly different interpretation see Sutton, *Aubrey Beardsley*, 41–3.
33. Susan McClary, *Feminine Endings: Music, Gender, and Sexuality* (Minneapolis, MN, and Oxford, 1991), 100.
34. Mitchell Morris, 'Tristan's Wounds: On Homosexual Wagnerians at the Fin de Siècle', in Sophie Fuller and Lloyd Whitesell (eds.), *Queer Episodes in Music and Modern Identity* (Urbana and Chicago, IL, 2002), 285f.
35. Karol Szymanowski, *Karol Szymanowski: Pisma Literackie*, vol. II, ed. Terersa Chylinska (Krakow, 1989), 151. This publication contains extant

fragments from the novel. My thanks to Dorota Zakrewska for pointing me to this passage and translating it.

36. Lawrence Kramer, *Music as Cultural Practice, 1800–1900* (Berkeley, CA, 1990), 164.
37. Bernard Grun (ed.), *Alban Berg, Letters to His Wife* (London, 1971), 24.
38. Thomas Mann, *Pro and Contra Wagner*, trans. Allan Blunden (Chicago, IL, 1985), 126.
39. Houston Stewart Chamberlain, *Richard Wagner*, trans. G. Ainslie Hight (London, 1897), 314.
40. Denis De Rougemont, *Love in the Western World*, rev. edn. (New York, NY, 1956), 231.
41. *Ibid.*, 227.
42. For additional allusions to *Tristan* and other Wagnerian operas see Steven Huebner, *French Opera at the Fin de Siècle: Wagnerism, Nationalism, and Style* (Oxford, 1999), 82–101.
43. See Michele Girardi, *Puccini: His International Art*, trans. Laura Basini (Chicago, IL, and London, 2000), 92f.
44. Norman Del Mar, *Richard Strauss: A Critical Commentary on his Life and Works*, vol. III (London, 1972), 183f.
45. François Lesure, *Claude Debussy: Biographie critique* (Paris, 1994), 446f.
46. David Code makes this point, as well as other insightful observations of the presence of *Tristan*, in his 'Hearing Debussy Reading Mallarmé: Music *après* Wagner in the *Prélude à l'après-midi d'un faune*', *Journal of the American Musicological Society*, 54 (2001), 526.
47. Letter to Willy, 10 October 1895, Debussy, *Correspondance 1884–1918*, ed. François Lesure (Paris, 1993), 114.
48. Major accounts include Léon Guichard, *La Musique et les lettres en France au temps du wagnérisme* (Paris, 1963); Erwin Koppen, *Dekadenter Wagnerismus* (Berlin and New York, NY, 1973); and Raymond Furness, *Wagner and Literature* (Manchester, 1982).
49. Elliott Zuckerman, *The First Hundred Years of Wagner's 'Tristan'* (New York, NY, 1964), vii.
50. Alberto Savinio, *Scatola sonora* (Milan, 1955), 119.
51. Friedrich Nietzsche, *Beyond Good and Evil* (section 229), in Walter Kaufmann (trans. and ed.), *Basic Writings of Nietzsche* (New York, NY, 1966), 348f.
52. Friedrich Nietzsche, *Ecce Homo* ('Why I am so clever', sec. 6), in *ibid.*, 706.
53. Marcel Proust, *La Prisonnière. À la recherche du temps perdu*, ed. Pierre-Edmond Robert (Paris, 1999), 1722.
54. For a reading of the resonances of *Tristan* in *À la recherche du temps perdu* that is particularly attentive to how Wagner's music interacts programmatically with the 'petite phrase', see Cormac Newark and Ingrid Wassenaar, 'Proust and Music: The Anxiety of Competence', *Cambridge Opera Journal*, 9 (1997), 163–83.
55. Thomas Mann, *Death in Venice – Tristan – Tonio Kröger*, trans. Kenneth Burke (New York, NY, 1924), 168.

56. *Ibid.*, 189.
57. Philip Rupprecht, *Britten's Musical Language* (Cambridge, 2001), 247–51.
58. See Robin Holloway, *Debussy and Wagner* (London, 1979), 60–142; Carolyn Abbate, '*Tristan* in the Composition of *Pelléas*', *19th-Century Music*, 5 (1981), 117–41. On the appeal of *Pelléas* to decadent subculture see Jann Pasler, '*Pelléas* and Power: Forces behind the Reception of Debussy's Opera', *19th-Century Music*, 10 (1986/7), 243–64.
59. For an extended discussion of this quotation in context, see George Perle, *Style and Idea in the 'Lyric Suite' of Alban Berg* (Stuyvesant, NY, 1995). Robert Gauldin discusses encoding of *Tristan* references as they apply to Helene Nahowski in 'Reference and Association in the Vier Lieder, Op. 2, of Alban Berg', *Music Theory Spectrum*, 21 (1999), 32–42.
60. For a more developed and slightly different interpretation see Elizabeth Morrison, *The Deadlly Feminine: Violence and Eroticism in Three Expressionist Operas* (PhD diss., McGill University, 2002).
61. DeVoto, 'The Strategic Half-Diminished Chord', 152.
62. Slavoj Žižek and Mladen Dolar, *Opera's Second Death* (New York, NY, and London, 2002), 129.
63. On Brangaene's scream see Michel Poizat *L'Opéra ou Le cri de l'ange* (Paris, 1986), trans. Arthur Denner as *The Angel's Cry: Beyond the Pleasure Principle in Opera* (Ithaca, NY, and London, 1992), 165f.
64. An incisive presentation of this view is Peter Dettmering, *Dichtung und Psychoanalyse: Thomas Mann – Rainer Maria Rilke – Richard Wagner* (Frankfurt/Main, 1976), 194–202.
65. For a developed discussion of *Tristan* in *Der Rosenkavalier*, see Walter Frisch, *German Modernism: Music and the Arts* (Berkeley, CA, 2005), 216–23.
66. Cited by Vincent d'Indy in a lecture given at the Concerts Pasdeloup, 8 April 1920, and published as a pamphlet in Paris later that year.
67. I am grateful to Kristin Taavola for this reference.
68. On this aspect of *Louise* see Huebner, *French Opera at the Fin de Siècle*, 436–55.
69. Hans Werner Henze, *Music and Politics: Collected Writings 1953–81*, trans. Peter Labanyi (London, 1982), 222.
70. *Ibid.*, 227.
71. *Ibid.*, 228f.

Select bibliography

Tristan and Isolde in legend and literature

Bechstein, Reinhold. *Tristan und Isolt in deutschen Dichtungen der Neuzeit* (Leipzig, 1876)

Bolz, Norbert. '*Tristan und Isolde* – Richard Wagner als Leser Gottfrieds', in Jürgen Kühnel *et al.* (eds.), *Mittelalter-Rezeption* (Göppingen, 1979), 273–93

Golther, Wolfgang. *Tristan und Isolde in den Dichtungen des Mittelalters und der neuen Zeit* (Leipzig, 1907)

Grill, Dorothee. *Tristan-Dramen des 19. Jahrhunderts* (Göppingen, 1997)

Grimbert, Joan Tasker (ed.). *Tristan and Isolde: A Casebook* (New York, NY, and London, 2002)

Hessler, Hans-Joachim. *Der 'Tristan'-Roman des Gottfried von Straßburg und Richard Wagners 'Tristan und Isolde': Eine Gegenüberstellung* (Dortmund, 2001)

Mertens, Volker. 'Der Tristanstoff in der europäischen Literatur', *wagnerspectrum*, 1 (2005), 11–42

Müller, Ulrich. 'The Modern Reception of Gottfried's *Tristan* and the Medieval Legend of Tristan and Isolde', in Will Hasty (ed.), *A Companion to Gottfried von Straßburg's 'Tristan'* (Rochester, NY, 2003), 285–306

Rosenband, Doris. *Das Liebesmotiv in Gottfrieds 'Tristan' und Wagners 'Tristan und Isolde'* (Göppingen, 1973)

Stein, Peter. 'Tristan', in Volker Mertens and Ulrich Müller (eds.), *Epische Stoffe des Mittelalters* (Stuttgart, 1984), 365–94

Guides to Wagner's *Tristan und Isolde*

Csampai, Attila, and Dietmar Holland (eds.). *Richard Wagner, Tristan und Isolde: Texte, Materialien, Kommentare* (Reinbek, 1983)

Druault, Alain and Michel Pazdro (eds.). *Wagner, Tristan et Isolde*, L'Avant-Scène Opera, 34/35 (Paris, 1981)

John, Nicholas (ed.). *Richard Wagner Tristan und Isolde*, English National Opera Guide, 6 (London and New York, NY, 1983)

Pahlen, Kurt, and Rosemarie König (eds.). *Tristan und Isolde: Textbuch, Einführung und Kommentar* (Mainz, 2006)

Genesis of the opera

Bailey, Robert. 'The Genesis of *Tristan und Isolde* and a Study of Wagner's Sketches and Drafts for the First Act' (diss., Princeton, NJ, 1969)

Bartels, Ulrich. *Analytisch-entstehungsgeschichtliche Studien zu Wagners 'Tristan und Isolde' anhand der Kompositionsskizze des zweiten und dritten Aktes* (Cologne, 1995)

Deathridge, John. 'Public and Private Life: Reflections on the Genesis of *Tristan und Isolde* and the *Wesendonck Lieder*', in *Wagner Beyond Good and Evil* (Berkeley, CA, 2008), 117–32

Kleinertz, Rainer. 'Liszt, Wagner, and Unfolding Form: Orpheus and the Genesis of *Tristan und Isolde*', in Christopher H. Gibbs and Dana Gooley (eds.), *Franz Liszt and His World* (Princeton, NJ, 2006), 231–54

Prüfer, Arthur. 'Novalis *Hymnen an die Nacht* in ihren Beziehungen zu Wagners *Tristan und Isolde*', in Ludwig Frankenstein (ed.), *Richard Wagner-Jahrbuch*, 1 (Leipzig, 1906), 290–304

Staehelin, Martin. 'Von den *Wesendonck-Liedern* zum *Tristan*', in Helmut Loos and Günther Massenkeil (eds.), *Zu Richard Wagner: Acht Bonner Beiträge* (Bonn, 1984), 45–73

Voss, Egon. 'Die "schwarze und die weiße Flagge": Zur Entstehung von Wagners *Tristan*', *Archiv für Musikwissenschaft*, 54 (1997), 210–27

The 'Tristan' chord

Bass, Richard. 'From Gretchen to *Tristan*: The Changing Role of Harmonic Sequences in the Nineteenth Century', *19th-Century Music*, 19 (1996), 263–85

Beeson, Roger. 'The *Tristan* Chord and Others: Harmonic Analysis and Harmonic Explanation', *Soundings*, 5 (1975), 55–72

Chew, Geoffrey. 'Ernst Kurth, Music as Psychic Motion and *Tristan und Isolde*: Towards a Model for Analysing Musical Instability', *Music Analysis*, 10 (1991), 171–93

Dahlhaus, Carl. '*Tristan* – Harmonik und Tonalität', *Melos/Neue Zeitschrift für Musik*, 4 (1978), 215–19

Danuser, Hermann. 'Der Rätselklang: Zur historischen Semiotik des Tristanakkordes', in Hermann Danuser and Herfried Münkler (eds.), *Zukunftsbilder: Richard Wagners Revolution und ihre Folgen in Kunst und Politik* (Schliengen, 2002), 151–60

DeVoto, Mark. 'The Strategic Half-Diminished Seventh Chord and the Emblematic *Tristan* Chord: A Survey from Beethoven to Berg', *International Journal of Musicology*, 4 (1995), 139–53

Giesl, Peter. 'Der *Tristan*-Akkord aus der Sicht der Clausellehre', in Ulrich Konrad and Egon Voss (eds.), *Der 'Komponist' Richard Wagner im Blick der aktuellen Musikwissenschaft* (Wiesbaden, 2003), 117–25

Gloede, Wilhelm. 'Zum Mythos "*Tristan*-Akkord"', *Musiktheorie*, 19 (2004), 69–81

Gostomsky, Dieter. 'Immer noch einmal: der "*Tristan*-Akkord"', *Zeitschrift für Musiktheorie*, 6 (1975), 22–7

Hartmann, Günter. 'Schon wieder: Der (?) *Tristan*-Akkord', *Die Musikforschung*, 42 (1989), 36–52

Hill, Cecil. 'That Wagner-*Tristan* Chord', *Music Review*, 45 (1984), 7–10

Holtmeier, Ludwig. 'Der Tristanakkord und die neue Funktionstheorie', *Musiktheorie*, 17 (2002), 361–5

Nattiez, Jean-Jacques. 'The Concepts of Plot and Seriation Process in Music Analysis', *Music Analysis*, 4 (1985), 107–18

Poos, Heinrich. 'Der 3. *Tristan*-Akkord. Zur Harmoniestruktur der Takte 1–16 der Einleitung von *Tristan und Isolde*', in Carl Dahlhaus *et al.* (eds.), *Bericht über den internationalen musikwissenschaftlichen Kongreß Bonn 1970* (Kassel, 1971), 539–42

Richey, John. 'History and the *Tristan* Chord', *The Music Review*, 5 (1994), 97–103

Rothgeb, John. 'The *Tristan* Chord: Identity and Origin', *Music Theory Online*, 1 (1995)

Schlotterer-Traimer, Roswitha. 'Akkorde, die einen Namen haben', in Bernd Edelmann and Manfred Hermann Schmid (eds.), *Altes im Neuen: Festschrift Theodor Göllner zum 65. Geburtstag* (Tutzing, 1995), 321–30

Ünlü, Altug. 'Der "*Tristan*-Akkord" im Kontext einer tradierten Sequenzformel', *Musiktheorie*, 18 (2003), 179–85

Vogel, Martin. *Der Tristan-Akkord und die Krise der modernen Harmonie-Lehre* (Düsseldorf, 1962)

Ziegler, Reinald. 'Der "Tristanakkord": Ein geschichtliches Phänomen', in Bernhard Appel *et al.* (eds.), *Musik und Szene: Festschrift fur Werner Braun* (Saarbrücken, 2001), 387–412

The Prelude

Amiot, Emmanuel. 'Pour en finir avec *le Desir*: La notion de symetrie en analyse musicale', *Analyse musicale*, 22 (1991), 87–92

Bailey, Robert. *Richard Wagner, Prelude and Transfiguration from 'Tristan und Isolde': The Authoritative Scores, Historical Background, Sketches and Drafts, Views and Comments, Analytical Essays* (New York, NY, 1985)

Burstein, L. Poundie. 'A New View of *Tristan*: Tonal Unity in the Prelude and Conclusion to Act I', *Theory and Practice*, 8/1 (September 1983), 15–41

'More on *Tristan*', *Theory and Practice*, 9/1–2 (July–December 1984), 125–8

Hindemith, Paul. 'Das Vorspiel zum *Tristan*', in Wieland Wagner (ed.), *Hundert Jahre 'Tristan'* (Emsdetten, 1965), 67–71

Jackson, Roland. 'Leitmotif and Form in the *Tristan* Prelude', *The Music Review*, 36 (1975), 42–53

Kerman, Joseph. '*Tristan und Isolde*: The Prelude and the Play', in *Write All These Down: Essays on Music* (Berkeley, CA, 1994), 335–49

Lorenz, Alfred. 'Die formale Gestaltung des Vorspiels zu *Tristan und Isolde*', in Gerhard Schuhmacher (ed.), *Zur musikalischen Analyse* (Darmstadt, 1974), 455–74

Maisel, Arthur. '*Tristan*: A Different Perspective', *Theory and Practice*, 8/2 (December 1983), 53–61

McKinney, Bruce. 'The Case against Tonal Unity in *Tristan*', *Theory and Practice*, 8/2 (December 1983), 62–7

Mitchell, William J. 'The Tristan *Prelude*: Techniques and Structure', *Music Forum*, 1 (1967), 162–203

Morgan, Robert P. 'Circular Form in the *Tristan* Prelude', *Journal of the American Musicological Society*, 53 (2000), 69–103

The 'alte Weise'/ cor anglais solo (Act III)

Deliège, Irène. 'Wagners "Alte Weise": Une approche perceptive', in 'Wagner, *Tristan und Isolde*, 'cor anglais' solo', *Musicae scientiae*, special issue (1998), 63–89

Forte, Allen. 'A Schenkerian Reading of an Excerpt from *Tristan und Isolde*', *Musicae scientiae*, special issue (1998), 15–26

Imberty, Michel. 'Du vide à l'infini: homologies structurales repérées dans *Tristan* à partir du solo de cor anglais du III° acte', *Musicae scientiae*, special issue (1998), 91–116

Labussière, Annie. '"Die alte Weise": une analyse sémiologique du *solo* de cor anglais du 3e Acte de *Tristan et Isolde*', *Analyse musicale*, 27 (1992), 30–53

Lerdahl, Fred. 'Prolongational Structure and Thematic Form in Tristan's *Alte Weise*', *Musicae scientiae*, special issue (1998), 27–41

Nattiez, Jean-Jacques. 'Le solo de cor anglais de *Tristan und Isolde*: essai d'analyse sémiologique tripartite', *Musicae scientiae*, special issue (1998), 43–61

'Der Dichter und der Geist der Musik', *wagnerspectrum*, 1 (2005), 43–62

Thorau, Christian. 'Untersuchungen zur "traurigen Weise" im 3. Akt von *Tristan und Isolde*', *Musik-Konzepte*, 57–8 (1987), 118–28

Early secondary literature (to *c.* 1940)

Allfeld, J. B. '*Tristan und Isolde' von Richard Wagner: Kritisch beleuchtet mit einleitenden Bemerkungen über Melodie und Musik* (Munich, 1865)

Chop, Max. *Richard Wagners 'Tristan und Isolde', Handlung in drei Aufzügen: Geschichtlich, szenisch, und musikalisch analysiert* (Leipzig, 1906)

Cleather, Alice Leighten and Basil Woodward Crump. '*Tristan und Isolde*': *An Interpretation Embodying Wagner's Own Explanations* (London, 1905)

Cotard, Charles. '*Tristan et Iseult': Essai d'analyse des leitmotifs* (Paris, 1895)

Frost, H. F. 'Some Remarks on Richard Wagner's Music Drama *Tristan und Isolde*', *Proceedings of the Musical Association*, 8 (1881/2), 147–67

Heintz, Albert. *Richard Wagners 'Tristan und Isolde'* (Berlin-Charlottenburg, 1891); trans. Constance Bache, *Tristan and Isolde by Richard Wagner, Explained According to the Musical Development of Its Motives* (London and New York, NY, 1892)

Kobbé, Gustav. *Richard Wagner's 'Tristan und Isolde': An Analysis* (New York, NY, 1886)

The Music-Dramas of Richard Wagner, With the Leading Motives in Notation (New York, NY, 1886) (rev. edn.: *Wagner's Music-Dramas Analyzed*)

Kufferath, Maurice. *Guide thématique et analyse de 'Tristan et Iseult'* (Paris, 1894)

Kurth, Ernst. *Romantische Harmonik und ihre Krise in Wagners 'Tristan'* (1923; repr. Hildesheim, 1985). Partial translation in Ernst Kurth, *Selected Writings*, ed. and trans. Lee Allen Rothfarb (New York, NY, 1991), 97–147

Lavignac, Albert. *The Music Dramas of Richard Wagner and His Festival Theatre in Bayreuth*, trans. Esther Singleton (New York, NY, 1898), 113–24, 284–315

Lehmann, Lilli. *Studie zu 'Tristan und Isolde'* (Wittenberg, 1906)

Lorenz, Alfred. *Der musikalische Aufbau von Richard Wagners 'Tristan und Isolde'* (Berlin, 1926)

Mayrberger, Karl. *Die Harmonik Richard Wagners an den Leitmotiven aus 'Tristan und Isolde' erläutert* (Chemnitz, 1882); repr. as 'The Harmonic Style of Richard Wagner, Elucidated with Respect to the Leitmotifs of *Tristan und Isolde*', in Ian Bent (ed.), *Music Analysis in the Nineteenth Century*, vol. I (Cambridge, 1994), 221–54

Mendès, Catulle. *L'Œuvre wagnérienne en France: 'Tristan et Iseult'* (Paris, 1899)

Nerthal. *'Tristan et Yseult': La passion dans un drame Wagnérien* (Paris, 1893)

Park, Rosemary. *Richard Wagners 'Tristan und Isolde' in der deutschen Literatur* (Jena, 1935)

Pfohl, Ferdinand. *'Tristan und Isolde': Handlung in drei Aufzügen von Richard Wagner* (Berlin and Leipzig, 1904)

Pfordten, Hermann Ludwig von der. *A Plain Handbook to the Plot and Text of Richard Wagner's 'Tristan and Isolde'*, trans. F. Speed (Berlin, 1892)

Porges, Heinrich. *'Tristan und Isolde' nebst einem Briefe Richard Wagners* (Leipzig, 1906)

Prüfer, Arthur. *Tristan und Isolde*, 3rd edn. (Bayreuth, 1928)

Reimann, Heinrich. *Musikalische Rückblicke: Modernes–Organistica* (Berlin, 1900), 41–7

Wolzogen, Hans von. *Thematischer Leitfaden durch die Musik zu Richard Wagner's 'Tristan und Isolde'*, 2nd edn. (Leipzig, 1877); trans. as *Guide through the Musical Motives of Richard Wagner's 'Tristan and Isolde'* (New York, NY, 1889)

Secondary literature (after 1945)

Abbate, Carolyn. 'Wagner, "On Modulation", and *Tristan*', *Cambridge Opera Journal*, 1 (1989), 33–58

Bermbach, Udo. 'Der tückische Tag: Überlegungen zu Wagners *Tristan und Isolde*', in Hanspeter Krellmann and Jürgen Schläder (eds.), *'Die Wirklichkeit erfinden ist besser': Opern des 19. Jahrhunderts von Beethoven bis Verdi* (Stuttgart, 2002), 123–31

Bernstein, David. 'Georg Capellen on *Tristan und Isolde*: Analytical Systems in Conflict at the Turn of the Twentieth Century', *Journal of Music Theory*, 37 (1993), 85–116

Bolz, Norbert. 'Isoldes Wunsch', in Olav Münzberg *et al.* (eds.), *Aufmerksamkeit, Klaus Heinrich zum 50. Geburtstag* (Frankfurt/Main, 1979), 70–74

Borchmeyer, Dieter. *Das Theater Richard Wagners: Idee – Dichtung – Wirkung* (Stuttgart, 1982); trans. Stewart Spencer, *Richard Wagner: Theory and Theatre* (Oxford, 1991), 326–67

'Love and Objectification in the Music Drama: Isolde and Her Sisters', in *Drama and the World of Richard Wagner*, trans. Daphne Ellis (Princeton, NJ, 2003), 157–79

Bork, Camilla. '"Tod und Verklärung": Isoldes Liebestod als Modell künstlerischer Schlußgestaltung', in Hermann Danuser and Herfried Münkler (eds.), *Zukunftsbilder: Richard Wagners Revolution und ihre Folgen* (Schliengen, 2002), 161–78

Brown, Jonathan. *'Tristan und Isolde' on Record: A Comprehensive Discography of Wagner's Music Drama with a Critical Introduction to the Recordings* (Westport, CT, 2000)

Brown, Matthew. 'Isolde's Narrative: From Hauptmotiv to Tonal Model', in Carolyn Abbate and Roger Parker (eds.), *Analyzing Opera: Verdi and Wagner* (Berkeley, CA, 1989), 180–201

Chafe, Eric. *The Tragic and the Ecstatic: The Musical Revolution of Wagner's 'Tristan und Isolde'* (New York, NY, 2005)

Chailley, Jacques. *Tristan et Isolde de Richard Wagner* (Paris, 1972)

Dahlhaus, Carl. '*Tristan*-Harmonik und Tonalität', *Melos/Neue Zeitschrift für Musik*, 4 (1978), 215–19

Richard Wagner's Music Dramas, trans. Mary Whittall (Cambridge, 1979), 49–64

'Wagners "Kunst des Übergangs": Der Zwiegesang in *Tristan und Isolde*', in *Vom Musikdrama zur Literaturoper* (Munich and Salzburg, 1983), 132–8

Deathridge, John. 'Wagner and the Post-Modern', *Cambridge Opera Journal*, 4 (1992), 143–61; repr. in *Wagner Beyond Good and Evil* (Berkeley, CA, 2008), 209–26

'Postmortem on Isolde', in *Wagner Beyond Good and Evil* (Berkeley, CA, 2008), 133–55

Döhring, Sieghart. 'Die Wahnsinnsszene', in Heinz Becker (ed.), *Die 'Couleur locale' in der Oper des 19. Jahrhunderts* (Regensburg, 1976), 279–314

Dorschel, Andreas. 'Die Idee der "Einswerdung" in Wagners *Tristan*', *Musik-Konzepte*, 57–8 (1987), 3–45

Ebbeke, Klaus. 'Richard Wagners "Kunst des Übergangs": Zur zweiten Szene des zweiten Aktes von *Tristan und Isolde*', in Josef Kuckertz *et al.* (eds.), *Neue Musik und Tradition: Festschrift Rudolf Stephan zum 65. Geburtstag* (Laaber, 1990), 259–70

Flechsig, Irmtraud. 'Beziehungen zwischen textlicher und musikalischer Struktur in Richard Wagners *Tristan und Isolde*', in Carl Dahlhaus (ed.), *Das Drama Richard Wagners als musikalisches Kunstwerk* (Regensburg, 1970), 239–56

Groos, Arthur. 'Appropriation in Wagner's *Tristan* Libretto', in Arthur Groos and Roger Parker (eds.), *Reading Opera* (Princeton, NJ, 1988), 12–33

'Wagner's *Tristan und Isolde*: In Defence of the Libretto', *Music & Letters*, 69 (1988), 465–81

Gut, Serge. 'Versuch einer androgynen Interpretation des Jagdmotivs in Wagner's *Tristan*', in *Festschrift Christoph-Hellmut Mahling zum 65. Geburtstag*, ed. Axel Beer *et al.* (Tutzing, 1997), 455–64

Hirsbrunner, Theo. 'Rebellion der Dekadenz: Eine Studie über Richard Wagners *Tristan und Isolde*', in *Von Richard Wagner bis Pierre Boulez* (Anif, 1997), 9–21

Huck, Oliver. 'Musik und Sprache in und zu Richard Wagners *Tristan und Isolde*', in Christian Berger (ed.), *Musik jenseits der Grenze der Sprache* (Freiburg, 2004), 157–72

Hutcheon, Linda and Michael Hutcheon. 'Eros and Thanatos: Richard Wagner's *Tristan und Isolde*', in *Opera: The Art of Dying* (Cambridge, MA, 2004), 45–72

Kerman, Joseph. 'Opera as Symphonic Poem', in *Opera as Drama*, 2nd edn. (London, 1989), 158–77

Kiem, Eckehard. 'Entwicklungsmotive: Ein Struktur- und Ausdrucksaspekt im *Tristan*', in Eckehard Kiem and Ludwig Holtmeier (eds.), *Richard Wagner und seine Zeit* (Laaber, 2003), 261–70

Kienzle, Ulrike. *– daß wissend würde die Welt!: Religion und Philosophie in Richard Wagners Musikdramen* (Würzburg, 2005), 157–72

Kinderman, William. 'Das Geheimnis der Form in Wagners *Tristan und Isolde*', *Archiv für Musikwissenschaft*, 40 (1983), 174–88

'Hans Sachs's "Cobbler's Song", *Tristan*, and the "Bitter Cry of the Resigned Man"', *The Journal of Musicological Research*, 13 (1993), 161–84

'Dramatic Recapitulation and Tonal Pairing in Wagner's *Tristan und Isolde* and *Parsifal*', in William Kinderman and Harald Krebs (eds.), *The Second Practice of Nineteenth-Century Tonality* (Lincoln, NE, 1996), 178–214

Kittler, Friedrich. '*Weltatem*: On Wagner's Media Technology', 1987, repr. in David Levin (ed.), *Opera Through Other Eyes* (Stanford, CA, 1994), 215–35

Knapp, Raymond. 'The Tonal Structure of *Tristan und Isolde*: A Sketch', *The Music Review*, 45 (1984), 11–25

'"Selbst dann bin ich die Welt": On the Subjective-Musical Basis of Wagner's *Gesamtkunstwelt*', *19th-Century Music*, 29 (2005), 142–60
Kramer, Lawrence. 'Musical Form and Fin-de-Siècle Sexuality', in *Music as Cultural Practice, 1800–1900* (Berkeley, CA, 1990), 135–76
Kropfinger, Klaus. 'Wagners *Tristan* und Beethovens Streichquartett Op.130: Funktion und Strukturen des Prinzips der Einleitungswiederholung', in Carl Dahlhaus (ed.), *Das Drama Richard Wagners als musikalisches Kunstwerk* (Regensburg, 1970), 259–71
Kühn, Hellmut. 'Brangänes Wächtergesang: Zur Differenz zwischen dem Musikdrama und der französischen großen Oper', in Carl Dahlhaus (ed.), *Richard Wagner: Werk und Wirkung* (Regensburg, 1971), 117–25
Lück, Heiner. 'Lehnrecht und Ehebruch: Das Beispiel Tristan', *wagnerspectrum*, 1 (2005), 80–97
Magee, Bryan. *The Tristan Chord: Wagner and Philosophy* (London, 2000)
Mahnkopf, Claus-Steffen. '*Tristan*-Studien', in Claus-Steffen Mahnkopf (ed.), *Richard Wagner: Konstrukteur der Moderne* (Stuttgart, 1999), 67–127
Maurer Zenck, Claudia. 'Komponierte Weiblichkeit: Rollenprofil der Isolde oder: Als Frau Isolde zuhören', in Susanne Vill (ed.), *'Das Weib der Zukunft': Frauengestalten und Frauenstimmen bei Richard Wagner* (Stuttgart, 2000), 95–117
Mayer, Hans. 'Der tragische Held und seine Freunde: Bemerkungen zu Wolfram, Brangäne, Kurwenal', in his *Richard Wagner*, ed. Wolfgang Hofer (Frankfurt/Main, 1998), 117–25
'Tristans Schweigen', *Richard Wagner*, ed. W. Hofer (Frankfurt/Main, 1998), 126–36
McCreless, Patrick. 'Isolde's Transfiguration in Words and Music', in Deborah Stein (ed.), *Engaging Music: Essays in Music Analysis* (New York, NY, 2004), 122–35
Metzger, Heinz-Klaus and Rainer Riehn (eds.). *Richard Wagner: Tristan und Isolde*, *Musik-Konzepte*, 57–8 (Munich, 1987)
Newcomb, Anthony. 'Ritornello Ritornato: A Variety of Wagnerian Refrain Form', in Carolyn Abbate and Roger Parker (eds.), *Analyzing Opera: Verdi and Wagner* (Berkeley, CA, 1989), 202–21
Newman, Ernest. *The Wagner Operas* (New York, NY, 1949; repr. 1983), 169–278 [published in the UK as *Wagner Nights*]
Poos, Heinrich. 'Zur *Tristan*harmonik', in Heinrich Poos (ed.), *Festschrift Ernst Pepping zu seinem 70. Geburtstag* (Berlin, 1971), 269–97
'Die *Tristan*-Hieroglyphe: Ein allegoretischer Versuch', *Musik-Konzepte*, 57–8 (1987), 46–103
Roch, Eckhard. 'Ein Geheimnis der Form bei Richard Wagner. Asymmetrische Periodenstruktur in Wagners *Tristan*', in Ulrich Konrad and Egon Voss (eds.), *Der 'Komponist' Richard Wagner im Blick der aktuellen Musikwissenschaft* (Wiesbaden, 2003), 105–15
Scharschuch, Horst. *Gesamtanalyse der Harmonik von Richard Wagners Musikdrama 'Tristan und Isolde': Unter spezifischer Berücksichtigung der Sequenztechnik des Tristanstiles* (Regensburg, 1963)

Schläder, Jürgen. 'Vom Gefühlsrausch zur intellektuellen Revolution: Zur Strategie des Liebesduettes in Wagners *Tristan*', in Hanspeter Krellmann and Jürgen Schläder (eds.), *'Die Wirklichkeit erfinden ist besser': Opern des 19. Jahrhunderts* (Stuttgart, 2002), 132–41

Schlagbauer, Sigrid. 'Die musikalische Darstellung der Natur in *Tristan und Isolde*', in *Richard Wagner und die Musikhochschule München* (Regensburg, 1983), 61–81

Schnapp, Friedrich. 'Robert Schumann's Plan for a *Tristan*-Opera', *The Musical Quarterly*, 10 (1924), 485–91

Scruton, Roger. *Death-Devoted Heart: Sex and the Sacred in Wagner's 'Tristan und Isolde'* (Oxford and New York, NY, 2003)

Siegele, Ulrich. '"Kunst des Übergangs" und formale Artikulation: Beispiele aus Richard Wagners *Tristan und Isolde*', in Ulrich Konrad and Egon Voss (eds.), *Der 'Komponist' Richard Wagner im Blick der aktuellen Musikwissenschaft* (Wiesbaden, 2003), 25–32

Steiger, Karsten. 'Liebe, Tod, Erlösung: Richard Wagners *Tristan* und der Einfluß Schopenhauers', *Schopenhauer-Jahrbuch*, 76 (1995), 103–32

Steinbeck, Wolfram. 'Die Idee des Symphonischen bei Richard Wagner: Zur Leitmotivtechnik in *Tristan und Isolde*', in Christoph-Hellmut Mahling and Sigrid Wiesmann (eds.), *Bericht über den Internationalen Musikwissenschaftlichen Kongreß Bayreuth 1981* (Kassel, 1981), 424–36

Stephan, Rudolf. 'Gibt es ein Geheimnis der Form bei Richard Wagner?', in Carl Dahlhaus (ed.), *Das Drama Richard Wagners als musikalisches Kunstwerk* (Regensburg, 1970), 9–16

Tanner, Michael. *Wagner* (Princeton, NJ, 1996), 140–55

Urmoneit, Sebastian. 'Untersuchungen zu den beiden "Todesmotiven" aus *Tristan und Isolde*', *Musik-Konzepte*, 57–8 (1987), 104–17

'Musik und Individualität: Die Tristanharmonik als philosophische Ideenreihe', in Oliver Schwab-Felisch *et al.* (eds.), *Individualität in der Musik* (Stuttgart, 2002), 257–71

Tristan und Isolde – Eros und Thanatos: Zur 'dichterischen Deutlichkeit' der Harmonik von Richard Wagners 'Handlung' 'Tristan und Isolde' (Sinzig, 2005)

Voss, Egon. *Studien zur Instrumentation Richard Wagners* (Regensburg, 1970)

'*Tristan*: Die Liebe als furchtbare Qual', in *'Wagner und kein Ende': Betrachtungen und Studien* (Zurich and Mainz, 1996), 91–104

'*Tristan* ohne Mythos', in *'Wagner und kein Ende'* (Zurich and Mainz, 1996), 110–17

Wagner, Wieland (ed.). *Hundert Jahre 'Tristan'* (Emsdetten, 1965)

Wapnewski, Peter. *Der traurige Gott. Richard Wagner in seinen Helden* (Munich, 1978)

'Rivale Faust: Beobachtungen zu Wagners Goethe-Verständnis', *Jahrbuch des Freien Deutschen Hochstifts* (1984), 128–56

Liebestod und Götternot: Zum 'Tristan' und zum 'Ring des Nibelungen' (Berlin, 1988)

Tristan der Held Richard Wagners, 2nd edn. (Berlin, 2001)

Weisstein, Ulrich. 'The Little Word *und*: *Tristan und Isolde* as Verbal Construct', in Leroy R. Shaw *et al.* (eds.), *Wagner in Retrospect: A Centennial Reappraisal* (Amsterdam, 1987), 70–90

Wesselmann, Katharina. 'Tristan – "der zage Held": Ein demontiertes Heldenbild und sein antikes Modell', *wagnerspektrum*, 1 (2005), 98–126

White, Andrew. 'Toward an Understanding of Wagnerian Music-Drama: An Examination of *Tristan und Isolde*', *Music Research Forum*, 14 (1999), 27–58

Winkler, Gerhard J. 'Wagners Erlösungsmotiv: Versuch über eine musikalische Schlußformel – Eine Stilübung', *Musiktheorie*, 5 (1990), 3–25

Staging and performance history

Appia, Adolphe. 'Die Inscenierung von *Tristan und Isolde*', in *Die Musik und die Inscenierung* (Munich, 1899), 237–54

Ashbrook, William. 'The First Singers of *Tristan und Isolde*', *Opera Quarterly*, 3/4 (1985–6), 11–23

Bahr-Mildenburg, Anna. *Darstellung der Werke Richard Wagners aus dem Geiste der Dichtung und Musik: 'Tristan und Isolde'. Vollständige Regiebearbeitung sämtlicher Partien mit Notenbeispielen* (Leipzig and Vienna, 1936)

Baragwanath, Nicholas. 'Anna Bahr-Mildenburg, Gesture, and the Bayreuth Style', *The Musical Times*, 148 (2007), 63–74

Bauer, Oswald Georg. *Richard Wagner: Die Bühnenwerke von der Uraufführung bis heute* (Frankfurt/Main, 1982), 124–53

'"... daß der Ausdruck Eindruck werde": Gustav Mahler und Alfred Roller – Die Reform der Wiener Wagner-Szene', *Jahrbuch der Bayerischen Akademie der Schönen Künste*, 11 (1997), 55–95

Carnegy, Patrick. 'The Staging of *Tristan und Isolde*: Landmarks along the Appian Way', *Tristan and Isolde*, English National Opera Guide, 6 (London, 1981), 29–35

Wagner and the Art of the Theatre (New Haven, CT, 2006)

Heldt, Brigitte. *Richard Wagner, 'Tristan und Isolde': Das Werk und seine Inszenierung* (Laaber, 1994)

Millington, Barry and Spencer, Stewart (eds.). *Wagner in Performance* (New Haven, CT, 1992)

Petzet, Detta and Michael Petzet. *Die Richard Wagner-Bühne König Ludwigs II.* (Munich, 1970), 33–74

Spencer, Stewart. '*Tristan und Isolde* in Great Britain', *wagnerspectrum*, 1 (2005), 145–63

Srocke, Martina. 'Die Entwicklung der räumlichen Darstellung in der Inszenierungsgeschichte von Wagners *Tristan und Isolde*', *Jahrbuch für Opernforschung*, 3 (1990), 43–68

Voss, Egon. 'Wagners Striche im *Tristan*', *Neue Zeitschrift für Musik*, 132 (1971), 644–47; repr. in *'Wagner und kein Ende': Betrachtungen und Studien* (Zurich and Mainz, 1996), 310–19

'Aufführungspraktische Konsequenzen der *Tristan*-Philologie' [Striche im *Tristan*, zweiter Versuch], in *'Wagner und kein Ende'* (Zurich and Mainz, 1996), 320–33

Wagner, Wieland. 'Gedanken zum Mythischen in Wagners *Tristan und Isolde*', in Oswald Georg Bauer (ed.), *Wieland Wagner: Sein Denken. Aufsätze, Reden, Interviews, Briefe* (Bayreuth, 1991), 49–53

Reception

Abbate, Carolyn. '*Tristan* in the Composition of *Pelléas*', *19th-Century Music*, 5 (1981), 117–41

Arlettaz, Vincent. '*Tristan* de Wagner critiqué par Berlioz', *Revue musicale de Suisse romande*, 49 (1996), 3–25

Baragwanath, Nicolas. 'Alban Berg, Richard Wagner, and Leitmotivs of Symmetry', *19th-Century Music*, 23 (1999), 62–83

Berger, Karol. 'King Roger's *Liebesleben*', in Michał Bristiger *et al.* (eds.), *Karol Szymanowski in seiner Zeit* (Munich, 1984), 101–12

Bittmann, Antonius. 'Aspekte der Wagner-Rezeption Max Regers', *Reger-Studien*, 6 (2000), 287–311

Christensen, Thomas. 'Schoenberg's Opus 11 No. 1: A Parody of Pitch Cells from *Tristan*', *Journal of the Arnold Schoenberg Institute*, 10 (1987), 38–44

Davidson, Audrey. *Olivier Messiaen and the Tristan Myth* (Westport, CT, 2001)

De Médicis, François. '"*Tristan* dans *Le Mer*": Le crépuscule wagnérien noyé dans le zénith debussyste?', *Acta musicologica*, 79 (2007), 195–251

Döge, Klaus. 'Die Wagner-Rezeption Hans Werner Henzes am Beispiel *Tristan*', in Petr Macek (ed.), *Richard Wagner – Nationalkulturen – Zeitgeschichte* (Brno, 1996), 85–90

Förger, Annette. '"... immer kommt das Erbe auf uns zu, fordernd, Antworten verlangend ..."', *wagnerspektrum*, 1 (2005), 127–44

Furness, Raymond. *Wagner and Literature* (Manchester, 1982)

Gauldin, Robert. 'Reference and Association in the Vier Lieder, Op. 2, of Alban Berg', *Music Theory Spectrum*, 21 (1999), 32–42

Guarnieri Corazzol, Adriana. *Tristano, mio Tristano: Gli scrittori italiani e il caso Wagner* (Bologna, 1988)

Huebner, Steven. 'A Tryst in Ernest Chausson's *Le roi Arthus*', in Annegret Fauser and Manuela Schwartz (eds.), *Von Wagner zum Wagnérisme: Musik, Literatur, Kunst, Politik* (Leipzig, 1999), 351–78

Janáček, Leoš. '*Tristan and Isolde* by Richard Wagner', in Michael Brim Beckerman (ed.), *Janáček and His World* (Princeton, NJ, 2003), 221–5

Jost, Christa. 'Von Wagner zu Schönberg: Anmerkungen zu Hans Werner Henzes Instrumentation der beiden "Studien für *Tristan und Isolde*"', in Petr Macek (ed.), *Richard Wagner – Nationalkulturen – Zeitgeschichte* (Brno, 1996), 76–84

Koppen, Erwin. *Dekadenter Wagnerismus: Studien zur europäischen Literatur des Fin de siècle* (Berlin and New York, NY, 1973)

Mann, Thomas. *Wagner und unsere Zeit: Aufsätze, Betrachtungen, Briefe*, ed. Erika Mann (Frankfurt/Main, 1963; repr. 1983); trans. Allan Blunden, *Pro and Contra Wagner* (Chicago, IL, 1985)

Müller, Heiner. 'Angst und Geometrie: Aus einem Gespräch über *Tristan und Isolde*', in Wolfgang Storch (ed.), *Der Raum Bayreuth: Ein Auftrag aus der Zukunft* (Frankfurt/Main, 2002), 215–20

'Notizen zu *Tristan und Isolde*: Während einer Probenarbeit Bayreuth 1993', *ibid.*, 221–37

Rauseo, Chris. 'Der Heldentenor und seine Rolle: Wagners *Tristan* und Wedekinds *Kammersänger*', *Euphorion*, 88 (1994), 156–68

Schäfer, Thomas. 'Wortmusik/Tonmusik: Ein Beitrag zur Wagner-Rezeption von Arnold Schönberg und Stefan George', *Die Musikforschung*, 47 (1994), 252–73

Schneider, Andrea. *Die parodierten Musikdramen Richard Wagners: Geschichte und Dokumentation Wagnerscher Opernparodien* (Anif, 1996)

Straus, Joseph N. '*Tristan* and Berg's Lyric Suite', *In Theory Only*, 8/3 (1984), 33–41

Truscott, Harold. 'Wagner's *Tristan* and the Twentieth Century', *The Music Review*, 24 (1963), 75–85

Vaget, Hans Rudolf. '"Ohne Rat in fremdes Land?": *Tristan und Isolde* in Amerika: Seidl, Mahler, Toscanini', *wagnerspectrum*, 1 (2005), 164–85

Zuckerman, Elliott. *The First Hundred Years of Wagner's 'Tristan'* (New York, NY, 1964)

Index